Linguistic Ethnography

Also by Julia Snell

BETTER THAN BEST PRACTICE
Developing Teaching and Learning through Dialogue (*co-authored*)

Also by Sara Shaw

FUNDING FOR PRIMARY CARE RESEARCH (*co-edited*)

HEALTH ECONOMICS (*co-edited*)

ISSUES IN PRIMARY CARE EPIDEMIOLOGY (*co-edited*)

HEALTH INFORMATICS AND PRIMARY CARE RESEARCH (*co-edited*)

PATIENT PARTICIPATION AND ETHICAL CONSIDERATIONS (*co-edited*)

RANDOMISED CONTROLLED TRIALS AND MULTI-CENTRE
RESEARCH (*co-edited*)

THE USE AND DESIGN OF QUESTIONNAIRES (*co-edited*)

STATISTICAL CONCEPTS (*co-edited*)

AN INTRODUCTION TO QUALITATIVE METHODS FOR HEALTH
PROFESSIONALS (*co-edited*)

Also by Fiona Copland

LINGUISTIC ETHNOGRAPY
Collecting, Analysing and Presenting Data (*co-authored*)

THE COURSEBOOK AND BEYOND (*co-authored*)

MATERIALS DEVELOPMENT (*co-authored*)

Linguistic Ethnography

Interdisciplinary Explorations

Edited by

Julia Snell
University of Leeds, UK

Sara Shaw
Queen Mary University of London, UK

and

Fiona Copland
University of Stirling, UK

First published 2015 by
PALGRAVE MACMILLAN

Palgrave Macmillan in the UK is an imprint of Macmillan Publishers Limited, registered in England, company number 785998, of Houndmills, Basingstoke, Hampshire RG21 6XS.

Palgrave Macmillan in the US is a division of St Martin's Press LLC, 175 Fifth Avenue, New York, NY 10010.

Palgrave Macmillan is the global academic imprint of the above companies and has companies and representatives throughout the world.

Palgrave® and Macmillan® are registered trademarks in the United States, the United Kingdom, Europe and other countries.

ISBN 978–1–137–03502–8 hardback

ISBN 978–1–137–52906–0 paperback

This book is printed on paper suitable for recycling and made from fully managed and sustained forest sources. Logging, pulping and manufacturing processes are expected to conform to the environmental regulations of the country of origin.

A catalogue record for this book is available from the British Library.

Library of Congress Cataloging-in-Publication Data
Linguistic ethnography: interdisciplinary explorations / edited by Julia Snell, University of Leeds, UK; Sara Shaw, Queen Mary, University of London, UK; Fiona Copland, Aston University, UK.

pages cm—(Palgrave Advances in Language and Linguistics)

ISBN 978–1–137–52906–0 (paperback)

1. Linguistics—Research—Methodology. 2. Linguistics—Research—Methodology—Case studies. 3. Sociolinguistics. 4. Sociolinguistics—Case studies. I. Snell, Julia, editor. II. Shaw, Sara, editor. III. Copland, Fiona, 1962– editor.

P126.L678 2015

306.44072—dc23   2015002841

Typeset by MPS Limited, Chennai, India.

*To Joe, Robert and Steve: thank you
for your support, patience and understanding*

Contents

List of Figures and Tables

Figures

Tables

Acknowledgements

Our thanks go to Jeff Bezemer, Adam Lefstein, Janet Maybin, Ben Rampton and Celia Roberts, all of whom were part of an advisory group set up to guide and steer the collection. All have been tirelessly supportive of the concept, the process and the work, giving their time and advice generously. Of course, in the end, the collection represents our vision and it is us alone who are responsible for any omissions, inaccuracies or inconsistencies.

We are also hugely grateful to the scholars who have written chapters for the book and who have been extremely patient with our somewhat unorthodox approach. Attending a workshop in Copenhagen, addressing a set of guiding questions in their chapters and taking on feedback, often in multiple redrafts, goes above and beyond what is normally expected of contributors to an edited collection. We have learnt a huge amount from engaging with all of you and feel honoured to have worked with you.

Special thanks go to Janet Maybin, Ben Rampton and Celia Roberts for their detailed, challenging and illuminating chapter on *Theory and Method in Linguistic Ethnography*. We can think of few scholars better placed to provide such a detailed introduction to linguistic ethnography and we are delighted with how their work sets the tone for the collection.

Chris Candlin, the editor for Advances in Language and Linguistics, fought our corner since our collection was accepted into the series. During the final editing stages of this book, Chris sadly passed away. It had been a pleasure to work with him: he was from the outset extremely enthusiastic about the volume and provided excellent guidance on the range of issues we discussed with him. He encouraged us to be confident and creative in our work, supported us through the thick and thin of editorial work, and was always prompt and wise in his comments. We have missed his support in recent weeks as we have finalised the collection but, under his initial guidance, we are sure he would have been as pleased as we are with the way the book has turned out. Chris was truly one of the giants of the applied linguistics world and will be sadly missed.

Finally, our thanks go to all the students and teachers on the first *Ethnography, Language and Communication* course in 2006/7. Working with you and learning from you made a huge impact on the way that we approach our own research and sowed the seeds for this collection. Meeting each other is another reason to be grateful to the course. All three of us have benefited hugely from an engaging and productive working relationship that has resulted in three Ethnography, Language and Communication conferences and this collection. Most importantly, we have become firm friends in the process.

Notes on Contributors

Jeff Bezemer is Co-Director of the Centre for Multimodal Research at the Institute of Education, University of London, and Deputy Director of Multimodal Methodologies for Researching Digital Data and Environments (MODE), a node of the National Centre for Research Methods funded by the UK's Economic and Social Research Council. He has published widely on language and communication, and teaching and learning, drawing on (mostly ethnographic) research across different settings, including schools and hospitals. He also writes about multimodal theory and methods, from the perspectives of social semiotics and conversation analysis. A detailed profile and access to publications can be found on jeffbezemer.wordpress.com and https://ioe-ac.academia.edu/JeffBezemer.

Adrian Blackledge is Professor of Bilingualism and Director of the MOSAIC Centre for Research on Multilingualism at University of Birmingham, UK. He is author of numerous articles and books based on his research on multilingualism in education and wider society. His books include *Heteroglossia as Practice and Pedagogy* (2014); *The Routledge Handbook of Multilingualism* (2012); *Multilingualism: A Critical Perspective* (2010); *Discourse and Power in a Multilingual World* (2005); *Negotiation of Identities in Multilingual Contexts* (2004); *Multilingualism, Second Language Learning, and Gender* (2001); and *Literacy, Power, and Social Justice* (2000). He is engaged in research funded through the Arts and Humanities Research Council's *Translating Cultures* theme, 'Translation and Translanguaging: Investigating Linguistic and Cultural Transformations in Superdiverse Wards in Four UK Cities'.

Sarah Collins has an interdisciplinary background in linguistics, social science, health care and education. Her research has included communication disability, cross-cultural studies, health care interaction and patient participation; and in her research she uses qualitative approaches, combining conversation analysis with ethnography and interviews. Sarah is Senior Lecturer in Communication at Manchester Medical School, University of Manchester, where she has a particular interest in novel applications of linguistics, social sciences and the humanities to communication training and professional education.

Fiona Copland is Professor of Teaching English to Speakers of Other Languages (TESOL), University of Stirling. She worked in the TESOL field in Nigeria, Hong Kong and Japan before returning to the UK to live and work. Fiona researches in a number of areas, including teacher education and teaching English to young learners, and has published widely in these areas. Fiona is co-author, with Angela Creese, of *Linguistic Ethnography: Collecting, Analysing and Presenting Data* and she was the convenor of the Linguistic Ethnography Forum between 2013 and 2014. A detailed profile can be found at: http://www.aston.ac.uk/lss/staff-directory/coplanf/

Angela Creese is Professor of Educational Linguistics at the School of Education, University of Birmingham. Her research interests are in linguistic ethnography, urban multilingualism and multilingual classroom pedagogy. Her publications include *Heteroglossia as Practice and Pedagogy* (with Adrian Blackledge, 2014); *The Routledge Handbook of Multilingualism* (with Marilyn Martin-Jones and Adrian Blackledge, 2012); *Multilingualism: A Critical Perspective* (with Adrian Blackledge, 2010); Volume 9: *Ecology of Language, Encyclopedia of Language and Education* (2009); *Teacher Collaboration and Talk in Multilingual Classrooms* (2005) and *Multilingual Classroom Ecologies* (2003). She has served as associate editor on the US-based *Anthropology & Education Quarterly* and is an editorial board member for Springer's *Educational Linguistics Series*.

Mirit Israeli is a doctoral student in Education at the Ben-Gurion University of the Negev in Israel. She researches classroom interaction and teacher learning, and serves as Coordinator of the Laboratory for the Study of Pedagogy.

Martha Sif Karrebæk is Associate Professor in the Department of Nordic Studies and Linguistics at the University of Copenhagen. Her PhD thesis was on language socialisation and (second) language acquisition in pre-school. She has led a project on mother tongue education financed by the Independent Research Council's elite grant for young research leaders, *Sapere aude*. Articles have appeared in the *International Journal of Bilingualism, Journal of Pragmatics, Journal of Sociolinguistics, Journal of Linguistic Anthropology, Food, Culture and Society, Language & Communication* etc. Prizes and awards include The Ton Vallen Award (2013), Einar Hansen Forskningsfond research grant (2012), Sapere Aude Research Leader (2013) and Young Elite Researcher prize (2010) from the Danish Independent Research Council. She is a reviewer for *NordAnd, Social Semiotics, Language and Education Quarterly* and other journals, and a member of the Urban Culture Lab at the University of Copenhagen.

Adam Lefstein is Senior Lecturer in Education at the Ben-Gurion University of the Negev in Israel, where he conducts research and teaches about pedagogy, classroom interaction, teacher learning and educational change. His book (with Julia Snell), *Better than Best Practice: Developing Teaching and Learning through Dialogue*, was published in 2014.

Lian Malai Madsen is an associate professor in the Department of Scandinavian Studies and Linguistics, University of Copenhagen. She received her PhD in 2008 based on a linguistic and ethnographic study among youth in a martial arts club. She has carried out postdoctoral research (2009–2012) on linguistic and social practices in school and leisure contexts among youth in culturally diverse settings and is involved in a project on language, globalisation and social stratification. Her main research interests involve: linguistic diversity, social positioning and categorisation; stylisation; peer-cultural activities in relation to language use; socialisation and education. She has published her work in journals including the *International Journal of Multilingualism*, *Linguistics and Education* and *Language in Society* and in international edited volumes on heteroglossia, sports, integration and societal cohesion, and European urban youth language. She has a forthcoming book with Multilingual Matters and is a member of the International Consortium on Language and Superdiversity (InCoLaS) and of the steering committee of Linguistic Ethnography Forum.

Janet Maybin is Senior Lecturer in Language and Communication at the Open University. Originally trained as an anthropologist, she has written extensively for Open University courses on English language and language arts. She combines ethnography and linguistics in research on adults' and children's informal language and literacy practices, focussing currently on narrative, creativity and voice. Publications include *Children's Voices: Talk, Knowledge and Identity* (2006), *The Art of English: Everyday Texts and Practices* (co-edited, 2006), a special issue of *Applied Linguistics* on creativity (co-edited, 2007), *Children's Literature: Approaches and Territories* (co-edited, 2009) and *The Routledge Companion to English Language Studies* (co-edited, 2010).

Ben Rampton is Professor of Applied and Sociolinguistics and Director of the Centre for Language Discourse and Communication at King's College London (www.kcl.ac.uk/ldc). He does interactional sociolinguistics, and his interests cover urban multilingualism, ethnicity, class, youth and education. He is the author of *Crossing: Language & Ethnicity among Adolescents* (1995/2005) and *Language in Late Modernity: Interaction in an Urban School* (2006), and a co-author of *Researching Language: Issues of Power and Method* (1992). He co-edited *The Language, Ethnicity & Race Reader* (2003) and edits *Working Papers in Urban Language and Literacy* (www.kcl.ac.uk/ldc). He was founding convener of the UK Linguistic Ethnography Forum (www.uklef.net), and is the Director of the King's Interdisciplinary Social Science Doctoral Training Centre (www.kcl.ac.uk/kissdtc) of the Economic and Social Research Council (ESRC).

Celia Roberts is Professor Emerita of Sociolinguistics at King's College London. Her interests are in language, migration and institutional disadvantage, and in the methodological implications of combining interactional sociolinguistics and ethnography. She also has a particular interest in the practical relevance of research and has directed many research projects, including on job interviewing, health communication, assessment and further education, all with practical outcomes such as training DVDs. Her publications include *Talk, Work and Institutional Order* (with Sarangi, 1999), *Language Learners as Ethnographers* (with Byram et al, 2001) and *Linguistic Penalties* (forthcoming).

Frances Rock is Senior Lecturer in the Centre for Language and Communication Research at Cardiff University. Her work investigates the mediation of experiences in social worlds by analysing written and spoken language, created when people make meaning together. Frances' research examines language and policing, workplaces and ecolinguistic topics. Publications include *Communicating Rights: The Language of Arrest and Detention* (2007) and the edited collection, *Legal-Lay Communication: Textual Travels in the Law* (2013). She is one of the editors of the *International Journal of Speech, Language and the Law*.

Jill Russell is Senior Lecturer in Health Policy and Evaluation in the Centre for Primary Care and Public Health at Barts and The London School of Medicine and Dentistry, Queen Mary University of London. Her methodological interests include linguistic ethnography, interpretive policy analysis and case study. Recent published work includes papers on the rationality of health care rationing practices, the timeliness of dementia diagnosis and the role of think tanks in shaping health policy.

Sara Shaw is Senior Lecturer in Health Policy Research and Director of the Unit for Social Policy & Practice in Health Care in the Centre for Primary Care and Population Health at Queen Mary University of London. She has a background in medical sociology and policy studies. Her research focuses on health policy and health care practices and she has a particular interest in discourse analysis and exploring how organisational processes, routines and decision-making are created through language/social interaction and shape health care. Sara has published widely on topics including health care commissioning, integrated care, patient experience and health research policy. She also writes about interpretive approaches to understanding and analysing policy. Her most recent work on the role of think tanks in shaping health policy has been published in *Sociology of Health & Illness* and *Critical Policy Studies*.

Julia Snell is Associate Professor in English Language at the University of Leeds. Her research focuses on linguistic and communicative processes in educational settings, and she has a particular interest in the relationship between language, social class and educational opportunities. She is the co-author, with Adam Lefstein, of *Better than Best Practice: Developing Teaching and Learning through Dialogue*, which was published in 2014. A detailed profile and access to publications can be found on www.snell.me.uk.

Deborah Swinglehurst is General Practitioner in Suffolk, UK and Senior Clinical Lecturer at Barts and The London School of Medicine, Queen Mary, University of London. Her PhD thesis (2012) was a linguistic ethnographic study of electronic patient records (EPRs) in general practice which explored how EPRs contribute to shaping working practices within the consultation and, more widely, within primary care settings. She has published widely on this work. Her research uses qualitative methods including ethnography, discourse analysis and narrative analysis to study working practices, technologies and interaction in health care settings. She is a Fellow of the Royal College of General Practitioners and a Fellow of the Higher Education Academy.

Jaspreet Kaur Takhi joined the University of Birmingham's School of Education in June 2010 as a bilingual Research Fellow on a project funded by the Humanities in the European Research Area Joint Research Project (HERA JRP), 'Investigating discourses of inheritance and identity in four multilingual European settings' with Adrian Blackledge and Angela Creese. She investigated linguistic repertoires and notions of inheritance and identity among young people living in Birmingham and attending a Panjabi complementary school. Publications include

Multilingualism and Superdiversity in Multilingual Urban Sites: Structure, Activity, Ideology (with Adrian Blackledge and Angela Creese) and *The Multilingual Turn: Implications for SLA, TESOL and Bilingual Education*. Her research interests include code switching, conflict between migrant generations and negotiating identity through language and popular culture.

Karin Tusting is Lecturer in Language and Literacy Studies in the Department of Linguistics and English Language, Lancaster University. She has published on a range of topics linked by an interest in the role of material texts in social processes, including literacy practices of accountability in educational settings, creativity in everyday literacies and literacies for learning in communities of practice. She has also contributed to publications dedicated to the development of linguistic ethnography as a field of study.

Tom Van Hout is an assistant professor in the Institute for Academic and Professional Communication at the University of Antwerp, Belgium and in the Department of Journalism and New Media at Leiden University, the Netherlands. His research examines public communication as sites of knowledge (re)production, representation and contestation. He recently guest-edited a special issue of *Discourse, Context & Media* on journalistic stance (with Gabrina Pounds and Bram Vertommen) and has published a methods handbook for journalism students (with Willem Koetsenruijter). His work on business journalism was published in the *Journal of Pragmatics*, *Text & Talk* and *Pragmatics*.

1

An Introduction to Linguistic Ethnography: Interdisciplinary Explorations

Sara Shaw, Fiona Copland and Julia Snell

The term 'linguistic ethnography' captures a growing body of research by scholars who combine linguistic and ethnographic approaches in order to understand how social and communicative processes operate in a range of settings and contexts. To date, linguistic ethnography has been described as an umbrella term: an area of shared interests where established research traditions interact (see Tusting and Maybin 2007; Rampton 2007a; Jacobs and Slembrouck 2010; Maybin and Tusting 2011). A great deal of research has been undertaken under this umbrella (see, for instance, the work of Jan Blommaert, Angela Creese, Marilyn Martin-Jones, Ben Rampton and Celia Roberts, and Table 1.1, below), building on the foundational work of scholars such as Frederick Erickson, John Gumperz and Dell Hymes, all of whom are cited throughout the collection. However, linguistic ethnography has yet to reach a position where we can claim it to be a clearly defined approach. Linguistic ethnographic work is dispersed among many different disciplinary areas and, currently, there is no dedicated journal to bring work together and support its development. We therefore thought it timely to publish a selection of contemporary linguistic ethnography work in one collection. Our aim is to take stock of linguistic ethnography: to invite readers to examine the breadth of disciplinary and methodological currents converging in linguistic ethnography, identify intelligible threads and consider opportunities and challenges.

Whether you are an established linguistic ethnographer with an interest in how the field is developing or you are new to linguistic ethnography and wondering what it's all about, we hope that there is something in the collection for you. We recount the historical, theoretical and methodological foundations of linguistic ethnography; present case studies of research written by experienced linguistic ethnographers;

and encourage readers to engage with these case studies and our interpretation of them. Our focus is on opening up the intellectual spaces in which those who are interested in linguistic ethnography are working, to engage with the range of approaches and interpretations they employ, and to encourage debate about linguistic ethnography.

We have structured the collection in such a way as to first provide readers with a basic outline of linguistic ethnography and an overview of some of the questions and challenges that readers (and researchers) may be grappling with (Chapter 1). We then give a detailed introduction to the assumptions, values, frameworks and techniques that currently characterise linguistic ethnography (Chapter 2); and finally, present 12 research studies (Chapters 3 to 14) that engage with current topics and approaches in linguistic ethnography. The studies that have been selected focus on different disciplinary areas and draw on a range of theories and methods.

Historical foundations

The foundations of linguistic ethnography lie in the work of scholars allied to the British Association for Applied Linguistics (BAAL). In the 1990s, BAAL provided an arena for debate among researchers interested in interactional sociolinguistics, literacy studies, critical discourse analysis, language and cognitive development, and interpretively oriented applied linguistics (Rampton, Tusting, Maybin, Barwell, Creese and Lytra 2004). In 2000, five BAAL members – David Barton, Angela Creese, Janet Maybin, Ben Rampton and Karin Tusting – established a new special interest group, the Linguistic Ethnography Forum (known then as UK LEF). The aim was to unite researchers who were interested in bringing together linguistic and ethnographic perspectives and, collectively, to engage in methodological and theoretical debate.

Linguistic ethnography has been influenced significantly by linguistic anthropology and shares many of the same theoretical underpinnings (Copland and Creese 2015). However, while linguistic anthropology has prospered in North America, this has not been the case in Europe where the idea of an 'institutionalized linguistic anthropology' (Rampton 2007b, p. 594) has not materialised (Flynn, Van Praet and Jacobs 2010; Jacobs and Slembrouck 2010; Copland and Creese 2015). Rather, the Linguistic Ethnography Forum has provided an intellectual and supportive home for those interested in exploring the disciplinary boundaries of linguistics and sociolinguistics. Members of the LEF have produced a position paper introducing the term (Rampton et al. 2004), a special journal edition (Rampton, Maybin and Tusting 2007), entries on linguistic ethnography to encyclopaedias and handbooks (Creese 2008; Maybin and Tusting 2010; Snell and Lefstein 2015) and a book to support researchers with doing linguistic ethnographic research (Copland and Creese 2015). All have emphasised the emergent state of the field.

The label 'linguistic ethnography' does not, of course, guarantee the quality of the research: as with any emerging field there is some excellent and some mediocre work. Nevertheless, the group of researchers aligning to linguistic ethnography has grown rapidly since the Linguistic Ethnography Forum was first set up. At the time of writing, it has over 600 members from more than 30 countries, many of whom attend LEF's biennial conference on Explorations in Ethnography, Language and Communication. A search of Google Scholar also indicates a growth in research and referencing of linguistic ethnography work, with citations growing steadily since the inception of LEF (Table 1.1).

Despite increasing interest, there remains a question about whether linguistic ethnography is a new interdisciplinary field or, whether, as Martin Hammersley has suggested, such growth reflects a wider 'obsession with re-branding and relaunching' (2007, p. 690) that is characteristic of the social sciences in the late 20th and early 21st centuries. This

Table 1.1 Citations of 'linguistic ethnography' on Google Scholar

Year	Citations
2013	171
2012	147
2011	128
2010	121
2009	104
2008	67
2007	58
2006	32
2005	28
2004	16
2003	27
2002	24
2001	7
2000	2

collection showcases a current of work which has appropriated linguistics, ethnography and linguistic anthropology in interesting ways and which share a number of commonalities (see below). Taken together, they suggest that linguistic ethnography should be considered as more than a simple rebranding exercise.

Editorial process

We came to linguistic ethnography in 2007 via a five-day course on *Key Concepts and Methods in Ethnography, Language and Communication*. The course introduced us to a range of perspectives and resources used to study language and communication ethnographically, drawn from the ethnography of communication, theories of social interaction, interactional sociolinguistics, linguistic anthropology, conversation analysis and social semiotics (see Chapter 2 for a detailed description). Our participation led us not only to continue our research using linguistic ethnography, but also to attempt to broaden discussions about the value, relevance and future of the field. In 2008, we established a conference on *Explorations in Ethnography, Language and Communication* (now the official conference for the Linguistic Ethnography Forum – see above). Impressed by the breadth and quality of contributions and also feeling that there were significant questions and issues about linguistic ethnography to be addressed, we decided on an edited collection. We sought a publisher and, together with our advisory group – Jeff Bezemer, Adam Lefstein, Janet Maybin, Ben Rampton and Celia Roberts – identified established and emerging researchers who were characterising their work as linguistic ethnography. We deliberately invited contributions from scholars working in a range of disciplines and settings. Our intention was to exhibit the breadth of research being undertaken and to invite debate about contemporary issues in linguistic ethnography. To aid this process we held a workshop for contributors in Copenhagen (at the same time as the *Explorations in Ethnography, Language and Communication* conference) with the intention of providing a forum for contributors to meet, explore connections and gain a sense of the aims and focus of the book. We discussed the proposed content and structure, asking contributors to provide case studies of current research (including detailed, worked analysis) and to address the following three questions:

1. In what ways did linguistic ethnography enable you to get to parts of the process you study which other approaches couldn't reach?

2. In what ways has appropriating linguistic ethnography led to changes in your work and the methods you use?
3. How has your own discipline influenced the concepts and emphases within linguistic ethnography?

Contributors provided a wealth of material from which we were able to draw to examine (at least a small part of) linguistic ethnographic research. As is the case with a broad area like linguistic ethnography, contributors' work varies in approach, focus and setting. There are, however, some commonalities. Our interpretation of the case studies in this collection is that they variously:

- adopt an interdisciplinary approach to research;
- use topic-oriented ethnography;
- combine linguistics with ethnography;
- bring together different sources of data; and
- aspire to improve social life.

Taken together, these commonalities may provide the basis for linguistic ethnography to be described as an emergent field. However, as we state above, linguistic ethnography cannot yet claim to be a clearly defined or established approach. We therefore adopt a questioning stance when describing commonalities and invite readers to do the same as they engage with the chapters in the collection. For us, the commonalities provide an interesting way of introducing the contributions to the collection, while pointing to the challenges facing linguistic ethnography that we are keen for readers to engage with.

Commonalities across the studies in this collection

Adopt an interdisciplinary approach

Over the past 20 years, there has been a gradual shift away from the organisation of academic knowledge in terms of disciplines to one that is based on interdisciplinarity (Gibbons et al. 1994; Rampton 2007b). Linguistic ethnography has embraced this shift, bringing together a community of scholars who are interested in joining debates about language and ethnography that cut across disciplines.

Scholars within a discipline tend to be socialised into a shared set of assumptions about the concepts and theories that underpin research in that area. However, disciplinary assumptions can become so ingrained as to be taken for granted (Bridges 2006). Authors in this collection are allied to diverse disciplines and professional contexts, including (but not limited to) medicine (Swinglehurst), sociology and social policy (Shaw and Russell), education (Lefstein and Israeli; Collins; Creese, Takhi and Blackledge), literacy studies (Tusting), social semiotics (Bezemer) and a range of sub-fields from within linguistics, including applied socio- and forensic linguistics, journalism studies and new media (Copland; Madsen and Karrebæk; Snell; Rock, Van Hout). Many have felt constrained by the paradigms in which they are working and describe how they have tried to extend disciplinary boundaries and bring in theories and methods that allow them to better answer their research questions. For example, Shaw and Russell's study (Chapter 7) of the role of think tanks in shaping health policy challenges traditional approaches to researching this area. They describe a shift in the way they work from their initial research training in medical schools where they were taught to look for 'themes' in interview data and to treat language as a 'transparent medium', to their finding and applying interpretative approaches.

Our contributors write eloquently about the value of interdisciplinarity to their own work. But such interdisciplinary working carries institutional risks. As Cerwonka and Malkii suggest, 'the promiscuousness of interdisciplinary scholars [might be] perceived to be unwise and, for some, dangerous to the academy because their work challenges the established divisions of authority and expertise that disciplinary borders conventionally reflect.' (2007, p. 9) Questions remain, then, as to how linguistic ethnographers should position their work within the academy: How can a scholar successfully defend linguistic ethnography in a viva examination or a bid for funding?

Each contributor to this collection draws on a range of theoretical and methodological perspectives to enable close, systematic analysis of language across social settings. For instance, Van Hout's analysis of business journalism (Chapter 4) extends linguistic analyses of news discourse by moving 'beyond the purely textual level'. Rock (Chapter 8) advocates for the need to 'burst the bonds of "mere" linguistics' in order to recognise the complexity of situated language use in routine police work. And Snell (Chapter 12) explains why traditional quantitative approaches to understanding working-class children's speech in sociolinguistics are problematic. None of our contributors explicitly mentions bricolage, but all make use of a range of methodological strategies in order to respond to research questions and 'the unfolding context of the research situation' (Kincheloe 2005, p. 324; see also Becker [1998]). This raises questions about what counts as rigour in linguistic ethnography and how linguistic ethnographers can deal with the potential shortcomings of combining methodological approaches. It also points to a wider question about whether or not linguistic ethnography is an established field with a range of underpinning theories and methods.

Use topic-oriented ethnography

Traditional anthropological work has tended to focus on 'making the strange familiar' (Hymes 1996, pp. 4–5), exploring and understanding different (and often distant) ways of life and cultural perspectives and illuminating these for others. But do linguistic ethnographers use ethnography to understand 'all of a way of life' as traditional anthropology tends to? The contributions to this collection suggest not, instead highlighting a concern with honing in on the institutions and practices that surround us in contemporary life and understanding how they are embedded in wider social contexts and structures. This kind of ethnography focuses on 'making the familiar strange', uncovering the routine and everyday, and capturing the way things unfold in real time (Heller 2011). It is topic-oriented (Rampton 2007b, drawing on Hymes 1996) and involves what Green and Bloome refer to as an 'ethnographic perspective', which encourages 'a more focused approach [in order] to study particular aspects of everyday life and cultural practices of a social group' (1997, p. 183).

Many of the studies in this collection are topic-oriented ethnographies. For example, Tusting (Chapter 3) investigates tutors' experiences of paperwork in a post-16 college and Swinglehurst (Chapter 5) examines General Practitioners' use of the Electronic Patient Record in medical consultations. Both demonstrate how increased centralisation of paperwork and other kinds of workplace documentation constrain the ways in which tutors, doctors and nurses perform their roles. Copland (Chapter 6) also focuses on one element of a teacher-training programme, the post-observation feedback conference.

For most contributors, understanding the everyday lives and practices of a particular social group involved periods of time spent 'lurking and soaking' (Werner and Schoepfle 1989) as participant observers in the field. But what does 'participation' mean for linguistic ethnographers? What length of time spent 'lurking and soaking' might be sufficient to study familiar and everyday practices? And in what ways does topic-oriented ethnography enable linguistic ethnographers to be systematic and rigorous in their research? The answers are far from straightforward. For instance, Madsen and Karrebæk (Chapter 13) stress the importance of long-term engagement with research sites over a number of years that allows them to dip in and out of sites over time and hone in on areas of specific interest. In contrast, Collins (Chapter 9) describes how visits to a cancer clinic over a five-month period allowed her to understand the different ways professionals and patients used clinical spaces. Like Collins, many of our contributors were not in a position to spend extended periods of time engaging with research sites and therefore adopted alternative strategies to gain depth in their research. For example, Bezemer (Chapter 11) describes his experience as an ethnographer 'in residence', becoming part of the hospital where he was researching surgeons' practices in the operating theatre; and Shaw and Russell (Chapter 7) draw on autoethnography to illuminate the work of think tanks in shaping health policy.

Combine linguistics with ethnography

If ethnography provides researchers with the means of opening up our understanding of everyday life, then it is the combination with linguistic analysis that provides a way of reaching 'deeper into the ethnographic description of social or institutional processes' (Chapter 2, page 18). The slow and intensive analysis of language and communication sheds light on small (but consequential) aspects of social practice, taking the ethnography into smaller and more focused spaces and drawing analytic attention to fine detail (for example, the gestures of surgeons – see Chapter 11). As Copland and Creese explain, it is the combination of linguistics and ethnography that 'links the micro to the macro, the small to the large, the varied to the routine, the individual to the social, the creative to the constraining, and the historical to the present and to the future' (2015, p. 26). But is it only the combination of linguistics and ethnography that makes these links? Are these kinds of connections made elsewhere? And if so, then what is it that makes linguistic ethnography appealing?

Linguistic ethnographers use the combination of ethnography and linguistics in ways that help them to understand the complexities of modern life (for example, focusing on processes of globalisation and superdiversity, see Blommaert [2013], Blommaert and Rampton [2011]). For linguists, the combination with ethnography represents a reorientation: a conscious effort to resist the perceived empirical rigour, neatness and certainty of linguistic analysis and embrace the openness and uncertainty of ethnography (see Copland's description of the development of her 'ethnographic sensibility' – Chapter 6). For ethnographers, the combination with linguistics presents an opportunity to hone in on specific instances of everyday life and to evidence analysis in small instances of social practice. This means that researchers employing linguistic ethnography are often not satisfied with one kind of data or one kind of analysis. They use ethnography to 'open up' linguistic analysis and linguistics to 'tie down' ethnographic insights (Rampton et al. 2004). To achieve this, they draw upon a wide variety of linguistic and discourse analytic traditions (for example, conversation analysis, textual analysis, quantitative variation analysis, corpus analysis, social semiotics) in combination with ethnography. This process of 'opening up' and 'tying down' may well distinguish linguistic ethnography.

Linking ethnography with language is not solely the territory of linguistic ethnography. Researchers in a range of areas have struggled to overcome the fundamental tension between openness and systematicity that is inherent in integrating the two disciplines. While there is clearly no one way of doing this kind of work, contributors to this collection provide examples that demonstrate how the linguistic and ethnographic come together in their analyses to ensure that tensions such as these are at least made explicit. For example, Bezemer (Chapter 11) explains how his analysis of linguistic and multi-modal data, alongside ethnographic field notes, revealed how surgeons use talk, their bodies, and other artefacts to make and communicate decisions in the operating theatre. And Snell (Chapter 12) uncovers the pragmatics of pronoun use amongst children by combining a rigorous quantitative analysis of the children's recorded talk with field notes which meticulously documented the children's actions. Both writers combine systematicity in ethnographic and linguistic data collection and analysis with an openness to the emic perspectives of the participants, enabling a synergy to emerge that in turn allows researchers to make plausible and nuanced interpretations of talk in context.

Established traditions and scholars have been influential in linguistic ethnography, guiding contributors to combine language and ethnography in ways that they find productive. The work of Dell Hymes, Erving Goffman and John Gumperz has been particularly influential. Their theoretically informed ways of working provide a catalyst for investigating language and communication and linking to wider social processes. This is evident in the use of Gumperz' work on 'contextualisation cues' and 'crosstalk' (Rock, Chapter 8); Goffman's work on 'co-ordinated task activity' (Bezemer, Chapter 11), footing (Swinglehurst, Chapter 5; Snell, Chapter 12), performativity (Shaw and Russell, Chapter 7) and face (Copland, Chapter 6); and in the use of Hymes's reminder that 'how something is said is part of what is said' (1972, p. 59), which is taken up by Creese, Takhi and Blackledge (Chapter 14). Contemporary scholars have also influenced the thinking and work of contributors to this volume. In particular, Silverstein's and Blommaert's work on indexicality (Rampton et al.; Chapter 2; Swinglehurst, Chapter 5; Snell, Chapter 12; Madsen & Karrebæk, Chapter 13) and Goodwin's work on 'professional vision' (Lefstein and Isreali, Chapter 10).

Bring together different sources of data

Linguistic ethnographers work with different types of data (for example, video- and audio-recordings of interactions, field notes, interview transcripts, policy documents, letters or photographs), which they bring together in order to understand the complexity of social events (Blommaert 2007). The emphasis is on 'making both academic and political generalisations about social life accountable to the kinds of small-scale everyday activity which we can observe, record and transcribe' (Rampton et al., Chapter 2, page 36). But what is the status of different kinds of data? What data can or should be treated as primary? And how might different sources of data be combined and analysed by those using linguistic ethnography?

The case studies in this collection demonstrate that there is no one fixed method or approach and no one 'correct' source of data. There are, however, productive tensions. In some linguistic ethnographic studies, the emphasis has been on collecting audio- and video-recordings of interaction for transcription and analysis, with field notes and other sources of data typically viewed as secondary (see Lefstein and Israeli, Chapter 10). In others, researchers maintain that field notes in particular are not simply useful for contextualising events but are as vital to linguistic ethnography as any other data. Creese, Takhi and Blackledge (Chapter 14) go further and argue that field notes should be subjected to the same rigorous linguistic analysis as interactional data.

Contributors to this collection stress the importance of bringing together different sources of data and demonstrate how and why they have focused on these within their analyses. For example, Madsen and Karrebæk (Chapter 13) combine fieldnotes, audio- and video-recordings, interviews and written texts in their study in order to make the case that (contrary to much research) hip-hop practices do not always challenge traditional educational models. Some also argue that there is a need for a diverse range of data to ensure that linguistic ethnographers are able to access areas of social life that may not be open to direct observation (Shaw and Russell, Chapter 7) or where 'ideal' data is simply not accessible (Rock, Chapter 8). Data sets that contributors have found valuable for linguistic ethnographic work include interviews (Copland), group meetings (Creese, Takhi and Blackledge), press releases (Van Hout), policy documents (Shaw and Russell), field notes and drawings (Collins), recorded interactions (Snell), letters (Rock), real time computer screen capture (Swinglehurst, Van Hout) and institutional forms (Tusting).

Aspire to improve social life

A significant amount of research now encompasses social or strategic goals, with government officials and policymakers increasingly focused on combining scientific, economic and social programmes (Shaw 2007). This reflects a shift away from mono-disciplinary research undertaken largely in universities with an emphasis on discovery towards interdisciplinary, market-oriented research increasingly undertaken within and outside of university settings and with an emphasis on the wider application of knowledge (Gibbons et al. 1994). For the linguistic ethnography community this means identifying and communicating 'beneficial societal impact' from linguistic ethnography research and strengthening efforts to advance its use. This is potentially challenging. However, an interest in the potential links between research and practical intervention runs deep in linguistic ethnography (Rampton et al., Chapter 2).

For many of our contributors this emphasis on 'beneficial societal impact' provides an opportunity to extend their research. Some work in partnership with professional groups (see, for instance, Bezemer's chapter on working with the medical profession). Others undertake research that comes from their own professional experience (see, for instance, Swinglehurst's description of how her experience as a family doctor using electronic patient records motivated her research); and/or start from 'real world' problems (see, for instance, Snell's chapter describing how reports in the press prompted her to examine specific issues relating to working class children's language). The challenge, neatly summarised by Lefstein and Israeli in their chapter exploring differences in the way linguistic ethnographers and teachers talk about classroom practice, is to 'adapt, complement and mediate linguistic ethnography in ways that are constructive, have integrity, and are recognised as helpful by practitioners' (Chapter 10, page 205). However, there remains a gap between the kind of robust and convincing analyses reported in this collection and significant impact in these areas.

How then might the findings from linguistic ethnographic work be used to bring about change? There is much more that we need to do as a community of scholars to think, work and collaborate differently with regard to change. We need to be ready to: 'persuade through numbers' (Rampton et al., Chapter 2, page 42) when required rather than rely on the 'telling case' (Mitchell 1984) as is more usual in linguistic ethnography; make productive use of diverse media to communicate more effectively with citizens, professionals and other groups; and better understand how our research findings and arguments are taken up in different settings.

Concluding remarks

When all of the chapters in this collection are taken together, we can see a clear role for linguistic ethnography in meticulously describing and analysing the complexity of social events (Blommaert 2007). However, questions remain about what it is that might distinguish linguistic ethnography as a new interdisciplinary field. We have identified five features of linguistic ethnography that are common across the case studies in this collection, and raised a series of questions relating to each of these. We now invite readers to consider for themselves the ways in which the following chapters address these questions, the extent to which these five features (individually or collectively) might characterise linguistic ethnography more broadly, and the status of linguistic ethnography as a new field.

References

Becker, H. S. (1998) *Tricks of the Trade* (Chicago: University of Chicago Press).

Blommaert, J. (2007) 'On scope and depth in linguistic ethnography', *Journal of Sociolinguistics*, 11(5) pp. 682–688.

Blommaert, J. (2013) *Ethnography, Superdiversity and Linguistic Landscapes: Chronicles of Complexity* (Critical Language and Literacy Studies) (Bristol: Multilingual Matters).

Blommaert, J. and Rampton, B. (2011) 'Language & superdiversity', *Diversities* 13(2) pp. 1–21.

Bridges, D. (2006) 'The disciplines and the discipline of educational research', *Journal of Philosophy of Education*, 40(2) pp. 259–272.

Cerwonka, A. and Malkii, L. H. (2007) *Improvising Theory: Process and Temporality in Ethnographic Fieldwork* (Chicago: University of Chicago Press).

Copland, F. and Creese, A., with Rock, F. and Shaw, S. E. (2015) *Linguistic Ethnography: Collecting, Analysing and Presenting Data* (London: Sage).

Creese, A. (2008) 'Linguistic Ethnography' in K. A. King and N. H. Hornberger (eds) *Encyclopaedia of Language and Education*, 2nd Edition (New York: Springer Science+Business Media LLC).

Flynn, P., Van Praet, E. and Jacobs, G. (2010) 'Emerging linguistic ethnographic perspectives on institutional discourses', *Text & Talk*, 30(2) pp. 97–103.

Gibbons, M., Limoges, C., Nowotny, H., Schwartzman, S., Scott, P. and Trow, M. (1994) *The New Production of Knowledge: The Dynamics of Science and Research in Contemporary Societies* (London: Sage).

Green, J. and Bloome, D. (1997) 'Ethnography and Ethnographers of and in Education: A Situated Perspective' in J. Flood, S. Brice Heath and D. Lapp (eds) *Handbook of Research on Teaching Literacy through the Communicative and Visual Arts* (New York: Macmillan).

Hammersley, M. (2007) 'Reflections on linguistic ethnography', *Journal of Sociolinguistics*, 11(5) 2007, pp. 689–695.

Heller, M. (2011) *Paths to Post-Nationalism: A Critical Ethnography of Language and Identity* (New York: Oxford University Press).

Hymes, D. (1972) 'What Is Ethnography?' in P. Gilmore and A. A. Glatthorn (eds) *Children In and Out of School: Ethnography and Education* (Washington DC: Centre for Applied Linguistics) pp. 21–32.

Hymes, D. (1996). *Ethnography, Linguistics, Narrative Inequality: Toward an Understanding of Voice* (London: Taylor and Francis).

Jacobs, G. and Slembrouk, S. (2010) 'Notes on linguistic ethnography as a liminal activity', *Text & Talk*, 30(2) pp. 235–244.

Kincheloe, J. L. (2005) 'On to the next level: continuing the conceptualization of the bricolage', *Qualitative Inquiry*, 11(3) pp. 323–350.

Maybin, J. and Tusting, K. (2011) 'Linguistic Ethnography' in J. Simpson (ed.) *Handbook of Applied Linguistics* (London: Routledge).

Mitchell, JC. (1984) 'Producing Data: Case Studies' in R. Ellen (ed.) *Ethnographic Research: A Guide to General Conduct* (London: Academic Press) pp. 237–241.

Rampton, B. (2007a) 'The micro-analysis of interactional discourse in linguistic ethnography: an illustration focused on the job interview', paper prepared for the ESRC Researcher Development Initiative, *Ethnography, Language and Communication*, Oxford.

Rampton, B. (2007b) 'Neo-Hymesian linguistic ethnography in the United Kingdom', *Journal of Sociolinguistics*, 11(5) pp. 584–607.

Rampton, B. (2011) *A neo-Hymesian trajectory in applied linguistics*, Working Papers in Urban Language & Literacies 78.

Rampton, B., Maybin, J. and Tusting, K. (2007) 'Special Issue: Linguistic Ethnography', *Journal of Sociolinguistics*, 11(5) pp. 575–716.

Rampton, B., Tusting, K., Maybin, J., Barwell, R., Creese, A. and Lytra, V. (2004) 'UK Linguistic Ethnography: A Discussion Paper', published at www.ling-ethnog.org.uk.

Shaw, S. E. (2007) 'Driving out alternative ways of seeing: the significance of neo-liberal policy mechanisms for UK primary care research', *Social Theory & Health*, 5 pp. 316–337.

Snell, J. and Lefstein, A. (2015) 'Moving from "Interesting Data" to "Publishable Research Article' – Some Interpretative and Representational Dilemmas in a Linguistic Ethnographic Analysis of an English Literacy Lesson' in P. Smeyers, D. Bridges, N. Burbules and M. Griffiths (eds) *International Handbook of Interpretation in Educational Research* (Dordrecht: Springer) pp. 471–496.

Tusting, K. and Maybin, J. (2007) 'Linguistic ethnography and interdisciplinarity: opening the discussion', *Journal of Sociolinguistics*, 11(5) pp. 575–583.

Werner, O. and Schoepfle, G. (1989) *Systematic Field Work* (Newbury Park, CA: Sage).

2
Theory and Method in Linguistic Ethnography

Ben Rampton, Janet Maybin and Celia Roberts

This chapter provides a sketch of the assumptions, values, frameworks and techniques that currently characterise linguistic ethnography. In keeping with the dynamic that makes it a productive and appealing perspective, we ground our account in a series of historical, institutional and/or methodological encounters, looking at the questions and possibilities that these interactions generate. So we consider the relationships between:

- linguistics and ethnography
- elements interacting in the communicative process
- linguistic ethnography and researchers from different disciplines
- linguistic ethnography and non-academic professionals

In the section titled 'Ethnography, linguistics and linguistic ethnography', we look at what is involved in the combination of linguistics with ethnography, and at some relatively recent historical changes that have influenced their relationship, strengthening the epistemological status of ethnography and sharpening the analytic relevance of linguistics. In the section titled 'Describing the elements interacting in communication', we turn to the communication process itself and describe key elements in the theory of language and society developed in linguistic anthropology. We emphasise the power of the contribution not just to linguistic ethnography but to practice theory more generally, with practice theory understood as a 'broad and capacious ... general theory of the production of social subjects through practice, and the production of the world itself through practice' (Ortner 2006: 16). In the section titled 'Linguistic ethnography in interdisciplinary training', we examine the interdisciplinary relevance of linguistic ethnography by reviewing a Linguistic Ethnography (LE) training programme for social scientists. This taught linguistic and discourse analytic tools embedded in an ethnographic epistemology, and we consider the pedagogy and its impact, positing heightened methodological reflexivity as the only way of responding to the inevitably very diverse ways in which LE gets appropriated. In the section titled 'Linguistic ethnography and non-academic professions', we explore more of this diversity, describing LE's encounter with the knowledge and experience of non-academic professionals in two ways. First, we discuss the challenges facing educators who take up LE research, and then we address the interaction between well-established linguistic ethnographers and health professionals in collaborative projects designed to improve institutional practice.

We begin with a discussion of the relations between ethnography and linguistics.

1.   Ethnography, linguistics and linguistic ethnography

To examine the dynamic relationship between linguistics and ethnography, there are at least three questions: Exactly how do we define these two perspectives? What kinds of potential emerge when they are put together? And what is the recent history of their combination? We can take each of these questions in turn.

There has always been disagreement across the social sciences about what exactly counts as ethnography, but from our perspective, the constitutive features are:

(a) *Regard for local rationalities in an interplay between 'strangeness' and 'familiarity'*: Ethnography typically looks for the meaning and rationality in practices that seem strange from afar or at first. It tries to enter the informants' life-world and to abstract (some of) its structuring features, and this entails a process of continuing alternation between involvement in local activity on the one hand, and on the other, an orientation to external audiences and frameworks beyond (cf. Todorov 1988 on making the strange familiar and the familiar strange). Ethnography tries to comprehend both the tacit and articulated understandings of the participants in whatever processes and activities are being studied, and it tries to do justice to these understandings in its reports to outsiders.

(b) *Anti-ethnocentricity and relevance*: Ethnography normally questions the oversimplifications in influential discourse, and interrogates prevailing definitions.

(c) *Cultural ecologies*: Ethnography focuses on a number of different levels/dimensions of socio-cultural organisation/process at the same time, and assumes that the meaning and significance of a form or practice involves an interaction between these (and other) levels/dimensions.

(d) *Systems and particularity:* Ethnography looks for patterns and systematicity in situated everyday practice, but it recognises that hasty comparison across cases can blind you to the contingent moments and the complex cultural and semiotic ecologies that give any phenomenon its meaning (see [c]). Ethnography seeks to produce theoretically 'telling' (rather than typical) cases, using 'the particular circumstances surrounding a case ... to make previously obscure theoretical relationships suddenly apparent' (Mitchell 1984: 239), and it demands our attention for the 'delicacy of its distinctions [rather than] the sweep of its abstractions' (Geertz 1973: 25).

(e) *Sensitising concepts, openness to data, and worries about idealisation*: Ethnographic analysis works with 'sensitising' concepts 'suggest[ing] directions along which to look' rather than with 'definitive' constructs 'provid[ing] prescriptions of what to see' (Blumer 1969: 148). Questions may change during the course of an enquiry, and the dialectic between theory, interpretation and data is sustained throughout (Hymes [1978] 1996: 10ff.). Although it recognises that selectivity and idealisation are intrinsic to data, ethnographic analysis tries to stay alert to the potential consequentiality of what gets left out.

(f) *Reflexivity and participation*: Ethnography recognises the ineradicable role that the researcher's personal subjectivity plays throughout the research process. It looks to systematic field strategies and to accountable analytic procedures to constrain self-indulgent idiosyncrasy, and expects researchers to face up to the partiality of their interpretations (Hymes [1978] 1996: 13). But the researcher's own cultural and interpretive capacities are crucial in making sense of the complex intricacies of situated everyday activity among the people being studied, and tuning into these takes time and close involvement.

(g) *The irreducibility of experience*: Ethnography's commitment to particularity and participation ([d] & [f]) combine with its concerns about idealisation ([e]) to produce a strong sense of what is unique and 'once-only' in situated acts and interactions (see Willis & Trondman 2001 on 'this-ness'). Ethnographic writing is often tempered by a sense of the limitations of available forms of representation, and it recognises that there is an important element in actions and events that eludes analysis and can only be intimated or aesthetically evoked (Hymes [1978] 1996: 12, 118).

Linguistics is also a highly contested field. There are a number of very robust linguistic sub-disciplines which treat language as an autonomous system, separating it from the social contexts in which it is used, and there are also varied, large and long traditions of research which have addressed language, culture and society together, using both linguistics and ethnography. But whatever their views on which aspects of language are worth studying, cursory inspection of any textbook or reference work (e.g. Crystal 2010) shows that among linguists, as well as among many linguistically oriented discourse analysts, it is widely accepted that:

- language is universal among humans, at the same time as changing over time and varying across social groups (of different sizes, durations and locations);
- it is possible to isolate and abstract structural patterns in the ways in which people communicate, and that many of these patterns are relatively stable, recurrent and socially shared (to different degrees);
- there is a wide range of quite well-established procedures for isolating and identifying these structures;
- the description and analysis of these patterns benefits from the use of technical vocabularies; and
- although there is certainly much more involved in human communication, these technical vocabularies can make a valuable contribution to our understanding of the highly intricate processes involved when people talk, sign, read, write or otherwise communicate.

When the tenets of linguistics and ethnography are set together like this, substantial differences stand out, both in method and aspiration. In linguistics, the empirical procedures – the elicitation techniques, the processes of idealisation and data preparation, and the rules of evidence – are relatively standardised and they are often taken more or less for granted, at least within particular schools and paradigms. The social and personal processes that have brought the researcher to the level of understanding where s/he could start to formulate linguistic rules are seen as relatively insignificant. In contrast in ethnography, participant-observation plays a major role, and the processes involved in learning and adjusting to different cultural practices are themselves regarded as potentially consequential for the analysis. The researcher's presence/ prominence in the field defies standardisation and it introduces a range of contingencies and partialities that really need to be addressed and reported.

The differences also often extend to the goals of research. Linguistics usually seeks to generalise about language structure and use, and typically only looks beyond what is actually said/signed/written when implied meaning is highly conventionalised (as in, for example, 'presupposition' and 'implicature'). In contrast, ethnography dwells longer in situated particularities, and this difference between them shows up in their finished products. Ethnographies involve rhetorical forms, such as vignettes and narratives (Hymes 1996:12–13), that are designed to provide the reader with some apprehension of the fullness and irreducibility of the 'lived stuff' from which the analyst has abstracted structure. Grammars normally don't.

Plainly, this book is founded on the belief that the differences between linguistics and ethnography certainly do *not* amount to incompatibility, and among its contributors there is a broad consensus that:

  (i) the contexts for communication should be investigated rather than assumed. Meaning takes shape within specific social relations, interactional histories and institutional regimes, produced and construed by agents with expectations and repertoires that have to be grasped ethnographically.
 (ii) analysis of the internal organisation of verbal (and other kinds of semiotic) data is essential to understanding its significance and position in the world. Meaning is far more than just the 'expression of ideas', and biography, identifications, stance and nuance are extensively signalled in the linguistic and textual fine-grain.

In fact, this formulation can also cover a much larger and older body of scholarship on language and culture, and it also allows differences in emphasis, so that in some research,

• ethnography serves as a way of enriching a fundamentally linguistic project, as in, for example, Eckert's research on language change (2000), or Levinson's cultural model of cognition (1996);

while in other work,

• linguistics can be a way of helping researchers with a range of different backgrounds to reach deeper into the ethnographic description of social or institutional processes (cf. Sapir 1929/1949: 166; Hymes 1996: 8).

But whichever way the balance tilts, a number of processes have added impetus to the integration of linguistics and ethnography in recent years, and it is worth describing these in more detail.

Although the history of their relationship reaches back much further, Gumperz and Hymes' seminal 1972 edited collection, *Directions in Sociolinguistics: The Ethnography of Communication*, provides a useful reference point from which to sketch these recent developments. The volume brought contributors together from very different backgrounds in linguistics, anthropology, sociology and psychology, and Hymes' first chapter explained that '[i]n order to develop models, or theories, of the interaction of language and social life, there must be ... an approach [to description] that partly links, but partly cuts across, partly builds between ... the disciplines' (1972: 41). Some of the chapters used socio-cultural methods to enhance the analysis of linguistic structure (e.g. Labov), and others drew linguistics into the examination of principally cultural questions (e.g. Bernstein). But since then, much has changed, both in the organisation of academic knowledge and in real-world experience, and there have been at least three major shifts which have affected the linguistics/ethnography relationship.

First, the development of post-structuralism has weakened the authority of formal structural linguistics as an epistemological reference point. During the post-war hey-day of structuralism, there was widespread anxiety that the humanities and social sciences were 'pre-scientific' (Hymes 1983:196), and linguistics was held up as a model for the scientific study of culture as an integrated system – indeed, suggests Hymes, the intensity of US anthropologists' interest in linguistics as a key to the organisation of culture was matched by linguists' lack of regard for ethnography. But since the 1970s, there has been a decline in the cross-disciplinary significance of formal linguistics as a model of knowledge production. With the emergence of post-structuralism, burgeoning interest in agency, fragmentation and contingency has weakened the linguist's traditional assumption that system and coherence were there in their data, just waiting to be discovered. Linguists' claims to the scientific status of their knowledge have also been relativised by growth in the belief that knowledges are situated and plural, and indeed it is now quite commonly felt that the natural sciences have themselves been worryingly 'pre-social', with ethnography and other forms of contextual study being invoked as necessary correctives (Gibbons et al. 1994:99).

Second, the critique associated with post-structuralism has of course entailed much more than just dislodging linguistics from its former pre-eminence. Received notions like 'society', 'nation', 'community', 'gender' and 'ethnicity' have also been the subject of extensive reassessment, so that now, rather than being seen as natural and unchangeable entities or identities, the default position in a great deal of social science is that these are social constructions, produced in discourse and ideology (see e.g. Foucault 1972; Anderson 1981). In addition, beyond the academy, established categories in social analysis and policy have been profoundly challenged by the material, real-world changes associated with globalisation, with massively increased population mobility and rapid developments in communication technology (Vertovec 2007; Platt 2008; Blommaert & Rampton 2011). The implications of these changes for empirical research are at least twofold:

(a) Ethnography becomes an invaluable resource. One of ethnography's key characteristics is its commitment to taking a long hard look at empirical processes that make no sense within established frameworks, and if right now we are experiencing a period where traditional frameworks are actually looking a lot less well-established than they used to, then ethnography is one important option to turn to. But, at the same time,

(b) if we relax the strictures of formalist theory and draw instead on its power as a resource for describing the patterns in communication, linguistics comes to the fore as a vital ingredient in the development of empirical analyses tuned to the contemporary material and philosophical environment. With post-structuralist critiques of essentialism firmly in place, it is conceptually now rather hard to justify any project that sets out to analyse particular peoples, groups and communities. Rather, the challenge is to understand how these group identities get constructed in culture, discourse and ideology, and how humans come to inhabit these social categories in ways that are both similar and different. So instead of, for example, setting out to study the Roma in Hungary, the aim should be to analyse how 'Roma' circulates as a representation in Hungarian discourse, how it settles on particular humans, how it comes to channel and constrain their activity and material position (cf. Tremlett 2008; see also Moerman 1974: 62). Once we make these commitments, linguistics becomes highly relevant. Categories and identities get circulated, taken up and reproduced in textual representations and communicative encounters, and so if we want to understand the social and cultural construction of identities, persons and groups, linguistics will help us take a serious look at the discursive processes.

Third, at least in the UK, the social sciences have seen a substantial shift in the dynamics of interdisciplinary knowledge production itself, moving from what researchers have termed 'Mode 1 interdisciplinarity' to 'Mode 2' (Gibbons et al. 1994). In Mode 1 interdisciplinarity, focal problems are identified within a particular (sub-)discipline, and there is cross-referencing to other paradigms or lines of research in order to get past a bottle-neck that researchers have reached using only the concepts and methods available within their own discipline. The rationales for cross-referencing, and the parameters of what to include and leave out, are set fairly clearly, and there is a well-defined sense of exactly what kinds of methodological borrowing and combination are in order. In contrast, in 'Mode 2' interdisciplinarity, 'real-world' issues of social, technical and/or policy relevance provide the starting point; there may be non-academic 'stake-holders' involved throughout; and it is the multi-dimensional complexity of the problem that motivates the mixing. Quite a high tolerance for ambiguity is required, and it is important not to commit too quickly to the specification of the key methods and dimensions of analysis. In the 1972 Gumperz and Hymes collection, there was a strong awareness of real-world issues (e.g. pp. 10, 13, 38, 53), but the interdisciplinary project was itself formulated in principally Mode 1 terms: linguistics was thought to have reached a cul-de-sac; there was a considerable discussion of methods for future work (e.g. pp. 23ff., 36); and the goal was to create 'a basic science that does not yet exist' (Hymes 1972: 38). In contrast, over the last 15 years in the UK (and elsewhere), the research and higher education funding councils have increased the emphasis on interdisciplinary work that takes real-world problems as a starting point, that involves collaboration with stakeholders and that reckons explicitly with impacts beyond the academy. The upshot is that in, for example, a recent study by Abreu et al. (2009), 60% of British social scientists were reported working with public sector partners, 45% with the third sector, 45% with both, and around 40% with the private sector (*Times Higher Education*, 25/6/09). This shift towards interdisciplinary research involving non-academic impacts and collaboration looks increasingly well-embedded (Gibbons et al. 1994; Bernstein 1996: 68; Strathern 2000), and if ethnography is characterised by a commitment to dialogue and to adaptive sensitivity to feedback from different audiences (e.g. Hymes 1996: 7), then Mode 2 interdisciplinarity may be especially compatible with an ethnographic sensibility.

These three shifts – the philosophical shifts associated with post-structuralism, the real-world changes effected by globalisation, and the emphasis on Mode 2 interdisciplinarity in research funding policy – impact on ethnography's status in the relationship with linguistics. Before, ethnography could simply be seen as an additional method of data-collection, supplementing the otherwise standard procedures of elicitation and analysis in linguistic science. But as we become more conscious of the social and historical particularity of knowledge, ethnography gains foundational weight as a way of seeing, building on dialogue and on a reflexive recognition of the researcher's own positioning. Instead, it is linguistics that becomes the operational resource, prized for its capacity to spotlight even the very smallest moves in the practical negotiation of social relations, but no longer revered as the path from interpretation to objective science. At the same time, perhaps somewhat paradoxically, this decline in the epistemological authority of linguistics opens the door to fuller interdisciplinary engagement, increasing the scope for combining its powerful techniques and findings on communication with the pursuit of issues and agendas formed elsewhere. This is something that Duranti reports in a historical survey of linguistic anthropology in the US:

> In contrast to earlier generations ... students today typically ask "What can the study of language contribute to the understanding of this particular social/cultural phenomenon (e.g. identity formation, globalisation, nationalism)?" ... for many young scholars today linguistic anthropology is a tool for studying what is *already* being studied by scholars in other fields, for instance, race and racism.
>
> (2003: 332–3)

Duranti's characterisation is compatible with a great deal of the work in linguistic ethnography in Britain and Europe, and this perspective also seems to be growing more influential in sociolinguistics more generally. In their Introduction to the 2nd edition of *The New Sociolinguistics Reader* (2009), Coupland and Jaworski see contemporary sociolinguistics as 'a broad and vibrant interdisciplinary project working *across* the different disciplines that were its origins [sociology, linguistics, social psychology, interactional sociolinguistics, discourse analysis]', and of the papers they include in the collection, 'a clear majority ... favour more open-ended, observational research methods and smaller-scale data ... This is the *ethnographic* research design that has considerable momentum in modern Sociolinguistics' (2009: 19; original emphasis).

So far, then, we have offered an outline of the fundamental characteristics of ethnography and linguistics, and described recent processes that have given momentum to their combination in linguistic ethnography. Gumperz and Hymes' (1972) volume featured as the starting point for our historical comments, and in fact it also serves as an excellent point of departure for the next section of this chapter, in which we review some key concepts for linguistic ethnography, focusing on the elements interacting in communication.

2.   Describing the elements interacting in communication

In the preface to their 1972 collection, Gumperz and Hymes took the view that the 'ready currency of the term *sociolinguistics* ... does not reflect fundamental agreement on common problems, sources of data, or methods of analysis ... [R]ecent publications ... have, so far, not been integrated into any general theory of language and society' (pp. vi–vii). Since 1972, however, the study of language, culture and society has undergone a huge process of disciplinary consolidation and refinement, especially in linguistic anthropology in North America (cf. Duranti 2003), and these developments have provided invaluable theoretical resources for contemporary linguistic ethnography, certainly in the UK and Europe. Following in Gumperz and Hymes' path, scholars such as Ochs, Silverstein, Bauman, the Goodwins, Hanks, Briggs, Blommaert and Agha have produced a remarkably coherent vocabulary that is not only congruent with ethnography but is also capable of producing detailed descriptions of the processes that are of central concern to theories of social practice, with practice understood as the 'production and reproduction of society ... as a skilled [but by no means wholly conscious] performance on the part of its members' (Giddens 1976: 160; Bourdieu 1977; Ortner 2006).

Blommaert provides an encapsulation of the perspective, tracing it back once again to Gumperz and Hymes. In sociolinguistics, he says, there is 'a very long tradition in which language, along with other social and cultural features of people, was primarily imagined relatively fixed in time and space ... Gumperz and Hymes (1972: 15), however ... destabilized these assumptions ... they defined social and linguistic features not as separate-but-connected, but as *dialectic*, i.e. co-constructive and, hence, *dynamic*' (Blommaert 2012: 11–12). This emphasis on the dynamic co-construction of social order and linguistic meaning can be found in Gumperz's call for 'closer understanding of how linguistic signs *interact* with social knowledge in discourse' (Gumperz 1982: 29 [emphasis added]), and it also matches Silverstein's succinct formulation of the 'total linguistic fact': '[t]he total linguistic fact, the datum for a science of language is irreducibly dialectic in nature. It is an unstable mutual interaction of meaningful sign forms, contextualised to situations of interested human use and mediated by the fact of cultural ideology' (1985: 220; see also Hanks 1996: 230). This contrasts sharply with structuralist linguistics, in which the formal properties of language are treated independently of their use (as in Saussure's 'langue' and Chomsky's 'competence'). But there is no surrender in analytic precision, and a flourishing linguistic anthropological literature has done much to achieve another of the goals outlined in 1972: 'to explain the meaning of language in human life ... and not in the abstract, not in the superficial phrases one may encounter in essays and textbooks, but in the concrete, in actual human lives' (Hymes 1972: 41).

So what are the central concepts and perspectives in the 'general theory of language and society' that has now emerged? Fuller exposition of a much wider range of ideas can be found in textbooks such as Duranti (1997), Blommaert (2005), Agha (2007) or Ahearn (2012), but to give an indication of the scope and tenor of this apparatus, it is worth outlining three sets of concepts, which in turn illustrate or engage with:

- dynamic contingency, reckoning with human agency and interpretation – the concepts of inferencing, indexicality and reflexivity;
- convention, structure and the building blocks of institutions, pointing to patterns and expectations of regularity ingrained in our practical consciousness and everyday activity – the notions of genre and register; and
- histories, outcomes and material processes beyond, before and after specific communicative encounters, expanding the spatio-temporal horizons of empirical description – multimodality, textual trajectories and contextual processes of different scales.

'Inferencing' refers to the interpretive work that people perform in trying to reconcile the stuff that they encounter in any given situation with their prior understanding. It refers to the normally effortless sense-making that occurs when people work out the significance of a word, an utterance, an action or an object by matching it against their past experience, against their expectations of what's coming up, their perceptions of the material setting and so forth. The term 'indexicality' is complementary, though it shifts the focus from sense-making to the utterances, things and actions that are treated as signs, and it refers to the fact that these signs are always taken as pointing beyond themselves, to something else in the past, the future or the surrounding environment. So for example, when a word, phrase or sentence is used in communication, it is always taken as a lot more than just its dictionary definition or literal meaning, important though these are. In addition, it will be assessed for, for example, its fit to the visible location, its stylistic elegance, its consistency with the speaker's usual ways of talking etc.

This process of assessment, calibrating the words you hear with your sense of the (dynamically evolving) situation, is referred to as 'meta-pragmatic' reflexivity, and it is a feature of speaking as well as listening. When someone formulates an utterance, it is more than just the semantic proposition that they construct. They also produce a whole host of small vocal signs that evoke, for example, a certain level of formality (selecting 'request' rather than 'ask'), or that point to the presence of bystanders (talking quietly), and this non-stop process of contextualisation may either reassure their listener that they're operating with a broadly shared understanding of the situation, or it can nudge the recipient's inferences in another direction. A lot of this processing is relatively tacit, with participants constantly engaged in low-key monitoring of how all the details of verbal communication fit with their grasp of the propositions being expressed, with their sense of the speaker's intent, with their understanding of the activity they are in and how it should proceed etc. But it only takes a slight deviation from the habitual, a small move beyond expected patterns of variation in the way that somebody speaks or acts, to send recipients into inferential over-drive, wondering what's going on when a sound, a word, a grammatical pattern, a discourse move or bodily gesture doesn't quite match: should I ignore or respond to this? Is it a joke or serious? What ties these apparently unconnected ideas together? Does the speaker still have their institutional hat on or are they now suddenly claiming solidarity with a particular group? (cf. E.M. Forster: 'A pause in the wrong place, an intonation misunderstood, and a whole conversation went awry' [1924] 1973: 267).

There are two general points to draw out from this account. The first concerns the relationship between language and context. As we have seen, word denotation, the formal structures of grammar and the propositional meaning of sentences still count, but they lose their traditional supremacy in linguistic study, and instead become just one among a large array of semiotic resources available for the local production and interpretation of meaning (cf. Hanks 1996; Verschueren 1999). At the same time, the conceptualisation of 'context' also changes. Rather than being 'separate-but-connected' as the relatively static, external and determining reference point traditionally added to language analysis as something of an afterthought – what Drew and Heritage call the 'bucket' theory of context (1992: 19) – context is conceived as dynamic, interactively accomplished, and intrinsic to communication. Language is pervasively indexical, continuously pointing to persons, practices, settings, objects and ideas that never get explicitly expressed. As people try to make sense to each other, contexts are constantly invoked, ratified and shifted by semiotic signs.

Second, context here is an understanding of the social world activated in the midst of things, an understanding of the social world that is also interactionally ratified or undermined from one moment to the next as the participants in an encounter respond to one another. In fact, when people engage with one another, there is considerable scope for social difference in the norms and expectations that individuals orient to, as well as in the kinds of thing they notice as discrepant, and there can also be a great range in the indexical interpretations that they bring to bear ('good' or 'bad', 'right' or 'wrong', 'art' or 'error', 'call it out' or 'let it pass', 'typical of this or that'). But the normative expectations and explanatory accounts activated like this in the interactional present seldom come from nowhere. Instead, they instantiate discourses that the participants have picked up through prior involvement in socio-communicative networks that can range in scale from intimate relationships and friendship groups to national education systems and global media. In this way, the notions of inferencing, indexicality and reflexive evaluation offer us a way of seeing how more widely circulating ideologies infuse the quick of activity in the here-and-now, even though this is integrated with an acute sensitivity of the participants' skilled agency.

With inference, indexicality and reflexivity, analytic attention leans towards agency in the ceaseless interplay of agency and structure, even though normative expectations and their social currency and origins follow very closely in the account. With **genre**, the balance tilts towards stability, structure and convention, though here too, there is an inextricable role for both agentive action and unpredictable contingency.

In the tradition associated with Bakhtin ([1953] 1986; Hanks 1987; Bauman 2001), a genre is a distinct set of conventionalised expectations about a recognisable type of activity that is also often named – for instance, an argument, a sales transaction, a committee meeting, a game of poker, reading the newspaper. These expectations include a sense of the goals and possible tasks on hand, the roles and relationships typically involved, the ways the activity is organised, and the kinds of resource suited to carrying it out. Genres help us construe what is happening in interaction and to work out the direction of activity from one moment to the next, and they channel the kind of inferences we make (e.g. laughing or being alarmed by some drastic report, depending on whether or not it's told in a joke): 'Genres guide us through the social world of communication: they allow us to distinguish between very different communicative events, create expectations for each of them, and adjust our communicative behaviour accordingly' (Blommaert nd; Gumperz 1972: 16–18).

In their potential for stability, genres are one of the building blocks of institutions – think of lessons, detentions, and assemblies in a school, or consultations and ward rounds in a hospital. While genres provide the larger bearings that orient our moment-to-moment micro-scale actions on the one hand, they also constitute some of the smallest units in the structural organisation of large-scale institutions on the other. Indeed Bakhtin saw genres as 'the drive belts from the history of society to the history of language' (1986:65). But the stability of genres is only ever temporary: '[a] genre ... [cannot] be viewed as a finished product unto itself, but remain[s] partial and transitional ... Because they are at least partly created in their enactment, ... genres are schematic and incomplete resources on which speakers necessarily improvise in practice' (Hanks 1987: 681,687). Genres have to be 'accomplished' or 'brought off' in interaction, and participants have to keep checking that they're all tuning to the same stage in the activity, giving and noting indexical signs that, for example, an event should now be moving to a close. There is plenty of scope for failures in generic coordination, and for the participants to be judged as socially insensitive, awkward or incompetent (or maybe just as the unlucky victims of disruptive intrusions from outside). Knowledge and expertise in different genres is of course very unevenly spread among individuals and across social groups, and properly genred performance is a central concern in socialisation throughout the lifespan, whether this involves learning to 'behave nicely at the dinner table' or to 'write a history essay'. As encapsulated visions of the social world tuned to practical action in recurrent situations, projecting particular kinds of conduct and relationship, promising the participants with particular types of personhood, genres are crucial to social reproduction, and they can become the focus of intense struggle as people and institutions try to fix or change their own and others' practice or potential (as can be seen, for example, in repeated UK government attempts to reformat classroom pedagogy and interaction [Rampton & Harris 2010]). But because there is no 'timeless closure' or 'unlimited replication' intrinsic to any genre (Bauman 2001: 81), a great deal of ideological work (for instance, training, publicity, penalties, consultant advice) is often needed if the preferred genres are to remain steadily in place.

With **'register'** (or 'style'), we move from the conventionalisation of situations and the arrangements for communicative interaction in genre to relatively stable patterning among the signs in speech and discourse (Gumperz & Hymes 1972: 21; Agha 2007; Auer 2007; Eckert 2008). Among other things, register covers accent and dialect, which are very commonly seen as reflections of social structure, marking differences in ethnicity, class, region, generation and/or gender. Conceptually, register is quite close to the well-established sociolinguistic notion of 'variety', but whereas sociolinguistics has traditionally treated the relationship between varieties and social structure as a 'separate-but-connected' correlation, the linguistic anthropological notion of register or style is once again aligned with the interaction of form, ideology and situated action identified in Silverstein's total linguistic fact.

Registers are distinctive sets of linguistic and other semiotic signs that get indexically associated with different types of person, group, activity or situation (they can also contribute to the differentiation of genres). The typification process that is crucial to the recognition of a register involves inferring e.g. that someone's from the north of England because of the way they pronounce 'bath' and 'one', that they've had an expensive private education when they say 'yaaa' rather than 'yeh' or 'yes', or that they've got a medical background because of the words they use to talk about bodies. Of course this linkage depends on our perceptions of stratified and segmented social space, which are themselves an aspect of ideology (Bourdieu 1991; Irvine 2001: 23–4). So whenever we make a spontaneous link between a speech sound and a social type, ideology is once again integral to locally situated sense-making, often with subsequent interactional effects (maybe increasing the participants' rapport, or alternatively undermining their self-confidence). The 'language ideological' practices that forge or reproduce these links between ways of speaking and social types can vary a great deal in their scale, explicitness and intensity, ranging from curriculum instruction and mass-mediated impersonations to fleeting self-corrections in conversations face-to-face. And register is often a resource for agentive action, as when, for example, pupils in a working-class urban school respond to being patronised by their teacher with a very exaggerated upper-class accent, even though they hardly ever refer to social class explicitly (Rampton 2006: Part III). More generally, though, register draws our attention to the fact that in the stream of linguistic expression that people produce together, they are continuously vulnerable to a reflexive process of low-key socio-ideological observation and coding, in ways that are far more enacted than declared (cf. G. B. Shaw's '[i]t is impossible for an Englishman to open his mouth without making some other Englishman hate or despise him' [1916: Preface]).

When other social scientists read sociolinguistic accounts of interactional practice, they are sometimes struck by the agility and speed with which participants adjust or shift their stance, position or self-projection, and this sometimes leads to talk of identities being 'multiple, fluid and ambiguous'. There is at least some justification for this if these accounts of interactional positioning are compared with static demographic identity ascriptions of the kind often used in studies which treat language and society as separate-but-connected, and plainly, the production, interpretation and reflexive monitoring are all agentive processes. But communication entails close and continual attunement among the participants, calibrating what's produced with the range of patterns one has hitherto come to expect, and there is often considerable socio-ideological investment in these expectations. This was clear in the discussion of genre and register, referring to the patterns of expectation for, respectively, the arrangements of activity and the stream of signs, and the proprieties regimenting communicative conduct reach much further. Yes, the normative expectations orienting our interaction certainly do shift as we move from one scene to another in our daily routine, and the opportunities for individual innovation can certainly be greater in some than in others. But there are pressures and constraints all the same, reaching right down into the way we formulate the smallest pieces of language. Rather than exemplifying the inherent fluidity of identity production, creativity is more aptly seen as the fleeting exploitation of what Erickson (2001) calls 'wiggle-room' – just a little bit of space for innovation within what's otherwise experienced as the compelling weight of social expectation (see also Rampton 2009).

It should be clear by now that although the perspective we are outlining offers an exceptionally sharp view of activity 'on-line' in the present, it also implies longer temporalities. Nevertheless, Gumperz and Hymes' early research programme centred on the 'speech event', and expansion in the spatio-temporal horizons of theory and analysis has been one of the most important developments since Gumperz and Hymes (1972).

Following scholars like Goffman and the Goodwins, there has been systematic attention to non-linguistic sign systems and to the fact that communication is always 'multimodal' with bodies, places and visual perception playing a major part. As C. Goodwin explains, 'the [human] body [is] an unfolding locus for the display of meaning and action' (2000: 1517), and eye gaze, hand gestures, head movement and the posture, movement and positioning of bodies all contribute to this. Obviously, these are themselves affected by material objects and the natural and built environment – compare the scope for expression in a cinema and a dinner table or a park bench – and although the material substance and surround is often treated as irrelevant (as when e.g. the readers of this chapter take the font and paper quality for granted), there are innumerable occasions when our level of attention to it increases (referring to objects, changing location, getting dressed, cleaning, clearing away). In addition, even though we are often only dimly aware of them (if that!), much of our material environment bears the traces of past designs, efforts and resource expenditures (Blommaert 2013).

When the relative durability of physical matter is combined with our capacity to inscribe it with meaning, individual events are positioned within much longer spans of time. The production and interpretation of meaning in the here-and-now becomes just one stage in the mobility of signs and texts, and participants are seen as themselves actively orienting backwards and forwards to the 'trajectories' through which their semiotic products travel (Briggs 2005). Whereas event-centred sociolinguistics had earlier focused on the local use-value of a particular communicative sign or practice, studying its effect within a given encounter, the 'exchange value' of a sign, text or semiotic object now enters the reckoning, and '*en*textualisation' and '*re*contextualisation' become key terms, addressing (a) the (potentially multiple) people and processes involved in the design or selection of textual 'projectiles' which have some hope of travelling into subsequent settings, and (b) the alteration and revaluation of semiotic objects as they are subsequently taken up in different settings (Bauman and Briggs 1990; Silverstein and Urban 1996; Agha and Wortham 2005).

Interest in the projection and circulation of texts and signs across different events and settings invites comparative analysis of the scale of the networks, media, materials and processes in which these signs travel – their spatial scope, temporal durability and social reach (Scollon & Scollon 2004; Pennycook 2007, 2010; Blommaert 2008, 2010a). Earlier, we discussed the shift away from context-as-'bucket' to context-as-process, but this itself now needs to be conceptualised as layered and 'multi-scalar' (Hymes 1972: 53; Cicourel 1992; Blommaert 2010a). The contexts in which people communicate are partly local and emergent, continuously readjusted to the contingencies of action unfolding from one moment to the next, but they are also infused with information, resources, expectations and experiences that originate in, circulate through, and/or are destined for networks, media and processes that can be very different in their reach and duration. This is vividly illustrated in Tusting's account of a few minutes in the work of a nursery nurse in an nursery, attending to small children while also trying to fill in a form she has been given for recording her observations of individuals:

> The process of writing the observation integrates the immediate activities in the room into broader social systems, and to systems at longer timescales. These broader and longer-term systems include (among others) the interpersonal relationships in the room; the Early Years Centre and its planning procedures; Thea's lifespan, career and training; and government policy and inspection. Each of these is associated with different goals and plays out at different timescales. This is an example of a situated activity which locally produces and reproduces broader social orders.
>
> (Tusting 2010: 85)

Gumperz emphasised the importance of embedding interactional encounters within broader spatio-temporal processes when he called for a 'dynamic view of social environments where history, economic forces and interactive processes ... combine to create or to eliminate social distinctions' (1982: 29). Notions like multimodality, textual trajectory and multi-scalar context increase our capacity to provide this. Admittedly, the job of describing the processes at play in any layered notion of context is challenging, requiring engagement with, if not expertise in, not just linguistics but potentially also history, economics, sociology, cultural studies, international relations and so forth. But it is worth reflecting on the account of ideology that this apparatus can bring to interdisciplinary research. In a great deal of policy and interview discourse analysis, ideology gets treated only as sets of explicitly articulated statements, but compare this with our portrait of tacit power emerging from ideology's links to inference and indexicality, or of ideological investment and struggle over genres and registers, both of them potentially inscribed in practical consciousness. Equally, if we take up the notion of textual trajectories and study what actually gets entextualised and what subsequently succeeds in carrying forward – or even translates into higher scale processes – then we can bring considerable empirical precision to political notions of 'hearability' and 'voice' (Hymes 1996; Mehan 1996; Briggs 1997; Blommaert 2005). In short, the apparatus developed in linguistic anthropology allows us to trace the palpable mundane reality of wide-spread societal ideologies through close scrutiny of discursive and contextual processes, and there is a good case for saying that this layered, multi-scalar and empirically grounded understanding of ideology is one of the most sophisticated in current social science (Blommaert & Rampton 2011: 13).

So that is a glimpse of the *instrumentarium* of contemporary linguistic anthropology, and it immediately gives rise to a question about our own disciplinary positioning: if linguistic anthropology is such a rich resource for the theory and description of communication in contemporary conditions, how come this book and chapter refer to linguistic *ethnography*, not anthropology, in their titles? There are two reasons. First, because for the most part, we are not anthropologists ourselves (and there hasn't been a great deal of interest in the details of communication in British or European anthropology [cf. Rampton 2007: 586]). Second, like Hymes, Gumperz and many others, we are convinced that the concepts and methods we are describing have potential relevance that reaches much further than anthropology – relevance both for other disciplines such as sociology, psychology or management studies, and for engagement with professionals such as teachers, doctors and social workers.

We will address this relevance in the next two sections. The section titled 'Linguistic ethnography in interdisciplinary training' discusses linguistic ethnography's interdisciplinary relevance, using the example of an interdisciplinary training programme to show that this is much more than only a token claim. And then the section titled 'Linguistic ethnography and non-academic professions' reflects on the encounter between linguistic ethnography and non-academic professionals, considering processes of re-socialisation and collaborative research in educational and medical settings.

3.   Linguistic ethnography in interdisciplinary training

In the previous section, we outlined some central concepts developed in linguistic anthropology, and argued for the distinctiveness of their contribution to contemporary debates about social process. Words like 'contingent', 'fluid' and 'unstable' are now frequently repeated in the social sciences, and there is widespread recognition that in order to grasp the new complexities of the contemporary period, the vocabularies of empirical analysis need to be extensively refurbished. We have claimed that through our alignment with linguistic anthropology, we have access to a set of very robust tools that can help repair this deficit in the resources for empirical analysis, and it is worth now showing that this claim to interdisciplinary relevance isn't just an empty boast.

To do so, we will describe a research training programme that we have been running for doctoral and post-doctoral researchers across the social sciences since 2007, originally funded by the UK Economic and Social Research Council (the tutors have been Jeff Bezemer, Jan Blommaert, Carey Jewitt, Adam Lefstein, Ben Rampton (director), Celia Roberts, and Julia Snell). The programme is entitled *Ethnography, Language & Communication* (ELC); it is targeted at researchers facing the challenge of analysing the data they have collected – it is advertised with the headlines *'Is "qualitative data analysis" too vague for you? Are you wondering how to do justice to your data?'*; it has consisted of intensive two- to five-day summer schools, master-classes (with distinguished US researchers such as Elinor Ochs and Ray McDermott), data sessions and day workshops variously thematising education, asylum, health and new media; and in the period 2007–10, there were 650–700 participants in the programme, coming from, *inter alia*, applied and sociolinguistics, health, education, management, psychology, sociology, anthropology. The participants generally responded to the programme very positively in their formal evaluations of it, and our belief in the cross-disciplinary resonance of concepts from linguistic anthropology has been considerably strengthened by our own first-hand experience of the teaching. Indeed within this general context of interdisciplinary interaction, it is worth dwelling longer on the programme (i) because it offers illumination of our approach to enriching ethnography with linguistics; (ii) because we have found a form of teaching that seems to avoid reification, even though pedagogic simplification often threatens to extinguish the kinds of interactive dynamism that we are identifying at the heart of linguistic ethnography; and (iii) because this will allow us to address some of the criticisms of linguistic ethnography as an interdisciplinary endeavour.

In the ELC programme curriculum, we capitalise on ethnography's wide dispersion across the social sciences by assuming that the participants already know about it, and our teaching focuses on the analytic resources offered by sociolinguistics and linguistic anthropology. There are no sessions on ethnographic interviewing or participant observation, and instead we get students to engage with authors or traditions like Goffman, Gumperz, conversation analysis, Goodwin and Goodwin, Briggs and Mehan. This points to a pattern of hybridisation that is likely to occur much more widely in linguistic ethnography. Although we see the LE enterprise as fundamentally ethnographic in character, bringing the priorities and perspectives sketched in the section titled 'Ethnography, linguistics and linguistic ethnography' (a)–(g) to bear on a range of different topics, it is the linguistics that makes our own contribution really distinctive. What our programme offers students are analytic tools from linguistics and discourse analysis embedded in an ethnographic epistemology (cf. the section titled 'Ethnography, linguistics and linguistic ethnography' above; Blommaert 2007). This means that the apparatus of linguistics and of discourse analysis are treated as a set of 'sensitising' concepts, and these have to be applied with reflexive understanding of the researcher's own participation in the circulation of power/knowledge. Once the linguistic apparatus is epistemologically repositioned like this – repositioned as just the extension of ethnography into intricate zones of culture and society that might otherwise be missed – then linguistics offers a very rich and empirically robust collection of frameworks and procedures for exploring the details of social life, also providing a very full range of highly suggestive – but not binding! – proposals about how they pattern together.

So how do we teach linguistics as a set of sensitising concepts? Indeed, how do we prevent students from forgetting the dialectical dynamism encapsulated in the 'total linguistic fact'? There are two steps.

First, focussing on what we have categorised as 'micro', 'genre', 'multimodal' and 'transcontextual' analysis, we provide an accessible distillation of key frameworks and methods, extracting ideas like 'adjacency' and 'entextualisation' from the intellectual traditions in which they gather so much (doctrinal) weight and authority. Of course we acknowledge that sub-disciplinary disputes between, say, Critical Discourse Analysis and Conversation Analysis, do matter, but we tell course participants that these are for later, once they have decided that these analytic perspectives are really worth pursuing. Instead, in regular stock-taking discussions, we push students to be realistic and reflexive in their appropriation of what we are offering, getting them to consider, for example, 'What are the limitations of Linguistic Ethnography?'; 'Could I successfully defend this approach in my viva examination or a job talk?'

Second – and this is also particularly important for students who already have some background in linguistics – we put the apparatus to use in data sessions, quite often working on data that the course participants have provided themselves. In each roughly two hour session, we immerse the students in a recording and its accompanying transcript, running with their interests and interpretations while at the same time pointing to the insights afforded by the new perspectives, and pushing them to make their claims accountable to evidence, with an eye on the perils of under- and over-interpretation (cf. Erickson 1985). The format partly resembles the traditional data-session in conversation analysis – there is emphasis on the aesthetic of 'slowness' and 'smallness' (Silverman 1998), and there are the insistent questions like 'why this now?', 'what next?' etc. (ten Have 1999). But instead of prioritising a drilling down into the sequential machinery of interaction, we also work outwards to larger scale processes, reflecting for example on the data's implications for the next steps in ethnographic fieldwork (see also Scollon & Scollon 2007: 615, 619). In some ways, the data in these sessions functions in a similar way to the vignette in anthropology, where there is always more going on than the analysis discloses. The sessions generate a huge surplus to what any researcher can actually use in their argument, but there is also a much clearer sense of what is going on, and what you can and really can't say about the episode in focus. By the end, participants' initial ideas often look either crude or just plain wrong, and there is a much sharper idea of which aspects of the interaction are amenable to plausible interpretation, as well as a much stronger sense of the dimensions that remain opaque, even though intriguing.

These sessions are highly accessible to people with different disciplinary backgrounds, involving interpretative processes that draw both on their ordinary sense-making capacities as language users, and on their biographical experience, including their knowledge of the sites where the data comes from and their sense of the relevant life worlds. But beyond the enjoyment of the sessions themselves, what can they get out of them?

For many participants, the process of slow, intensive analysis is itself a revelation, disclosing vivid empirical details in the processes of social construction that they had hitherto had little or no conception of. As this ontological re-gearing takes effect, students become clearer about the potential relevance to their own projects of the apparatus we are offering. Of course there are sure to be some people who decide not to make any further use of these tools, but our hope is that their intensive exposure to the tangible, on-line moment-to-moment co-production of social relations has at least put them in a different position intellectually. Even if they revert to the content analysis of field-notes or interview transcripts as their main analytic strategy, we still hope that they retain some residual sense of what they are glossing over. To encourage a degree of more active adoption, we do tell the participants that if there is a small stretch of interaction that forms the crux of an argument that they want to develop, then it is worth double-checking with the concepts and procedures learnt in the data sessions, using them as a safety measure to ensure that they haven't jumped the gun in their first interpretations. More than that, data-session procedures can help to work up a thesis chapter with data they'd initially viewed as poor, insufficient and destined for the bin. And then at the highest level of interdisciplinary engagement, our aim is to provide the participants with the resources for varying the magnification in their analyses, moving flexibly across processes of different scales in line with the development of their arguments and questions. There is no retreat from larger generalisations about contemporary society in linguistic ethnography, and plainly, participants with non-linguistic backgrounds bring a range of sophisticated vocabularies that are very well tuned to the description of historical, political, institutional and other processes. But our overall commitment is to making both academic and political generalisations about social life accountable to the kinds of small-scale everyday activity which we can observe, record and transcribe, and data sessions represent a first arena in which to explore the analytic practices that this entails.

As we have said, when one alters the magnification and shifts from one process to another in a layered and multiscalar view of context, it is necessary to draw on different sets of analytic resources, reading different literatures. This is very well accepted in ethnography (cf. e.g. Burawoy 1998; Hammersley 2007: 694; Scollon & Scollon 2007: 617; Rampton 2006: 390), but the mixing of perspectives is obviously not straightforward, and it can often give rise to some discomfort. Bricolage and eclecticism can sometimes amount to 'factitious amalgamation of dissimilar ideas or theses that look compatible only insofar as they are not clearly conceived' (Angenot 1984: 159, cited in Hammersley 1999: 577). Indeed, we ourselves have been scolded for failing to realise that, for example, 'post-structuralist theory ... sociolinguistic quantitative empirical studies, [and] qualitative conversation analytical work ... are not of the same epistemological status, and therefore they cannot be added up to a single argument' (Koole 2007, reviewing Rampton 2006). But the point is that paradigms don't have to be swallowed whole. Sociolinguistic quantitative studies and conversation analysis can be mixed if one is careful and willing to separate findings and methods from the explanations and interpretations with which they are conventionally packaged. So it is, for example, perfectly possible to work with the fact that there are systematic quantitative differences in the extent to which speakers use particular sounds in particular settings *without* having to buy into the idea that these are produced by variations in 'attention to speech' (cf. Labov 1972). Similarly, it is easy to make very productive use of CA findings on the sequential organisation of talk *without* refusing to consider the participants' ideological interpretations (Wetherell 1998; Schegloff 1999).

In fact this denaturalisation of paradigms is hard to avoid in interdisciplinary dialogues of the kind instantiated in our training programme, and it generates a methodological reflexivity that has to be embraced. In the interdisciplinary regions oriented to real-world problems – 'Mode 2' discussed in the section titled the section titled 'Ethnography, linguistics and linguistic ethnography' – definitions and assumptions are repeatedly relativised and there is 'a continuous process of negotiating authority and relevance' (Roberts and Sarangi 1999:475). There is incessant pressure to account for the particularity of the angles and occlusions that different methods and approaches entail, and one is forced back to fundamentals to try to work out how different things fit together. In the ELC programme, there has been no question of trying to establish the kind of orthodoxies one might expect in a singular discipline like anthropology. As a programme team based outside the institutions and disciplines where individual participants are doing their research, we have had no control over what our short course graduates eventually do with the training we provide; we haven't been able to impose any uniformity in the theoretical questions driving them; and since there are no assessed assignments and they soon return home to the diverse disciplinary departments where their PhDs are examined, we have made no attempt to standardise criteria and monitor the adequacy of their data analyses (Rampton 2007: 594–5; contrast Hymes 1972: 52). Indeed, the training itself could be characterized, albeit a little flippantly, as (a) 'coming together' (b) 'getting down to basics' in the sessions, and then afterwards (c) 'anything goes'. Heightened methodological reflexivity is the only option here, tuned to the task with encouragement from Hymes: '[p]roductive scholars know that problems lead where they will and that relevance commonly leads across disciplinary boundaries' (1969: 44–45).

We turn now to linguistic ethnography's encounter with non-academic professions, where some similar issues emerge but where LE is also likely to face a range of doubts and resistances that are firmly grounded in specific institutions.

4.   Linguistic ethnography and non-academic professions

Interest in the potential links between research and practical intervention runs deep in linguistic ethnography. Carrying across the Atlantic, US linguistic anthropology was welcomed within a very active tradition of applied linguistics in Britain (cf. Rampton 2007: 586–90), and this commitment to practical intervention in real-world processes has gathered momentum with development of Mode 2 interdisciplinarity. So in this section, we look at LE's encounter with non-academic professionals from two perspectives. First, we consider the shifts in orientation involved when, in an experience of re-socialisation, people with backgrounds in education become LE researchers. Second, we discuss what linguistic ethnography looks like when, in contexts of collaborative research, it encounters the very well-established perspectives of professionals in health.

In **research in educational settings**, the stimulus for engaging with linguistic ethnography often starts from an educator's professional experience and practice. But the theoretical questions which they subsequently explore as linguistic ethnographers are shaped at least in part by ideas and insights from a rather different body of knowledge, of the kind outlined in the sections titled 'Ethnography, linguistics and linguistic ethnography' and 'Describing the elements interacting in communication'. This involves some substantial shifts – from a teaching, advisory or educational management role to that of researcher, from a professional school gaze to the ethnographic scrutiny of phenomena and their meaning between, around and cross-cutting official activity (e.g. Maybin 2006) – and these entail radical changes in the perception of what's happening in the classroom and how it is significant. Educationalists can face quite formidable ontological and epistemological challenges achieving this: 'it takes a tremendous effort of will and imagination to stop seeing only the things that are conventionally "there" to be seen ... [I]t is like pulling teeth to get [researchers] to see or write anything beyond what "everyone" knows' (Becker 1971: 10). The authoritative, knowledge-full professional who is responsible for guiding students through a particular curriculum has to become a novice researcher, striving to immerse her/himself in 'the moment to moment interactional implementation of locally instantiated social organisation' (Cicourel 1993: 89). While the educational focus has to incorporate national targets, pre-determined curriculum goals and the measurement of individual competencies, the researcher's gaze needs to open to a more holistic understanding of what is going on within the local constructions of meaning on the one hand, and the configuring of the school environment by broader linguistic and sociopolitical processes on the other. To the educator, the school may serve primarily as a site for inculcating particular skills and bodies of knowledge, currently specified in England and Wales as a National Curriculum. The linguistic ethnographer, however, has to set aside these institutional lenses, and there can be a very uncomfortable disjuncture between, on the one hand, the individual psychological model of students and learning in school (which may also have structured the educational researcher's own professional training), and on the other, the social constructionist, poststructuralist perspectives underpinning contemporary research in linguistic ethnography.

This contrast between educational and ethnographic perspectives stands out especially clearly when language and literacy are in focus.

In schools in England, for instance, English language in the National Curriculum is largely codified through rather formal descriptions of grammar and genre. Terms like 'context', 'speaker', 'listener', 'meaning', and 'function' are relatively fixed concepts in the analysis and evaluation of speech and writing. Students' individual progress is measured against specified language targets, and their results are treated as the indicators of the success of teaching and learning, on which teacher careers and school survival depend. This is in stark contrast to linguistic ethnography, which emphasises the complexity of contextualisation, the dynamics of dialogue, the multi-scalar implications of language functions and the contingency and ideological saturation of meaning. Thus, researchers moving from language education to linguistic ethnography have to engage with at least three kinds of epistemological shift. First, they need to move from an educational view of language and literacy as skills and competencies to a more anthropological focus on how language is used as part of social practice, deeply connected with relationships, identity, power and cultural values. Second, there is a shift from seeing language as produced by individuals, reflecting their knowledge and competence, to focussing on language as produced between people, providing a site for their exploration and negotiation of knowledge and positioning. And third, there is a shift from treating language as a coherent product, a system which needs to be learnt, to studying it as part of a dynamic ideological communicative process emerging in everyday life and experience. In terms of fieldwork practice, these moves often entail a shift of empirical gaze, looking beyond students' spoken language and literacy in official classroom activities, to collecting data from different sites across the school, investigating the meaning and significance of their different language practices for the individuals themselves. And data is no longer analysed in terms of how it speaks to an educational framework of skills, competencies and improvement – instead it is examined in terms of emergent meanings and significance for participants' (different) perspectives, generating a far richer understanding of context and contingency.

But although they are often very disconcerting initially, these shifts are worth making. The move beyond a lens disciplined by education policy and priorities leads to fresh perspectives on, for example, the potential of students' different language resources for learning, or on the disjunctions and connections between students' literacy practices in and out of class. Combined within fine-grained analysis of specific interactions, linguistic anthropological concepts re-orient the researcher to the dynamic intersection of language with activity, with cultural ideology and with other semiotic resources. There is scope for repairing the under-theorisation of context and the neglect of cultural/ historical process that have characterised the psychologically based approaches dominating educational research. For instance, the analysis of processes of contextualisation and indexicality can highlight how a classroom's local institutional imperatives, its affordances for particular kinds of learning, and its recurrent sites of cultural struggle, are configured by larger scale structures and processes and by social categories grounded in ideology. In this way, linguistic ethnography can complement and extend neo-Vygotskian and dialogic research in schools, offering more ideologically sensitive insights about the situated dialogues between teachers and students that constitute key mediating communicative patterns of learning. It can map out the social, cultural and historical dimensions of students' zones of proximal development, and bring out their implications for students' engagement in school language and literacy practices. Or alternatively, in the context of multilingual education, linguistic ethnography can show how struggles over authority and legitimation reveal fault-lines and fractures in the wider society, often related to past colonial histories that are played out through educational processes in class (Heller and Martin-Jones 2001).

In reality of course, there is a good deal of variation in how far people travel along the route from education into linguistic ethnography (see Green and Bloome 1997), and hybridisation also occurs when well-established and experienced LE researchers work with professionals side-by-side (see e.g. Hymes 1980). But collaboration is itself by no means simple, and we can illustrate this by now turning to LE work on **health communication** (for an educational case, see Lefstein and Snell 2011).

In research on health communication, there are some people with medical training who develop expertise in linguistic ethnography in order to address issues that concern them professionally (cf. Swinglehurst et al. 2011, chapter in this book), but most of the LE research has been driven by academic social scientists without health backgrounds. Instead of involving the process of de-familiarisation described in the educational case above, the initial challenge bears closer resemblance to the classic anthropological task of becoming familiar with the strange. But the work doesn't end there: when researchers take on advisory and consultancy roles, they also have to show the professionals that their own perspective has practical relevance in a process that involves problematising the issues rather than attempting easy solutions (Roberts et al. 2000).

This requires perspectival shifts – and can generate resistances – that can be quite considerable.

First, language is not generally an object of gaze within the health professions, except in its narrowest, deficit formulation as 'poor language'. When communication is addressed as 'communication skills', this is done normatively, using social psychological terms or prescriptive nostrums like 'use open questions'. So there is a substantial distance between this position, where language is treated as a transparent medium for referring and for achieving actions, and the linguistic ethnographic view of situated language practices playing a major role constructing healthcare and shaping the medical (Freeman and Heller 1987; Candlin and Candlin 2003; Swinglehurst et al. 2011; Chapter 5). There are also substantial differences in approaches to research, and the move to joint problematisation requires the professionals to abandon the stance of a research consumer, shifting into a more collaborative relationship (Roberts and Sarangi 2003). Alongside the positivist and statistical perspectives rated most highly within medicine, medical professionals need to make space for findings that derive from long periods in the field and from the slow and protracted examination of what initially looks small and banal, eventually coming to integrate these with wider ideologies and processes.

We can illustrate the kinds of process involved by referring to Roberts' work with the Royal College of General Practitioners (RCGP). In an involvement that has proved long-term, Roberts was first approached in the 1990s and then invited in again 15 years later, with a request to investigate the selection processes that the RCGP used to license family doctors in the UK, in order to see whether they involved practices that might account for a persistent gap in the success rates of white British candidates and candidates from migrant or ethnic minority backgrounds (Roberts et al. 2014). The mix of health, 'race' and exclusion is a potent one, and made more complex and political by (sometimes productive) tensions around credibility and authority. During the project, there were debates around what counted as language, about the extent to which language and cultural processes were wired together, and about where indeed 'language' actually was in the simulated consultations which were the centre-piece of the licensing exam. Much of this debate focused on the way that candidates were rated for 'data gathering', 'clinical mmanagement' and 'interpersonal skills'. While the professionals treated these as unproblematic categories, Roberts and Atkins sought to analyse the encounters more holistically and to draw out the taken-for-granted assumptions about language use and linguistic competence which permeated the exam.

Another central debate focused on the ways of thinking that governed the design and implementation of the examination. The RCGP evaluated the exam within a definition of reliability and validity, which among other things, excluded consideration of the effect of simulated consultations on candidate behaviour, and of the degree of linguistic and cultural diversity within the population of patients that they would be serving as GPs. RCGP colleagues could recognise and approve of the science in the linguistic analysis, the detailed transcripts and the effort to seek patterns across relatively large amounts of data, but there were some tensions when (i) researchers tried to link the linguistic detail to the wider issues of exam validity; when (ii) they used small and highly detailed examples to make telling points rather than persuade through numbers (see also Bezemer Chapter 11); and when (iii) they introduced new classificatory systems which focussed on how local inferencing processes combined broad normative judgements (e.g. 'the candidate was clunky') with the evaluation of micro-linguistic features that operated below the level of conscious awareness. Within the RCGP's regime of thought, it was generally very hard to understand the perspective of linguistic ethnography, and if the researchers weren't actually regarded as mad or bad, it was easy to see them as just sad, spending so much time on what looked irrelevant to the professionals, either all too obvious or really rather meaningless (Foucault 1971: 12–16). With the researcher acting both as ethnographer and critical consultant, there was also considerable scope for suspicion. In the examination centre, the associate researcher on the project initially referred to the spaces where she wasn't permitted as 'sacred places' – as areas where she needed to go as a researcher working in partnership with the RCGP, but wasn't seen as 'one of us'.

The researchers also found that the interpretations, findings and conclusions produced in reports and papers often seem overly tentative and open when compared with the styles of research communication that medical professionals are used to. Over the course of Roberts' relationship with the RCGP, which has now involved a good deal of data collection and analysis working across several scales, there has been a lot of productive discussion about how categorical a particular stance or interpretation ought to be, and whether it is possible to acknowledge multiple interpretations. What may seem to be a healthy and realistic interpretive plurality in linguistic ethnography may look like 'dormouse valour' to professionals, and in the end, a consensus on new ways of looking at institutional and professional problems – in this case, a new analytic language for talking about the oral examination – can itself require both professionals *and* researchers to embrace impurity, seeking productive compromises. So although it is important to acknowledge the complexity of interaction and its relationship to broader themes such as assessment, standards and fairness, there are limits to how far one could expect any professional institution to embrace the dynamic contingency involved in something like the 'total linguistic fact' (see Section 2). In purely academic terms, correlational approaches to communication which treat the ingredients as only separate-but-connected clearly lead to an impoverished understanding of meaning-making in human interaction, but if language is to be used in any kind of institutional measurement or assessment, a stabilised system has to be established in which some dimensions of communication are given priority over others. For linguistic ethnographers who seek to engage with these institutional regimes practically, there is no question of standing outside the ideological processes that this fixing entails. Instead, the task is to try to understand them as fully as possible, to appreciate reflexively the strengths and limits of their own position, and to nudge the standardisation process in directions that seem more defensible.

This health communication case also throws light on joint data-sessions and the different kinds of understanding they make possible among professionals and LE researchers. Engaging professionals in data-sessions focused on interactions relevant to their work interests can either serve as part of the ethnographic data-collection process itself (Lefstein and Snell 2011), or as a post-research activity, providing opportunities to examine and debate professional policies and practices with research informants and their colleagues (Bloor 1997: 320–321; Bezemer chapter in this book). Responses to these data may be anywhere on the spectrum from *ad hoc* and immediate reactions to a specific incident, to feedback in formal group sessions where data illustrate the researcher's likely findings, and there are traps and affordances in the process of joint analysis that relate to stance, to values and to purposes.

The encounter between the ethnographer, professionals and the data can spark the renegotiation of subject positions around authority, credibility, trust, status and expertise. Exposing professionals to video recordings of their own practice can have quite wide organisational ramifications, independent of the researcher's perspective (Iedema and Carroll 2011), while in Mey's disturbing metaphor (Mey 1987), the researcher may him/herself be seen as 'the poet' handing out knowledge to 'the peasants', since the researcher's justification for these joint sessions resides in claims to expertise which prioritise their own ways of looking and knowing over the practical knowledge of the professional group. There can be tensions around what counts as analysable and whether and how that matters, and data sessions are also places where learner/teacher relationships can be renegotiated, with institutional and professional knowledge trumping the researcher's interpretations, producing new and more ecologically valid analysis (Cicourel 2007). In the discussion of the interdisciplinary training courses in the section titled 'Linguistic ethnography in interdisciplinary training', the data sessions had a principally pedagogic function, but in the interaction with professionals, they can serve a much wider range of purposes. Some of these relate to knowledge and understanding: using data sessions to persuade, to discover about the insiders' perspective, to demonstrate new ways of seeing, to see language as a topic in itself (and not just take it for granted), to move through the micro to more macro processes. But data sessions also play an important part in the management of field relations: gaining trust and access to opportunities for more 'lurking and soaking', satisfying curiosity, justifying the time that informants have had to give to the project and appeasing their concerns. On matters such as these can depend the outcomes of research, their authority, credibility and usefulness.

Judged by the textual standards expected in purely academic work, the written products of collaborative linguistic ethnography undertaken with professionals in fields such as education, health or law often look relatively low-key, conceptually and/or methodologically. But the work and experience that underpins this can in fact seriously enhance linguistic ethnography if we can guarantee that, within LE, there is always open movement between theoretical, descriptive and interventionist work, and that there is ongoing dialogue or indeed active teamwork between people with these different but complementary leanings.

5.   Conclusion

The collective consolidation of linguistic ethnography in the UK started in 2000, but in a review of developments in 2007, Rampton denied that LE was a paradigm or cohesive school, and instead described it as a 'discursive space' and a 'site of encounter', bringing people with fairly mixed interests and backgrounds together in broad alignment with the two tenets cited on page 18 above – contexts for communication should be investigated rather than assumed, and to grasp the significance of semiotic data, its internal organisation has to be addressed (2007: 585). Since then, this trajectory has gathered momentum, and in recent years, the collective energies in LE have been dedicated rather more to outreach and new recruitment than to methodological standardisation among core affiliates, as intimated in the section titled 'Linguistic ethnography in interdisciplinary training'. In line with this, membership of the Linguistic Ethnography Forum has grown from around 200 in 2007 to over 600 in 2014.

But whatever its organisational success, any approach claiming space in the academy needs to show that it produces good research. Of course, academic discourse communities differ a great deal in what they mean by 'good research', and as sites of knowledge production, universities now also accommodate a range of missions – pure, mixed and applied. But bearing these caveats in mind, we can suggest that:

(a) good research should be careful, logical, accountable, explicit, sceptical, well-informed, comparative and original, leading to the production of interesting claims that people (in some determinate discourse community) can trust, and

(b) that the present collection allows us to take stock of the character and quality of work that self-identifies as linguistic ethnography.

Working as individuals or in small teams, all of the authors in this volume get published outside an LE framing, and there is also a steady stream of research that is well-received in linguistic anthropology. But what does linguistic ethnography look like when these authors are gathered together in a collection like this? When LE participates in interdisciplinary interaction, what kinds of position does it occupy – partnership, challenge or ancillary support? Is it really true that LE uncovers hitherto hidden dimensions of social process, or throws new light on old topics? Just how coherent as a way of seeing does LE seem to be, and does it matter if it's not? As the editors explain, it is questions like these that motivate this collection, and in the pages that follow, there is an opportunity to look for some answers.

References

Abreu, A. Grinevich, V., Hughes, A. & Kitson, M. 2009. *Knowledge Exchange between Academics and the Business, Public and Third Sectors*. Cambridge: UK IRC. At http://www.cbr.cam.ac.uk/pdf/AcademicSurveyReport.pdf.

Agha, A. & Wortham, S. (eds) 2005. *Discourse across Speech Events*. Special issue of *Journal of Linguistic Anthropology*. 15/1.

Agha, A. 2007. *Language and Social Structure*. Cambridge: Cambridge University Press.

Ahearn, L. 2012. *Living Language: An Introduction to Linguistic Anthropology.* Malden MA: Wiley-Blackwell.

Anderson, B. 1983. *Imagined Communities.* London: Verso.

Auer, P. (ed.) 2007. *Style and Social Identities.* Berlin: Mouton de Gruyter.

Bakhtin, M. [1953] 1987. *The Dialogic Imagination.* Austin: Texas University Press.

Bakhtin, M. 1984. *Problems in Dostoevsky's Poetics.* Minneapolis: University of Minnesota Press.

Bakhtin, M. 1986. The problem of speech genres. In *Speech Genres and Other Late Essays.* Austin: University of Texas Press. 60–102.

Bauman, R. & Briggs, C. 1990. Poetics and performance as critical perspectives on language and social life. *Annual Review of Anthropology* 19: 59–88.

Bauman, R. 2001. Genre. In A. Duranti (ed.) *Key Terms in Language & Culture.* Oxford: Blackwell.

Becker, H. S. 1971. Footnote. In M. Wax, S. Diamond & F. Gearing (eds) *Anthropological Perspectives on Education.* New York: Basic Books. 3–27.

Bernstein, B. 1996. Pedagogizing knowledge: Studies in recontextualisating. In *Pedagogy, Symbolic Control and Identity.* London: Taylor and Francis. 54–81.

Blommaert, J. 2005. *Discourse: A Critical Introduction.* Cambridge: Cambridge University Press.

Blommaert, J. 2007. On scope and depth in linguistic ethnography. *Journal of Sociolinguistics* 11/5: 682–688.

Blommaert, J. 2008. *Grassroots Literacy.* London: Routledge.

Blommaert, J. 2010a. *The Sociolinguistics of Globalization.* Cambridge: Cambridge University Press.

Blommaert, J. 2012. *Chronicles of Complexity: Ethnography, Superdiversity & Linguistic Landscapes. Tilburg Papers in Culture Studies 29.* At http://www.tilburg university.edu/research/institutes-and-research-groups/babylon/tpcs/

Blommaert, J. nd. Genre. MS.

Blommaert, J. & Rampton, B. 2011. Language & superdiversity. *Diversities* 13/2: 1–21.

Bloor, M. 1997. Addressing social problems through qualitative research. In D. Silverman (ed.) *Qualitative Research: Theory, Method and Practice.* London: Sage. 221–238.

Blumer, H. 1969. *Symbolic Interactionism: Perspective and Method.* Berkeley: University of California Press.

Bourdieu, P. 1991. *Language and Symbolic Power.* Oxford: Polity.

Bourdieu, P. 1977. *Outline of a Theory of Practice.* Cambridge, UK: Cambridge University Press.

Briggs, C. 1997. Notes on a 'confession': On the construction of gender, sexuality, and violence in an infanticide case. *Pragmatics* 7: 519–546.

Briggs, C. 2005. Communicability, Racial Discourse, and Disease. *Annual Review of Anthropology* 34: 269–291.

Burawoy, M. 1998. The extended case method. *Sociological Theory* 16/1: 4–33.

Candlin, C. and Candlin, S. 2003. Health Communication: A problematic site for applied linguistic research. *Annual Review of Applied Linguistics* 23: 134–154.

Cicourel, A. 1992. The interpenetration of communicative contexts: Examples from medical discourse. In A. Duranti & C. Goodwin (eds) *Rethinking Context.* Cambridge: Cambridge University Press. 291–310.

Cicourel, A. V. 1993. Aspects of structural and processual theories of knowledge. In C. Calhoun, E. LiPuma & M. Postone (eds) *Bourdieu: Critical Perspectives.* Cambridge, UK: Polity Press. 89–115.

Cicourel, A. 2007. A personal retrospective view of ecological validity. *Text and Talk* 27 (5/6): 735–752.

Coupland, N. & Jaworski, A. (ed.) 2007. *The New Sociolinguistics Reader.* Basingstoke: Palgrave Macmillan.

Crystal, D. 2010 (3rd edn). *The Cambridge Encyclopedia of Language.* Cambridge: Cambridge University Press.

Drew, P. & Heritage, J. 1992. Analyzing talk at work: An introduction. In P. Drew & J. Heritage (eds) *Talk at Work.* Cambridge: Cambridge University Press. 3–65.

Duranti, A. 2003. Language as culture in US anthropology (including comments from Laura Ahearn, Jenny Cook-Gumperz and John Gumperz, Regina Darnell, Dell Hymes, Alan Rumsey, Debra Spitulnik, Teun van Dijk). *Current Anthropology.* 44: 323–347.

Duranti, A. 1997. *Linguistic Anthropology.* Cambridge, UK: Cambridge University Press.

Duranti, A. (ed.). 2001a. *Key Terms in Language and Culture.* Oxford, UK: Blackwell.

Eckert, P. 2008. Variation and the indexical field. *Journal of Sociolinguistics.* 12/4: 453–476.

Eckert, P. 2000. *Linguistic Variation as Social Practice.* Cambridge, UK: Cambridge University Press.

Erickson, F. 1986. Qualitative methods in research on teaching. In M. Wittrock (ed.) *Handbook of Research on Teaching: 3rd Edition.* New York: Macmillan. 119–61.

Erickson, F. 2001. Co-membership and wiggle room: Some implications of the study of talk for the development of social theory. In N. Coupland, S. Sarangi & C. Candlin (eds) *Sociolinguistics & Social Theory.* London: Longman. 152–181.

Forster, E.M. [1924] 1973. *A Passage to India.* Harmondsworth, Middlesex. Penguin Modern Classics: 267.

Foucault, M. 1971. Orders of Discourse. *Social Science Information* 10/2: 7–30.

Foucault, M. 1972. *The Archaeology of Knowledge.* London: Tavistock Publications.

Freeman, S. & Heller, M. (eds) 1987 . *Medical Discourse.* Special Issue of *Text* 7 (1).

Geertz, C. 1973. *The Interpretation of Cultures.* London: Hutchinson.

Gibbons, M., Limoges, C., Nowotny, H., Schwartzman, S., Scott, P. & Trow, M. 1994. *The New Production of Knowledge: The Dynamics of Science and Research in Contemporary Societies.* London: Sage.

Giddens, A. 1976. *New Rules of Sociological Method.* London: Hutchinson.

Goffman, E. 1964. The neglected situation. *American Anthropologist.* 66/6: 133–6.

Goodwin, C. 2000. Action and embodiment within situated human interaction. *Journal of Pragmatics* 32: 1489–522.

Green, J. & Bloome, D. 1997. Ethnography and ethnographers of and in education: A situated perspective. In J. FLood, S. Brice Heath & D. Lapp (eds) *Handbook of Research on Teaching Literacy through the Communicative and Visual Arts.* New York: Macmillan. 181–202.

Gumperz, J. & Hymes, D. (eds) 1972. *Directions in Sociolinguistics: The Ethnography of Communication.* Oxford: Blackwell.

Gumperz, J. 1972. Introduction. In J. Gumperz & D. Hymes (eds) *Directions in Sociolinguistics: The Ethnography of Communication.* Oxford: Blackwell. 1–25.

Gumperz, J. 1982. *Discourse Strategies.* Cambridge, UK: Cambridge University Press.

Gumperz, J., Jupp, T. and Roberts, C. 1979. *Crosstalk.* Southall, Middx, UK: BBC/ National Centre for Industrial Language Training.

Hall, S. 1980. Encoding/decoding. In S. Hall, D. Hobson, A. Lowe & P. Willis (eds) *Culture, Media, Language.* London: Unwin Hyman. 128–138.

Hammersley, M. 1999. *What's Wrong with Ethnography.* London: Routledge.

Hammersley, M. 2007. Reflections on linguistic ethnography. *Journal of Sociolinguistics.* 11/5: 689–95.

Hanks, W. 1987. Discourse genres as a theory of practice. *American Ethnologist.* 14/4: 668–92.

Hanks, W. 1996. *Language and Communicative Practices.* Boulder, CO: Westview Press.

Harris, R. 2006. *New Ethnicities and Language Use.* London: Palgrave.

Heller, M. & M. Martin-Jones (eds) 2001. *Voices of Authority: Education and Linguistic Difference.* Westport, CT: Ablex.

Hymes, D. 1980 *Language in Education: Ethnolinguistic Essays.* Washington DC: Centre for Applied Linguistics.

Hymes, D. 1972. Models of the interaction of language and social life. In J. Gumperz & D. Hymes (eds) *Directions in Sociolinguistics: The Ethnography of Communication.* Oxford: Blackwell. 35–71.

Hymes, D. 1983. *Essays in the History of Linguistic Anthropology.* Amsterdam: John Benjamins.

Hymes, D. 1996. *Ethnography; Linguistics, Narrative Inequality: Toward an Understanding of Voice.* London: Taylor and Francis.

Hymes, D. 1969. The use of anthropology: Critical, political, personal. In D. Hymes (ed.) *Reinventing Anthropology.* Ann Arbor: University of Michigan Press. 3–82.

Iedema, R. & Carroll, K. (2011) The clinalyst: Institutionalising reflexivity and flexible systematisation in health care organisations. *Journal for Organizational Change Management.* 24/2: 175–90.

Irvine, J. 2001. 'Style' as distinctiveness: The culture and ideology of linguistic differentiation. In P. Eckert & J. Rickford (eds) *Style and Sociolinguistic Variation.* Cambridge: Cambridge University Press. 21–43.

Koole, T. (2007) review of Ben Rampton (2006) Language in Late Modernity. Interaction in an urban school, *Journal of Pragmatics,* 39/4: 778–80.

Labov, W. 1972. *Sociolinguistic Patterns.* Oxford: Blackwell.

Lefstein, A. & Snell, J. 2011. Professional vision and the politics of teacher learning. *Teaching and Teacher Education* 27: 505–514.

Levinson, S. 1996. Relativity in spatial conception and description. In J. Gumperz & S. Levinson (eds) *Rethinking Linguistic Relativity.* Cambridge: Cambridge University Press. 177–202.

Maybin, J. 2006. *Children's Voices: Talk, Knowledge and Identity.* Basingstoke, UK: Palgrave Macmillan.

Mehan, H. 1996. The construction of an LD student: A case study in the politics of representation. In M. Silverstein & G. Urban (eds) *Natural Histories of Discourse.* Chicago: University of Chicago Press. 253–276.

Mey, J. 1987. Poet and Peasant: A pragmatic comedy in five acts. *Journal of Pragmatics* 11: 281–297.

Mitchell, J. C. 1984. Case studies. In R. Ellen (ed.) *Ethnographic Research: A Guide to General Conduct.* London: Academic Press. 237–41.

Moerman, M. 1974. Accomplishing ethnicity. In R. Turner (ed.) *Ethnomethodology*. Harmondsworth: Penguin. 54–68.

Ortner, S. 2006. *Anthropology and Social Theory: Culture, Power and the Acting Subject*. Durham: Duke University Press.

Pennycook, A. 2007. *Global Englishes and Transcultural Flows*. London: Routledge.

Platt, L. 2008. *Ethnicity and Family: Relationships within and between Ethnic Groups: An Analysis using the Labour Force Survey*. Equality and Human Rights Commission.

Rampton, B. & Harris, R. 2010. Change in urban classroom culture and interaction. In K. Littleton & C. Howe (eds) *Educational Dialogues: Understanding and Promoting Productive Interaction*. London: Routledge. 240–64.

Rampton, B. 2006. *Language in Late Modernity: Interaction in an Urban School*. Cambridge: Cambridge University Press.

Rampton, B. 2007. Neo-Hymesian linguistic ethnography in the United Kingdom. *Journal of Sociolinguistics*. 11/5: 584–607.

Rampton, B. 2010. An everyday poetics of class an ethnicity in stylisation and crossing. *Working Papers in Urban Language & Literacies # 59*. At www.kcl.ac.uk/ldc.

Roberts, C. & Sarangi, S. 1999. Hybridity in gatekeeping discourse: Issues of practical relevance for the researcher. In S. Sarangi & C. Roberts (eds) *Talk, Work and Institutional Order*. Berlin: Mouton. 473–503.

Roberts, C., Sarangi, S., Southgate, L., Wakeford, R. & Vass, W. 2000. Oral examinations – equal opportunities, ethnicity and fairness in the MRCGP. *British Medical Journal*. 320: 370–374.

Roberts, C. and Sarangi, S. 2003. Uptake of discourse research in interprofessional settings: Reporting from medical consultancy. *Applied Linguistics*. 24/3: 338–359.

Roberts, C., Atkins, S. and Hawthorne, K. 2014. *Performance Features in Clinical Skills Assessment*: Linguistic and Cultural Factors in the MRCGP GPs examination. Centre for Language, Discourse and Communication, King's College London.   http://www.kcl.ac.uk/sspp/departments/education/research/ldc/publications/index/aspx

Sapir, E. [1929] 1949. The status of linguistics as a science. In D. Mandelbaum (ed.) *Edward Sapir: Selected Writings in Language, Culture and Personality*. Berkeley: University of California Press. 160–6.

Schegloff, E. 1999. Naivete vs sophistication or discipline vs self-indulgence: A rejoinder to Billig. *Discourse and Society*. 10: 577–582.

Scollon, R. & Scollon, S. 2007. Nexus analysis: Refocusing ethnography on action. *Journal of Sociolinguistics*. 11/5: 608–25.

Scollon, R. & Scollon, S. 2004. *Nexus Analysis: Discourse and the Emerging Internet*. London: Routledge.

Shaw, G. B. 1916. Preface to Pygmalion. At http://www.bartleby.com/138/0.html

Silverman, D. 1998. *Harvey Sacks: Social Science and Conversation Analysis*. Oxford: Polity Press.

Silverstein, M. & Urban, G. (eds) 1996. *Natural Histories of Discourse*. Chicago: University of Chicago Press.

Silverstein, M. 1985. Language and the culture of gender. In E. Mertz and R. Parmentier (eds) *Semiotic Mediation*. New York: Academic Press. 219–59.

Strathern, M. (ed.) 2000. *Audit Cultures*. London: Routledge.

Swinglehurst, D., Roberts, C. & Greenhalgh, T. (2011). Opening up the 'black box' of the electronic patient record: a linguistic ethnographic study in general practice. *Communication and Medicine.* 8/1: 3–16.

ten Have, P. 1999. *Doing Conversation Analysis.* London: Sage.

Todorov, T. 1988. Knowledge in social anthropology. *Anthropology Today.* 4/2: 2–5.

Tremlett, A. 2007. *Representations of the Roma: Public Discourse & Local Practices.* PhD dissertation, King's College London.

Tusting, K. 2010. Eruptions of interruptions: Managing tensions between writing and other tasks in a textualised childcare workplace. In D. Barton & U. Papen (eds) *The Anthropology of Writing: Understanding Textually Mediated Worlds.* London: Continuum. 67–89.

Verschueren, J. 1999. *Understanding Pragmatics.* London: Arnold.

Vertovec, S. 2007. Super-diversity and its implications. *Ethnic and Racial Studies* 30/6: 1024–54.

Vygotsky, L. 1978. *Mind in Society.* Cambridge, MA: Harvard University Press.

Wetherell, M. 1998. Positioning and interpretative repertoires: Conversation analysis and post-structuralism in dialogue. *Discourse and Society* 9: 431–56.

Willis, P. & Trondman, M. 2000. Manifesto for *Ethnography. Ethnography.* 1: 5–16.

3
Workplace Literacies and Audit Society

Karin Tusting

A range of ethnographic research in literacy studies has focused on workplace literacy practices, particularly increased textualisation and changing writing demands (Gee, Hull, & Lankshear, 1996; Farrell, 2006; Brandt, 2009). The volume and complexity of workplace paperwork have increased in many workplaces. Work intensity has also increased as paperwork is co-ordinated with other tasks. This has an impact on time and space available for other activities at work, such as caring and emotional work (Davies, 1994), 'hands-on' tasks (Lamvik, Naesje, Skarholt, & Torvatn, 2009) or workplace learning (Arthur & Tait, 2004). Increased centralisation of paperwork demands means that the sources and purposes of paperwork can become unclear (Ball, 2003). Professional identities and relationships are transformed when goals of accountability and performance management seem to change the nature and purpose of the work (Farrell, 2001; Iedema & Scheeres, 2003; Karlsson, 2005).

Power (1997, 2000) argues that a set of interrelated social changes in the 1990s caused an 'audit explosion'. These included New Public Management in the public sector, political demands for greater accountability in service providing organisations, and the extension of quality assurance practices from industry across the public and private sector. Such practices – regular monitoring against quantitative performance measures, fed back to management – have changed how organisations are regulated. Workers produce their own auditable measures of performance. External audits check that these internal control systems are in place. Performance measures are designed not just in terms of how well they *measure* performance, but perhaps predominantly by how well they make performance *visible*, creating a 'window' on the organisation thereby making monitoring and intervention possible. This shapes how 'auditable performance' is produced and interpreted.

For Power, these practices have unintended consequences. Auditable accounts of performance do not necessarily produce transparency, particularly when auditing becomes defensive. Auditees learn 'creative compliance'; finding ways of performing well on auditable measures, without changing performance. Relationships alter where audit demands are predicated on, and create, mistrust.

Such processes are very visible in educational workplaces. Education is governed by policy frameworks, inspection bodies, examining boards, funding agencies, and various other authorities, who all have different reporting demands. Studies in schools (Troman, 2000; Williams, Corbin, & McNamara, 2007) and in further education (Hamilton, 2009) have linked policy-mandated audit practices to increased levels of stress.

This chapter draws on examples from a study which explored the impact of such demands on people's workplace experiences and identities in two contrasting educational workplaces (Tusting, 2010a, 2012). The genesis of the work was in previous research carried out in adult literacy, numeracy and ESOL classes, shortly after the introduction of a new national strategy (Barton et al. 2007). Paperwork and management practices were not the focus of attention in that study. However, tutors' experiences of new curricula, performance measurements and associated paperwork emerged as a key factor shaping their experience (Tusting 2009).

The study reported on here was designed to explore tutors' experiences of paperwork in more depth, in two sites: a college, and an Early Years centre. These were both places where changes in national policy and inspection regimes had recently changed the nature of paperwork demands. My interest was in the experiences of front line staff around the literacy practices associated with 'paperwork': broadly, reading and writing tasks (paper-based or digitally-mediated) directly associated with people's work. I worked with nine tutors at the college, mainly teaching in non-vocational areas, and 12 staff at the nursery. This chapter will focus on two staff from the college, describing the specifics of their situation. (The two settings have been compared elsewhere, for example in Tusting 2012. For more detail on the Early Years site see Tusting 2010a.)

I will first outline the importance of literacy studies within linguistic ethnography. I will discuss the textually mediated nature of the contemporary social world, and the need to address this within the linguistic ethnographic enterprise. I will then draw on examples from the study data to illustrate the impact of audit society in participants' working lives.

Literacy studies

'Literacy studies' approaches reading and writing as situated social practices (Barton, Hamilton, & Ivanič, 2000; Barton, 2007). Rather than focusing on literacy as an individualised cognitive skill, a practice perspective on literacy focuses on what people do with reading and writing. People engage in 'literacy events' (Heath 1983) – events in which written texts play a part – in characteristic ways in different domains of life. These patterned ways of engaging with texts can be called 'literacy practices'. While literacy practices cannot be directly observed, they can be inferred from observing literacy events over time and developing understandings of the routinised ways in which literacy is used in social domains. Literacy practices are shaped by, and shape, the histories, institutions and power relationships in which they are situated. This is one specific development of the approach to understanding social life known as practice theory (Gherardi 2009).

Literacy studies shares perspectives with linguistic ethnography more generally, as outlined in Rampton et al. (2004) and the introduction and Chapter 1 of this collection: an understanding of language in terms of practices specific to social groups and domains, rather than as universal systems; an appreciation of recurrent and relatively stable patterns in how people use language, learned and continued in interaction; drawing on established procedures and relatively technical vocabularies for isolating and identifying these structures.

Literacy studies also shares the orientation towards 'close knowledge through first hand participation [which] allows the researcher to attend to aspects of lived experience' (Rampton et al., 2004). By employing ethnographic methods (Tusting & Barton, 2005), participating in settings and observing literacy events over time, understandings have been developed of how literacy practices are situated within and shaped by context, domain, historical setting and person (Barton & Hamilton, 2000; Martin-Jones & Jones, 2000). Studies of people's everyday literacies (such as Barton & Hamilton, 1998) make visible 'vernacular' practices which make up most of people's literacy lives and yet are undervalued and backgrounded in dominant discussions of literacy in terms of skills and levels.

Theoretical traditions are also shared with linguistic ethnography. Foundational works in literacy studies come from anthropology (Street 1984), and the key concept of the 'literacy event' (Heath, 1983) was adapted from the ethnography of communication. A recent collection edited by Barton and Papen (2010) orients explicitly to this anthropological tradition.

Textually mediated society

Addressing people's practices around texts is important, because social institutions are co-ordinated in large part by what people do with material (paper and digital) texts. As Smith (2001) has demonstrated, texts and documents are 'essential to the objectification of organizations and institutions and to how they exist' (p. 160). Linguistic ethnography's interest in 'interactional and institutional discourse' (Rampton et al., 2004, p. 6) must therefore include a focus on the textual flows and practices by means of which this is constituted. This is evidenced in recent work exploring, for instance, the role of computerised patient record systems in shaping interaction between doctors and patients (Swinglehurst, 2012 and this collection); the practices by means of which a police officer tries to change how police and members of the public communicate, by rewording letters sent to complainants (Rock, 2012); and the ways decisions about insurance claims are shaped by the insurance professional's practices using computerised forms (van Hout, 2012).

Literacy studies offers one way for linguistic ethnography to address the textual practices involved in mediating, co-ordinating, regulating and authorizing activities. This enables ethnographies to be extended beyond the scope of the events under observation, exploring how macro and institutional levels are instantiated and co-ordinated in local language practices.

Methods in literacy studies

There is variation in how far work in linguistic ethnography balances the 'contradictory pulls of linguistics and ethnography' (Rampton et al., 2004, p. 4). Some work orients more to the ethnographic pole and some more to the technical linguistic one. Literacy studies has for the most part been less directly influenced by the interactional sociolinguistic tradition than other areas of linguistic ethnography. While research into literacy practices *may* draw on audio- or video-recordings of interaction analysed in detail (Bloome 2005; Maybin 2007; Lefstein 2008), this is not necessarily the case. Technical linguistic tools can also come into play in the analysis of the texts with which people interact (Burgess, 2008), or in 'text-oriented ethnography', combining ethnographic data around the processes of text production and interpretation with linguistic analysis of the texts produced (Lillis, 2009). Or fieldnotes, interview data and photographs can form the central data set, rather than recordings of interaction. These data can still be analysed to address sociolinguistic questions about language and literacy practices on the basis of the literacy events observed and discussed (Papen, 2005; Blommaert, Collins, & Slembrouck, 2005; Juffermans, 2011; see Tusting 2013 for a more extended discussion). That is to say, literacy studies which does not draw on interactional sociolinguistics in analysing recorded interaction is still linguistic analysis from a different perspective, in exploring sociolinguistic questions around literacies and language use.

The contribution of linguistic ethnography

Linguistic ethnography has informed the understandings developed in the research described here in several ways. From a theoretical perspective, linguistic ethnography sensitised me to the role of local language and literacy practices in the instantiation of culture and structure. This supports interpretation of the data at different levels, drawing together local observations and accounts with people's histories and broader institutional positionings, and with theory and empirical work on wider social and historical trends such as audit society and transformations in adult education. An ethnographic stance also validates drawing on individuals' accounts of their experiences to illuminate social structural processes from an emic perspective.

Linguistic ethnography has also added sensitivity to participants' language use in representing their experience. The accounts below will draw out particularities of teachers' descriptions of their experience, including the metaphors drawn on to represent teaching process; the use of 'vague' referents for sources of paperwork; consistent use of directive modality to frame descriptions of paperwork as obligations; constructions of risk and self-protection; and contrasting stances adopted on the location of responsibility for difficulties in completing paperwork.

Paperwork and pressure in educational workplaces

In the study reported here I worked in depth with nine staff at a post-16 college and 12 staff at an early years centre, combining interviews with observations of their work, and recording informal conversations with additional people as opportunities arose, in fieldnotes and where possible audio-recorded. I carried out general interviews discussing participants' working practices, and more focused interviews structured around a free-form log they kept to record the paperwork they encountered over the course of a week. All the interviews were semi-structured, guided by open interview schedules oriented towards opening up conversations about participants' experiences and engaging with and responding to their perspectives. I started with a general interview schedule which was the same for all interviewees. Subsequent discussions followed up on points from the first interviews, so schedules were specific to each participant.

Interviews were transcribed using a broad orthographic transcription. Minimal responses ('Mmm', 'Right' and so on) were included in the data used for analysis but have been edited out in extracts reproduced below as they are not relevant to the level of detail addressed here. Where data has been elided this is represented with [...]. Pauses I interpreted as communicatively significant are represented with [,] for a shorter pause and [...] for a longer one.

I participated in and observed classes and worked with people in various ways to get an understanding of their practices – visiting some people's homes to see their home offices, or being taken through examples of their filing systems. At the end of the data collection period, I generated a set of preliminary emergent ideas and themes and discussed these with participants.

This work generated a broad and varied data set, bringing together data of several different kinds to enable analysis of the kinds of paperwork people were working with (document collection; interviews), how this was synchronised, organised and co-ordinated in their working lives (observation of teaching, offices, and filing systems; logs; interviews), and people's accounts of their experiences and responses (interviews). The data set was initially analysed using qualitative coding, with the support of the software ATLAS.ti. I approached the data set with the goal of coding it exhaustively and comprehensively (Silverman 2001), to record and map an interpretation of the data set overall, within which to situate a focus on particular extracts of data.

An initial broad list of codes was adopted, framed by the original research questions of the project, which addressed the nature of participants' paperwork literacy practices, and the effects of these on their experiences, identities, relationships and social practices. I then read through each of the documents in the data set several times, assigning codes to relevant extracts, adding and developing codes whenever necessary. As the numbers of codes used proliferated, I organised them by adding pre-modifiers to code names (Woolf, 2007) to group them, eventually into the following categories: paperwork and practices;

education; evaluation; experiences; factors influencing responses; function; identity; nature; relationships; source; strategies.

Interpreting the research simply in terms of the numbers of data extracts coded under each code would be inappropriate. The data were collected in ways responsive to the particular setting and situation of each individual, so the amount of data collected from each participant differs. I used multiple coding of individual data extracts, so each extract could be coded with one or many codes. The data imported into ATLAS.ti was also only a part of the full data set; additional handwritten fieldnotes, interviewees' paperwork logs, and examples of paperwork from the settings were kept separately, and returned to when developing analysis of specific points. I am also aware that my coded interpretation was informed by tacit lived understandings built up through being in the settings, which are not easy to quantify. The systematic coding process is a tool to support thinking about the data, providing ways of collecting data extracts together in new ways, and also making it easier to find extracts and returning to consider them in their discursive context. It does not provide a means of understanding the data on its own.

Nevertheless, coding across the digital part of the data set in this way does provide a way into identifying commonalities and differences in interpretations of data from different individuals and different settings. It provides a means of checking my sense of the patterns which analysis constructed across the data set as a whole, and whether individual data extracts identified as being of interest are like other extracts, or are unusual in some way.

The memoing function of ATLAS.ti was used to collect together quotations of relevance for specific topics and reflect on them in writing, and to make links between the coded data set and the other kinds of data collected. For instance, quotations relating to aspects of a particular individual's role were linked to memos summarising that aspect. Figure 3.1 illustrates this, showing how a memo illustrating 'Megan's paperwork demands' is linked to quotations from the data. The screenshot also illustrates the coding process, with the transcript of the interview 'underneath' the memo list window and the margin down the right hand side recording codes attached to particular segments.

In this chapter, I focus on two of the college participants, Aidan and Megan. (Both names are pseudonyms, and certain details have been left imprecise to avoid identifying participants.) I have chosen these individuals because of their work situations, commonalities and contrasts. Both worked in community education, full-time or close to full-time hours, and were operating with a degree of autonomy. However their

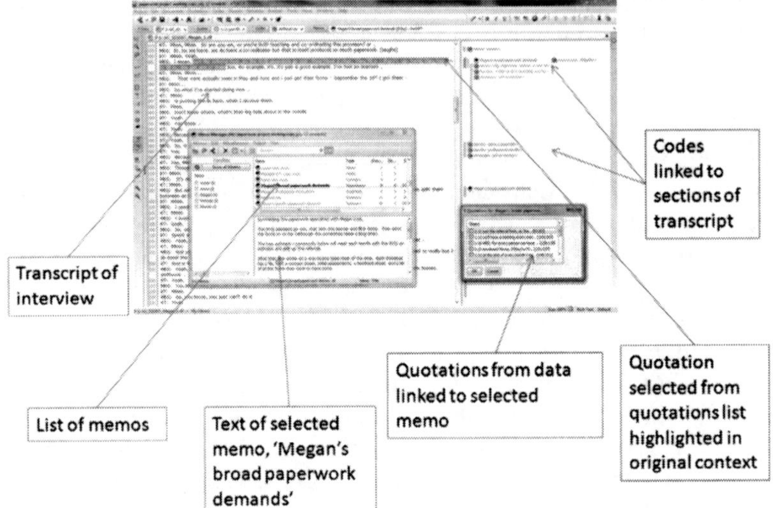

Figure 3.1   ATLAS.ti screenshot showing memo about Megan's paperwork demands

contrasting histories, positionings and responsibilities mean that the broad themes emerging from the analysis play out rather differently for each of them.

I began by considering the patterns which emerged from the data set as a whole, and then looked at the patterns of coding across the data from just these two people. I generated lists of data extracts under codes of particular interest, whether because they were represented in data from both people, or because they were more characteristic of the data from one than from the other. These codes of particular interest formed the basis of the points made in the analysis below. Extracts from the data which illustrate these points well have been selected from these quotation lists.

I will begin with 'pen portrait' summaries of Megan and Aidan (Barton and Hamilton 1998) and their paperwork demands, drawing on the memos described above. I will then draw out themes – amount of paperwork; purpose; obligation; and identity – which emerged from the study overall, and illustrate how they were oriented to by these two participants.

Aidan: role and responsibilities

Aidan had been working in his current role as a community development tutor for nearly three years. He was experienced in adult education and well qualified, with a degree and several post graduate qualifications. A lot of his work was designed to encourage people from socially excluded groups into education, providing the first step towards courses more focused on specific skills, employment or qualifications. He worked with a wide range of groups, including people with learning difficulties, mental health issues, histories of drug and alcohol addiction, and carers. He set up educational activities including classes in college, outdoor field trips and activities, and outreach workshops held beyond the college.

About half his time was spent liaising with outside agencies, such as drug rehabilitation centres and the health service, to understand the needs of the people he was working with and to design appropriate courses. Some of these courses he delivered himself, some of them he managed, with other tutors doing the face to face teaching. The other half of his time was spent teaching.

Aidan's paperwork

A lot of Aidan's paperwork involved planning, because of his course design responsibilities. He had to put together a plan for each course he designed, including a rationale stating how the course contributed to the strategies of the institution and the region, tutor contracts, aims, objectives and learning outcomes, a scheme of work, lesson plans, risk assessments (his offsite courses required additional risk assessments), and details of student assessments. In order to fulfil RARPA (Recognizing and Recording Progress and Achievement) requirements introduced by the Learning and Skills Council to standardise measures of success in non-accredited courses, Aidan had to demonstrate outcomes of student learning through formative initial and final assessments, and have ways of tracking students' progress through the course and beyond.

Aidan's principal 'unit' of paperwork was therefore 'the course'. Other paperwork related to individual students. Each student had to sign an enrolment form and a learner contract form, in which the commitment between them and the college was made explicit. A profile of needs and goals was developed for each through the course, and each student had an individual learning plan, showing what they were learning each week. A group profile was also put together for each course. All of this was on standardised forms produced by the college.

Megan: role and responsibilities

Megan worked as a community and workplace outreach tutor, mainly in adult literacy and numeracy. Her initial training was as a school teacher, and she had less experience in adult education than Aidan. She worked mainly with community partners including the Probation Service, and with NVQ candidates in workplaces. She led workshop sessions and carried out initial assessments. She also ran short specialist courses at the college, and some staff development courses on embedding literacy and numeracy in other subject areas. But most of her work was on a one to one basis with students, in a range of locations: in libraries, workplaces, or a Probation hostel.

Megan's paperwork

Where Aidan's principal unit of paperwork was 'the course', Megan's was 'the student'. Her 'typical' file began with a referral form with the student's details, from an assessor or a referring agency. She would phone the student to set up a meeting and an initial literacy assessment. She filled in a feedback sheet with candidates' scores and an explanation, talked through with students at a second meeting. She then completed their individual learning plan, adding specific goals after a later, more detailed diagnostic assessment. Other pedagogic paperwork included a 'motivation sheet' in which learners reflected on how they would feel when they achieved a certificate, and a 'ground rules' health and safety sheet defining norms of behaviour. NVQ candidates had 'Train to Gain' forms, recording enrolment and tracking achievements. Some learners also had a dyslexia assessment.

There was also college administrative paperwork. Megan tracked all her contacts with students carefully, recording phone calls on contact sheets, with every appointment, date, time, learner's signature, and the date of the next appointment. This was particularly important for students on probation who had to attend sessions to avoid breaching their order. Each month, she drew on her attendance register and assessment records to feed back on students' progress at the community team monthly meeting. She also occasionally ran courses. For these, she had a similar list of course file paperwork to complete as Aidan, as listed in the checklist below (Figure 3.2).

Amount of paperwork

Most participants, across both sites, said they had difficulties with the amount of paperwork, reflecting Power's (2000) claim of an 'audit explosion'. Megan and Aidan both talked about excessive amounts of paperwork, but this was expressed in different ways. While Aidan could

Skills for Life Course File		
Name of tutor(s)		
Course		
Documents		
Course Information Sheet		
Venue information and Risk Assessment		
Syllabus for OCNW E1,2,3/Level1,2 tests Location of Core Curriculum and OCNW Guidelines *(as appropriate)*		
IV/EV reports *(as appropriate)*		
Course rationale (including use of Volunteer Supporters rationale)		
Scheme of Work		
Lesson Plans		
Workshop Plans *(if necessary)*		
Materials/Handouts used in course		
Course Record sheet including class profile and end of term tutor evaluation		
Progress records for whole class *(if appropriate)*		
Student evaluations		
Individual learner records:	Initial Assessment plus any diagnostic assessments *(evidence of and links with ILP)*	
	Updated student profiles *(for continuing learners)*	
	Evidence of induction *(especially for students who enrol after first 3 weeks)*	
	ILPs and Progress records *(showing evidence of regular reviews)*	
	Learning Support referrals	

Figure 3.2   College checklist summarising course paperwork required

see the purpose of each individual piece, he felt that there was much more than necessary. He had concerns about the paperwork being time consuming, and the knock-on effects on other things he was doing: 'you spend more time kind of recording and justifying what we do than actually kind of doing it'. He talked about the volume of paperwork as often disproportionate to the purposes it was trying to achieve: 'if you just teach a three hour course, you could well just spend the whole three hours just filling in forms'. He also felt that the practicalities of completing some of this paperwork were not considered, given the outdoor settings of a lot of his work.

Megan described a constant increase in the volume of paperwork requirements, particularly providing evidence of what she had done.

Every person she saw had to sign a piece of paper confirming she had seen them, 'to keep a track on what I'm doing'; this was a new requirement, as was the requirement that every professional development course she attended was logged in a legal document which could be made available for inspection.

Clashing purposes

Particular problems arose across the college participants when paperwork was evaluated as clashing with the tutor's teaching goals. Quality management processes at the college included mandated structures and associated forms to complete for schemes of work and lesson planning. Specific objectives had to be set for each session and for each student, and their achievement recorded – the process Power (1997) identifies of workers producing their own performance measures and regularly monitoring themselves against these, to produce auditable records, using a process which can be demonstrated to external auditors. Regular college 'quality management' observations ensured that these processes were in place for each tutor. Where production of these auditable records was not performed adequately, mentoring sessions were set up with managers to ensure compliance. We see here the process Power (2000) describes: extension of quality assurance practices from industry across to the very different setting of adult education.

Aidan spent a lot of his time producing planning framed in this way, but questioned whether these formats were useful for his activities. A requirement to plan sessions in detail as a list of timed activities with objectives set in advance to be assessed at the end (Figure 3.3) did not fit with his characterisation of the importance of flexibility. He consistently used the metaphor of 'flow' to describe 'good teaching', evoking a fluid responsiveness to the demands of the situation. He felt paperwork could be actively detrimental to this: 'if I had to sort of sit there referring to bits of paper all the time I'd just completely lose my flow'. This supports Power's (1997, 2000) concern about differences between what the auditable records are measuring, and what matters in the job.

Megan also expressed concerns about mismatches between the official paperwork and her practices, mainly to do with learners' understandings of the forms, and 'because what we do in college doesn't quite fit what we do out there'. Her solution was to generate additional paperwork of her own, like a feedback sheet explaining the meaning of learners' scores on their initial assessments, reframing 'weaknesses' as 'areas needing support', or a simplified individual learning plan for

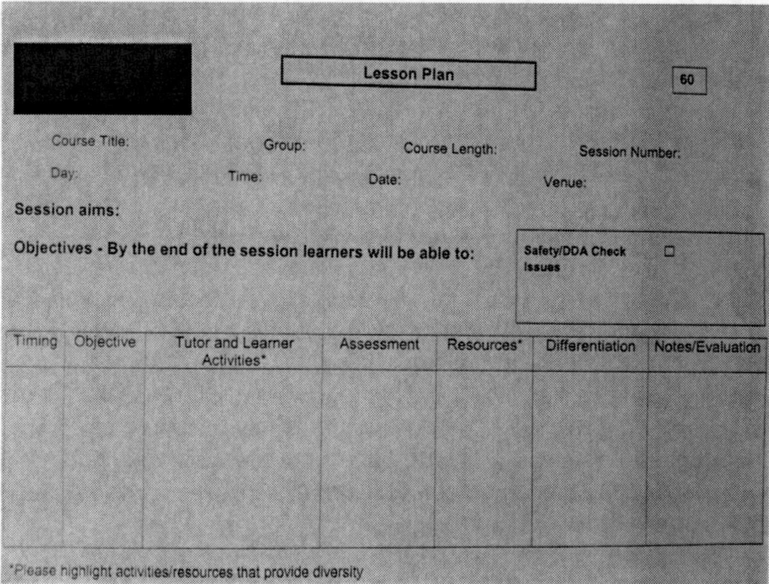

Figure 3.3 College format for lesson planning

learners on a pre-entry level course, which she then transferred onto the official plan herself. While this addressed one problem, it caused another in adding to her amount of paperwork – one of Power's (1997) unintended consequences.

Aidan and Megan described much of the paperwork as providing evidence about what they were doing, rather than fulfilling pedagogic purposes. Aidan said: 'you can have a nice course file full of these wonderful aims and objectives and things but does that bear any relation to what actually happens?' The evidence he had to provide was of various kinds, both of his activities and recording students' progress, individually and as a class. He minimised the impact of this requirement for himself and for students wherever possible. For instance, to record achievement he might 'just jot down a few things about what people have achieved' – reminiscent of Power's (2000) notion of 'creative compliance', in which ways are found to perform appropriately on the auditable measures while minimising their effect on performance.

Aidan had particular concerns about the impact of the paperwork on his relationship with students, supporting Power's (1997) claims about the effects of audit society on workplace relationships. For instance, he had to ask students direct questions on first meeting them about mental health, learning disabilities and any other concerns they had about their capacity to do the course, in order to complete their initial learner record forms. He found it difficult to ask these questions directly at this early point: 'I find if you sort of sit down it's kind of embarrassing the questions you have to ask'. The imperatives of the information required by the system clashed with his purposes of building up a relationship with students where mutual trust evolved over time.

Other forms he said were too challenging for students to complete without a lot of support. His principal strategy for addressing this was to actively mediate between the paperwork and the students. For instance, he provided structured support to help students write down their desired outcomes by doing an activity in class where they chose outcomes from a list, or by chatting with them during outdoor activities and then filling the form in with them later. An extract from fieldnotes taken during an observation of a class about the environment illustrates this point:

> Aidan gave out another set of handouts with pictures, entitled: 'What I would like to learn more about this term'. The pictures included photography, wild animals, finding your way, weather, trees, and a question mark entitled 'Anything else you would like to learn about?' [...] Aidan asked the students to look at the pictures and tick in the box 'if that's something you're interested in learning about. The last one is for if there is anything else you are interested in.'

Picture worksheets gave students a way of generating their own individual learning plans, which were more accessible to them than the standard form provided by the college. Their success depends on Aidan knowing his students well enough to be able to prepare a sheet of likely options. This activity came immediately after a more open discussion of what people would like to study, giving them the space to generate their own ideas rather than being constrained by the sheet; but most of the topics students raised as possibilities were in fact represented by the pictures. Aidan took the information from students' picture forms and transferred it onto their official learner progress record – another example of a self-generated paperwork task to address pedagogic goals.

Megan spoke more about the kinds of evidence needed to demonstrate she was doing the job. This included recording dates she received forms, all steps taken towards contacting learners (including unsuccessful calls), and taking learners' signatures each meeting. She explained this in terms of self-protection from implied threats: 'you have to cover your back'; 'if something happens I've got a fallback'; 'if somebody comes up and says well you've never contacted me [...] you've got your proof there'. This supports Power's (2000) claims that audit processes can generate mistrust and defensive practices. Again, we see unintended consequences: a feeling of constant surveillance, additional workload, and auditable measures which do not significantly improve performance.

Obligation – from where?

All participants in the study, including Aidan and Megan, described their experience of workplace paperwork using directive modality, as things that they 'have to' do. Aidan told me, 'you'd <u>have to</u> fill one of these in' ... 'you'd <u>have to</u> keep a log of that for each lesson' ... 'you <u>have to</u> fill in progress forms for learner support'. Megan explained 'we <u>have to</u> update the existing forms and we <u>have to</u> say who's achieved and who's withdrawn' ... 'there is a workshop planning sheet 'that I <u>have to</u> fill in'.

However, the source of this obligation was often unclear. Common across the college data was a vagueness about where paperwork demands were coming from and the purposes which they served. Tutors often spoke of paperwork requests as coming from an unspecified 'they' whose purposes were unknown and who were distant from the realities of teaching. This reflects Power's (1997) point that audit demands affect trust between managers and staff, when the requirement to feed records back to management is clear, but the purposes and consequences for staff can be less so.

Aidan was fairly clear about the link between funding and paperwork and the kinds of evidence funding bodies required, because of his dual position as manager and tutor. He appreciated the need for much of the tracking information requested, 'because if this isn't filled in [the college] won't get any money'. However, he was less clear when this did not relate to a course he organised directly, recommending that to understand demands linked to Learning and Skills Council funding (which funded most college activities at the time) I should talk to a manager higher up in the college. His description of a document required by the local council's adult learning department shows a more typical detachment from the purposes of the system: 'I think they have to have all this information to claim [...] I don't really get involved in all that you know, I just fill it in and hand it on'.

Megan's work was geared towards meeting (and recording) targets for the numbers of learners on courses and gaining qualifications. Most of her work was funded through the *Skills for Life* national literacy and numeracy strategy for which national targets had been set, broken down into regional targets to which every local provider had to contribute. She was not averse to working to targets, liking to have something to focus on, and understanding the relationship between meeting the targets and sustaining funding. However, targets were not always communicated clearly to her, and she said they could change without warning, 'moving the goalposts' and adding to her sense of uncertainty and threat.

Identity

Responses to paperwork were influenced by people's professional identities, histories and situations. Many tutors described a feeling of their autonomy having been eroded over time, as more and more of the paperwork had to be in particular, prescribed formats. They described this as a lack of trust in their professional capabilities. Aidan had a long history of working in adult education, relatively autonomously. He felt the mandated planning structure was too detailed, more appropriate for a new teacher than for someone with his extensive experience, supporting Power's (2000) point that audit systems are both predicated on and can create mistrust.

Megan did not interpret the paperwork as a challenge to her professional identity in the same way. Where Aidan critiqued the system, Megan interpreted her struggles to keep on top of it as personal failings. She described herself as 'really not good at paperwork', having 'awful habits', and having 'a haphazard way of doing things' – self-criticisms which were not supported by the files she showed me, which seemed to show a well organised personal system for keeping track of a very complex set of obligations. While difficulties in keeping on top of the paperwork arose for many participants, some people including Megan personalised and individualised these issues more than others, internalising the mistrust built into the audit system.

The instantiation of audit society in workplace literacy practices

So we see both Aidan and Megan described increased demands to provide an account of their work. They were both concerned with the requirement to produce auditable records – 'evidence' – which were fed back to management, for purposes which were not fully clear to them. They both, Aidan in particular, made distinctions between these auditable records and what 'really' counted in their teaching. Unintended consequences of these measures included finding ways to minimise the amounts, 'creative compliance' (Aidan); the production of additional self-generated paperwork which added to workload (Megan); damage to teacher-student relationships (Aidan); overwhelm and self-criticism (Megan); and describing a distance between the realities of their teaching and requests from management (both).

These patterns are inflected by their specific situations. It made a difference that Aidan had management responsibilities as well as a teaching role, giving him a better understanding of the source and purpose of some of the paperwork he faced. Their professional histories shaped their responses too. Aidan drew on a clearly articulated values system from his long history of working in adult education to frame a critique of the paperwork as clashing with the purpose of the role: responding to students' needs as an autonomous professional. Megan had less experience in adult and community education, framing her concerns more in terms of ensuring that paperwork and teaching were all completed in the time she had available. When this became difficult, she tended to blame herself rather than the system.

Their experiences were also set within different national policy structures. Megan worked within a target driven framework, and was concerned with providing evidence that she had done everything she could to meet these targets. Aidan's work was not driven by externally set targets at this point, though he thought these might be introduced. The concerns he expressed were mainly around constraints on responding to the specific needs of the students he was working with.

Despite these differences, Aidan and Megan's experiences illustrate trends across the data set more broadly. Across both sites, key issues were how possible it was to complete the paperwork; the extent to which paperwork fulfilled the purposes of the job or not; the expression of a sense of obligation to an unspecified and distant source of demands; and how far the nature of the paperwork fitted or clashed with people's descriptions of their own professional identities (Tusting 2010b). By engaging closely with people's experiences and everyday literacy practices, this study provides concrete empirical evidence of the issues raised by Power (1997) in his analysis of audit society. Addressing this question from a linguistic ethnographic perspective has enabled more detailed focus on the meaning-making processes by means of which the audit society is instantiated and experienced in people's working lives.

References

Arthur, L., & Tait, A. (2004) 'Too Little Time to Learn? Issues and Challenges for Those in Work', *Studies in the Education of Adults, 36*(2), 222–234.

Ball, S. J. (2003) 'The Teacher's Soul and the Terrors of Performativity', *Journal of Education Policy, 18*(2), 215–228.

Barton, D. (2007) *Literacy: an Introduction to the Ecology of Written Language (2nd edn)*, Oxford: Blackwells.

Barton, D., & Hamilton, M. (2000) 'Literacy Practices', in D. Barton, M. Hamilton, & R. Ivanič (eds), *Situated Literacies*, London and New York: Routledge, pp. 7–15.

Barton, D., Hamilton, M., & Ivanič, R. (2000) *Situated Literacies: Reading and Writing in Context*, London: Routledge.

Barton, D., & Papen, U. (2010) *The Anthropology of Writing: Understanding Textually Mediated Worlds*, London: Continuum.

Blommaert, J., Collins, J., & Slembrouck, S. (2005) 'Spaces of Multilingualism', *Language & Communication, 25*(3), 197–216.

Bloome, D. (2005) *Discourse Analysis and the Study of Classroom Language & Literacy Events: A Microethnographic Perspective*, Mahwah, N.J.; London: Lawrence Erlbaum Associates.

Brandt, D. (2009) *Literacy and Learning: Reflections on Writing, Reading, and Society*, San Francisco, CA: Jossey-Bass.

Burgess, A. (2008) 'The Literacy Practices of Recording Achievement: How a Text Mediates between the Local and the Global', *Journal of Education Policy, 23*(1), 49–62.

Creese, A. (2008) 'Linguistic ethnography', in K. A. King & N. H. Hornberger (eds), *Encyclopedia of Language and Education 2nd edition, Volume 10: Research Methods in Language and Education*, New York: Springer Science and Business Media LLC, pp. 229–241.

Davies, K. (1994) 'The Tensions between Process Time and Clock Time in Carework: The Example of Day Nurseries', *Time and Society, 3*(3), 277–303.

Farrell, L. (2001) 'Negotiating Knowledge in the Knowledge Economy: Workplace Educators and the Politics of Codification', *Studies in Continuing Education, 23*(2), 201–214.

Farrell, L. (2006) *Making Knowledge Common: Literacy and Knowledge at Work*, New York: Peter Lang.

Gee, J. P., Hull, G. A., & Lankshear, C. (1996) *The New Work Order: Behind the Language of the New Capitalism*, Sydney: Allen and Unwin.

Gherardi, S. (2009) 'Introduction: The Critical Power of the "Practice Lens"', *Management Learning, 40*(2), 115–128.

Heath, S. B. (1983) *Ways with Words: Language, Life, and Work in Communities and Classrooms*, Cambridge: Cambridge University Press.

Iedema, R., & Scheeres, H. (2003) 'From Doing Work to Talking Work: Renegotiating Knowing, Doing, and Identity', *Applied Linguistics, 24*(3), 316–337.

Juffermans, K. (2011) 'The Old Man and the Letter: Repertoires of Literacy and Languaging in a Modern Multiethnic Gambian Village', *Compare: A Journal of Comparative and International Education*, 41(2), 165–179.

Karlsson, A.-M. (2005) 'Goods, Services and the Role of Written Discourse', in B.-L. Gunnarson (ed.), *Communication in the Workplace*, Uppsala: Uppsala University.

Lamvik, G. M., Naesje, P. C., Skarholt, K., & Torvatn, H. (2009) Paperwork, Management, and Safety: Towards a Bureaucratization of Working Life and a Lack of Hands-on Supervision, in *Safety, Reliability and Risk Analysis: Theory, Methods and Applications, Vols 1–4*, pp. 2981–2986.

Lefstein, A. (2008) 'Changing Classroom Practice through the English National Literacy Strategy: A Micro-Interactional Perspective', *American Educational Research Journal*, 45(3), 701–737.

Lillis, T. M. (2009) 'Bringing Writers' Voices to Writing Research: Talk around Texts', in A. Carter, T. M. Lillis, & S. Parkin (eds), *Why Writing Matters: Issues of Access and Identity in Writing Research and Pedagogy*, Amsterdam: John Benjamins, pp. 169–188.

Martin-Jones, M., & Jones, K. (2000) *Multilingual Literacies: Reading and Writing Different Worlds*, Amsterdam: John Benjamins.

Maybin, J. (2007) 'Literacy under and over the Desk: Oppositions and Heterogeneity', *Language and Education*, 21(6), 515–530.

Maybin, J., & Tusting, K. (2011) 'Linguistic Ethnography', in J. Simpson (ed.), *Routledge Handbook of Applied Linguistics*, London; New York: Routledge, pp. 229–241.

Papen, U. (2005) 'Reading the Bible and Shopping on Credit: Literacy Practices and Literacy Learning in a Township of Windhoek, Namibia', in A. Rogers (ed.), *Urban Literacy*, Hamburg: UNESCO Institute for Education, pp. 211–235.

Power, M. (1997) *The Audit Society: Rituals of Verification*, Oxford: Oxford University Press.

Power, M. (2000) 'The Audit Society – Second Thoughts', *International Journal of Auditing*, 4(1), 111–119.

Rampton, B., Tusting, K., Maybin, J., Barwell, R., Creese, A., & Lytra, V. (2004) UK Linguistic Ethnography: a Discussion Paper. Retrieved from http://uklef.net/documents/papers/ramptonetal2004.pdf.

Rock, F. (2012) ' "I've looked at these letters for years and it just now occurred to me": Handling Hybridity in the Workplace', paper presented at *Explorations in Ethnography, Language and Communication 4*, Copenhagen, 13–14 September 2012.

Smith, D. E. (2001) 'Texts and the Ontology of Organizations and Institutions', *Studies in Cultures, Organizations and Societies*, 7(2), 159–198.

Swinglehurst, D. (2012) 'The Electronic Patient Record (EPR) in General Practice: New Methodologies, New Insights', paper presented at *Explorations in Ethnography, Language and Communication 4*, Copenhagen, 13–14 September 2012.

Troman, G. (2000) 'Teacher Stress in the Low-trust Society', *British Journal of Sociology of Education*, 21(3), 331–353.

Tusting, K. (2009) '"I am not a 'good' teacher, I don't do all their paperwork": Teacher Resistance to Accountability Demands in the English Skills for Life Strategy', *Literacy and Numeracy Studies*, 17(3), 6–26.

Tusting, K. (2010a) 'Eruptions of Interruptions: Managing Tensions between Writing and Other Tasks in a Textualised Childcare Workplace', in D. Barton & U. Papen (eds), *The Anthropology of Writing: Understanding Textually Mediated Worlds*, London and New York: Continuum, pp. 67–89.

Tusting, K. (2010b) Paperwork and Pressure in Educational Workplaces: the Textual Mediation of Target Culture, *ESRC Full Research Report*, RES-000-22-2036. Swindon: ESRC.

Tusting, K. (2012) 'Learning Accountability Literacies in Educational Workplaces: Situated Learning and Processes of Commodification', *Language and Education*, 26(2), 121–138.

Tusting, K. (2013) Literacy Studies as Linguistic Ethnography, paper 105 in *Working papers in urban language and literacies*, London: King's College. Retrieved from http://www.kcl.ac.uk/innovation/groups/ldc/publications/workingpapers/the-papers/WP105-Tusting-2013-Literacy-studies-as-linguistic-ethnography.pdf

Tusting, K., & Barton, D. (2005) 'Community-based Local Literacies Research', in R. Beach, J. Green, M. Kamil, & T. Shanahan (eds), *Multidisciplinary Perspectives on Literacy Research*, New Jersey: Hampton Press, pp. 243–263.

Van Hout, T. (2012) Analyzing Textual Flow: Lurking and Soaking in Real Time, paper presented at *Explorations in Ethnography, Language and Communication 4*, Copenhagen, 13–14 September 2012.

Williams, J., Corbin, B., & McNamara, O. (2007) 'Finding Inquiry in Discourses of Audit and Reform in Primary Schools', *International Journal of Educational Research*, 46(1–2), 57–67.

Woolf, N. (2007) 'Best Practices: a Little Structure in your Codes ...', *Inside ATLAS-ti*, 3–6.

4

Between Text and Social Practice: Balancing Linguistics and Ethnography in Journalism Studies

Tom Van Hout

Introduction

Digital media technologies have given (and continue to give) way to new genres, forms and practices of public communication. These include mobile news consumption, digitally mediated social protest, data journalism, machine-written news, massive databases such as Wikileaks and NSA leaks, and the metajournalism of linking, modifying, reposting and commenting on news stories. The promise and potential of these new technologies stand in sharp contrast to the moribund discourses surrounding traditional news media, in particular print and broadcast media. Their political economy is fraught with declining numbers: circulation, advertising revenue, staff count and market capitalization. In addition, there is widespread concern about the future, quality and diversity of journalism in the face of industrial concentration, precarious labour conditions, increased productivity demands, news aggregation and saturation. Taken together, these changes in news production, content and consumption have sparked public and academic interest in journalism.

Journalism studies is a fast-growing interdisciplinary project that spans journalism theory, practice and education. Four phases can be distinguished in its historical development (Wahl-Jorgensen and Hanitzsch, 2009). While the field's *prehistory* dates back to mid-19th century German social theory, the *empirical* study of journalism began after the Second World War with the foundation of journalism schools in the United States. A first generation of news scholars produced groundbreaking work on news values, agenda setting and gatekeeping in the 1950s (for instance, White, 1950). A wave of very productive and influential *sociological* studies then followed in the 1970s and 1980s (for a review, see Cottle, 2007), yielding important insights into news production at Anglo-American elite news organisations. The past two decades have witnessed a *global-comparative* turn in the study of journalism, with multinational research projects such as the *Worlds of Journalism Study* (Reich and Hanitzsch, 2013) or *Journalistic Role Performance around the Globe* (Mellado and Van Dalen, 2014).

This burgeoning field of journalism studies has drawn substantially from work in the two constituent domains of linguistic ethnography. However, work that combines linguistics and ethnography is rare in journalism studies. And yet, linguistic ethnography has much to offer to journalism studies. And vice versa. Linguistic ethnography offers journalism studies useful analytical frameworks for studying the shifting sands of contemporary news journalism. Journalism offers linguistic ethnography fertile ground for examining the representational practices which normalise ways of speaking about culture, ideology and identity (Spitulnik, 1993).

In this chapter I describe how my research on business journalism gradually appropriated the epistemology of linguistic ethnography. My ethnographic site is the business newsdesk of a Belgian newspaper. Here I analyse how a news story about government research funding makes its way into the newsroom, onto the reporter's computer screen, and into the newspaper. Before describing this case study in detail, I begin with a brief review of past and present work on the linguistics and ethnography of journalism.

Language and journalism

The instrumental relation between language and journalism has yielded productive lines of inquiry in critical discourse analysis, conversation analysis, corpus linguistics and sociolinguistics (for a recent overview, see O'Keeffe, 2012). These systematic and detailed studies have pointed to ways in which news texts make particular worldviews seem commonsense. They have taught us about the structure, form and functions of news discourse. They have described interactional aspects of broadcast news and multimodal aspects of online news. However, investigations of media language have tended to remain 'unpeopled' and primarily text-driven, with little focused attention paid to the production process. This analytical blind spot was first observed by Jef Verschueren, who in 1985 wrote that discourse analysis of journalism tends to ignore the 'structural and functional properties of the news gathering and reporting process' (1985). More recently, Philo (2007), has argued that purely text-based critical discourse analysis in the work of Fairclough (2003) and Van Dijk (1988) encounters a series of problems specifically in its ability to show: (1) the origins of competing discourses and how they relate to different social interests; (2) the diversity of social accounts compared to what is present (and absent) in a specific text; (3) the impact of external factors such as professional ideologies on the manner in which the discourses are represented; and (4) what the text actually means to different parts of the audience.

Although these critiques present something of a strawman argument as they overstate the absence of a production component in critical discourse analysis and predate the emergence of alternative approaches (Richardson, 2008; Krzyżanowski, 2011), they highlight the necessity of analysing news discourse beyond the purely textual level. A more encompassing, holistic approach to the language of journalism is exactly what one group of scholars belonging to a group called *NewsTalk&Text* advocates. Building on seminal work by Verschueren (1985), Bell (1991) and Jacobs (1999), and more recent work by Cotter (2010), Van Hout et al. (2011) and Perrin (2013), *NewsTalk&Text* prioritises 'ethnographic descriptions and [...] insider perspectives on the actual practices and values of news production, documenting how these often differ from the claims of theorists, while simultaneously exploring new theoretical frameworks to better understand and analyse news production practices' (Catenaccio et al., 2011). This small but growing network of language and media scholars has ventured into newsrooms to capture a sense of what contemporary newsmaking is and does. This brings me to the ethnography of journalism.

Ethnography and journalism

Ethnography is no stranger to media and journalism studies. In fact, much of what we know about journalism comes from the classic newsroom ethnographies conducted in the 1970s and 1980s (for a review, see Cottle, 2007). These studies focused attention on the structural and professional forces at play in the newsroom, for instance, how news production is a matter of managing the unpredictability of news through careful planning and resource allocation (Golding and Elliot, [1979]1999), or how reliance on elite sources is a strategic ritual (Tuchman, 1972) that allows journalists to frame their work as 'objective' and hence trustworthy. The theories generated by the first wave of newsroom ethnography are currently being reassessed in light of the cultural, technological and professional changes that journalism is going through (Paterson and Domingo, 2008; Paterson and Domingo, 2011). However, both past and present newsroom ethnography is rooted in a sociological tradition of realism that has 'emphasized the objective nature of data collection and thus clearly lean[s] toward observation and away from the emic-etic interpretative work necessitated when participation is given full partnership in methodological practice' (Murphy, 2011).

In contrast to newsroom ethnography, the anthropology of journalism (see for instance the excellent collection of work in Bird, 2010) is more reflective in its methods and critical in its analyses. For instance, Hannerz (2004) describes the lives of foreign correspondents by 'studying sideways' a craft that resembles ethnographers' tales from the field. In her ethnography of news production in modern day India, Rao (2010) ventures outside the newsroom to examine the politics of news reporting in a recently commercialised mediascape. Peterson (2003) sees the ethnography of journalism as 'an emergent effort [...] to talk about the agency of media producers within a cultural system while still recognizing their embeddedness in larger structures of power'. Such a view not only speaks to the practices, serendipity and creativity embodied in journalism as the journalist negotiates various sources, demands and constraints, but also to the analytical attempts at coming to grips with journalism's 'cultural system'. In practice, this means learning to see the 'structures of power' that bring reporters, editors and desk chiefs together to construct texts. In other words, this requires ethnographic fieldwork.

Balancing linguistics and ethnography in a study of business news

In the introduction to this edited volume, Rampton et al. (2015) write that ethnography may serve as 'a way of enriching a fundamentally linguistic project' (ethnographic linguistics) or 'alternatively linguistics can be a way of helping researchers with a range of different backgrounds to reach deeper into the ethnographic description of social or institutional processes' (linguistic ethnography). Work that combines linguistics and ethnography in journalism studies tends to blur the distinction between ethnographic linguistics and linguistic ethnography. My own research on business news (Van Hout and Jacobs, 2008; Van Hout and Macgilchrist, 2010; Van Hout, 2010; Van Hout et al., 2011) serves as a case in point.

Between October 2006 and March 2007, I made 47 research visits to the business newsdesk of *De Standaard*, the largest Dutch-language quality newspaper in Belgium. Overall, conditions of access were excellent.

I was granted a workspace next to one of two journalists whom I had met during preliminary research interviews. Upon simple request, I was given a guest account which gave me access to the editorial platform, the newsroom diary and mailbox. Moreover, I had all access to the various editorial meetings and was able to make extensive fieldnotes, collect newsroom documents such as press releases, internal memos and working documents, conduct formal and informal interviews and log reporters' writing processes in real time.

During my fieldwork, the business newsdesk employed thirteen professional journalists (one female, twelve male): a desk chief, a section editor and eleven 'editors' (Dutch: *redacteurs*), i.e. senior reporters assigned to fixed domains ('news beats') for the print edition of the newspaper: banking, finance, energy, transport, technology, labour, media, marketing and human resources. In addition, the economics newsdesk hired the services of a self-employed financial markets journalist and occasionally relied on freelancers and interns. Two editors from the online newsdesk were permanently assigned to the economics newsdesk to content manage the *.Biz* website, the online version of the print edition. Apart from the section editor and the two online editors, all business reporters were in their mid-thirties to early fifties and had considerable professional experience, some at other newsdesks, others at rival newspapers or broadcast media.

Business news comprises both 'hard' news about financial markets, corporate finance and government expenditure and 'soft' news about personal finance, consumer products, marketing and technology. Despite its prestige (cf. the Financial Times or the Wall Street Journal) and omnipresence in quality news media, business news remains an under examined practice of professional journalism. However, we do know that business newsrooms are flooded with company PR, government announcements, industry surveys, newswire messages and news alerts (Doyle, 2006) and that business journalists and business professionals form an increasingly interdependent relationship (Grünberg and Pallas, 2013). When I began the research for this project in 2006, I was primarily interested in how *preformulation*, i.e. the newspaper-like style of press releases (described at length in Jacobs, 1999), impacted business journalists' work and enlisted ethnography as 'method' (Lillis, 2008): a procedure for collecting talk around texts.

However, what captured my attention once I began fieldwork were not isolated discourse events – the act of reproducing preformulated texts – but rather the densely intertextual social practices 'of research, information selection, collegial coordination, and editorial conversation' (Boyer and Hannerz, 2006) that characterise newsmaking. Each time a journalist lifts a quote from a telephone interview and inserts it into a news story, a truth claim is reported and a journalistic stance is encoded. It is through this intertextual lens that I gradually learned to see journalism practice as a recursive and relatively stable process of textual organisation and coordination. This insight turned my gaze away from applied linguistic notions of text towards ethnographic approaches to context (Lillis, 2008), genre (Briggs and Bauman, 1992) and writing (Barton and Papen, 2010). In other words, by trying to make sense of what I was observing, my epistemological focus shifted from using ethnography as a methodological add-on (ethnographic linguistics) to embedding discourse analysis in an ethnographic framework (linguistic ethnography).

Ethnography privileges participant perspectives, speaks to theoretical claims made elsewhere and favours thick descriptions of worlds inhabited by informants – and their researchers. These tenets cast a wide net which I tried to haul in empirically by tracking newsroom text trajectories (Blommaert, 2005) across time and space. I started with the identification of newsworthy events via their selection and negotiation during editorial conferences and followed their transformation into newspaper articles. Embracing linguistic ethnography's openness towards data and methods, its commitment to participation, and its aesthetic of smallness and slowness, I combined discourse analysis and computer-assisted writing process analysis (Latif, 2008) to 'deepen' my ethnographic descriptions of business journalists at work.

More specifically, I used two software applications that recorded in real time what journalists did on their computer screens. Inputlog (Leijten and Van Waes, 2006) is a Windows based keystroke logging tool that records keyboard strokes and mouse movements. Camtasia Studio® is an online screen registration tool which records computer screen action (Degenhardt, 2006). Both applications ran in the background and did not interfere with normal computer operations. Collecting the keystroke logging data was preceded by a period of 'informant recruiting' in which I asked for reporters' informed consent. I offered them a written agreement detailing the objectives of my study, permission to use the data for scientific purposes and data veto right. Out of the twelve reporters (the desk chief did not write stories on a regular basis), I actively recruited nine. Four accepted my invitation to participate and two declined. Two computers were declared unresearchable and another reporter lost interest because the logging software slowed his computer down.

The software added contextual depth to my observations by contrasting retrospection and social action. I asked journalists to comment on excerpts from the screenvideos during so-called 'cue-based retrospective interviews' (Perrin, 2013). These authorial metacomments provided insights about journalists' understandings of news writing, journalism and power. The software made it possible to compare what journalists said about their writing practices and what they actually did on screen. Crucially, these contrastive observations enabled me 'to explore what's significant and at stake for writers at specific sociohistorical moments and, importantly, thus to engage with what is significant contextually' (Lillis, 2008).

Along the way, I developed a four step research protocol that involved (i) identification of stories within the news beats of my key informants; (ii) asking for reporter permission to record their writing process; (iii) data recording and storage; and (iv) conducting a retrospective interview as soon as the reporter had filed the story for copy-editing. From these data, I extracted a core set of 18 cases that document empirically how particular stories entered the newsroom, were discussed during staff meetings, and produced and filed for copy-editing. The cases were selected for their specificity and not as representative samples (Small, 2009). Every logged story comprised at least four data files: the Inputlog data file, the Camtasia screenvideo, an audiofile of the retrospective interview and copies of the source texts. In addition, relevant working documents, email messages, interview notes made by the reporters and fieldnotes were included. I made rough transcripts of the screenvideos and retrospective interviews and had Inputlog generate analytical files from the raw logging data. These analytical files range from detailed records of the recorded writing session, including input actions (keyboard, mouse click or movement, window nagivation) to linear (i.e. line by line) representations and descriptive statistics about the writing session (total number of characters and words produced, and average pause times).

Analytically, the challenge was 'to keep the research centred on the tension between text and social practice and not to drift into either a text-free analysis of social situations or a decontextualized analysis of text' (Scollon, 1998). In what follows, I illustrate this balancing act between text and professional practice by analysing how an unplanned news story made its way through the newsroom and into the newspaper.

Labouring in the field: talking, reading and writing business news

News management

One of my earliest field observations was that the daily newsroom operation at *De Standaard* bears a striking resemblance to the routines of news management that first-generation newsroom ethnographers described in the 1970s (Van Hout and Jacobs, 2008). For instance, Golding and Elliott's ([1979]1999) portrayal of broadcast news production as 'a highly regulated and routine process of manufacturing a cultural product on an electronic production line' applies remarkably well to a print context, even after 35 years. So does their claim that the newsroom diary and the story meeting are central mechanisms 'aimed at plotting the flow of events in the world and marking them for manufacture into 'stories'' (Golding and Elliot, [1979]1999).

The diary is a written record of events 'based on the knowledge that events will occur, not on observation of them unfolding' (Golding and Elliot, [1979]1999: 113). It pools events that have been judged newsworthy *a priori*, either on the grounds of previous coverage or on their perceived public weight. The diary manages the unpredictability of news by marking planned events for coverage. The entries are based on press releases, announcements and invitations that circulate in the newsroom. Reporters are free to add entries and do so regularly but usually in consultation with the desk chief. One of the journalists told me that reporters could pretty much 'autonomously decide whether or not to follow up a story lead' (DS_FN1_4). The diary represents the initial selection of news; the 'critical mass' of marked – and electronically inscribed – events that initiate the daily news cycle.

These events trigger another regulating mechanism: the story meeting (Van Hout and Van Praet, 2011). These staff meetings are literacy events par excellence. They are episodes of textual mediation that are ritualised (and hence discursively stable, repeated and observable) and feature two dominant literacy practices: talk about planned or spot news events; and inscription of mutually established decisions about story play and authorship. Four of these meetings are held daily and each serves a particular purpose in the production cycle (Figure 4.1).

Around 10:00am, the desk chiefs and one or two representatives from the chief editorial team assemble to review the previous day's paper and preview major stories for next day's paper. Reporters trickle in and work on planned stories, make phonecalls and read up on developing stories. At 2:00pm, the separate newsdesks convene to negotiate story selection, length, placement and authorship. Front page story suggestions are made. Immediately following the 2:00pm newsdesk meetings, the copy-editors, editor-in-chief and a representative from the affiliate title, *Het Nieuwsblad*, convene at 2:45pm for a front page editorial meeting. The main activity here is to pool and review front page story nominations and inside stories per newsdesk. On the newsroom floor, reporters

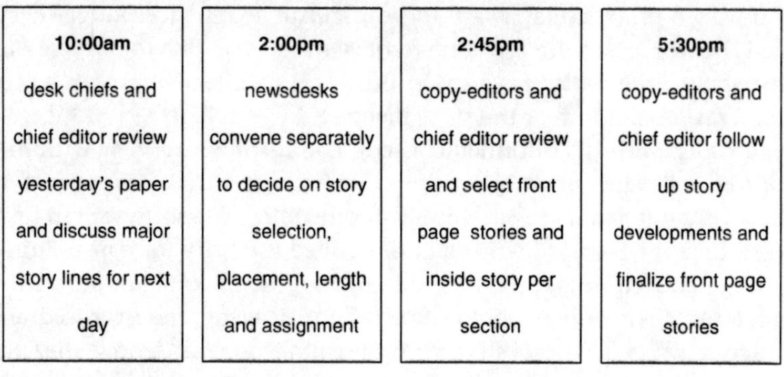

Figure 4.1   Editorial routine at *De Standaard*

write up their assigned stories. Final decisions regarding the front page layout are made during a 5:30pm meeting. The copy-editors announce which stories, photos and graphics will be displayed on the front page. Each news desk circulates their respective (and final) story selections. The front pages for *De Standaard* and *Het Nieuwsblad* are discussed, story updates since 2:45pm are reviewed and regional news stories are briefly summarised. Most stories are filed between 6:00pm and 8:00pm, after which time the copy-editors take over.

Introducing the VIB story

The story (henceforth: the VIB story) is concerned with increased government funding of biotechnology and nanotechnology research (Van Hout, 2010). Two Flemish research institutes, the *Flanders Interuniversity Institute for Biotechnology* (VIB) and the *Interuniversity Microelectronics Centre* (IMEC) are awarded five-year research contracts by the Flemish government. This was an unplanned story that was brought to the attention of senior reporter Rutger (a pseudonym). A spokesperson for the Flemish Minister of Science had called Rutger to ask if he was planning on attending the press conference. Hearing that he was not, the spokesperson then informed Rutger that a press release would be sent round and that the slides used during the press conference were also available. Rutger asked some questions about the story, made notes on a notepad and said he would have a look at the documents.

Rutger was one of my key informants. He enjoyed special status in the newsroom: during my fieldwork, he was promoted to adjunct desk chief

and won a professional award for journalistic excellence. Rutger occupied the workspace directly next to me and so I was able to observe him
throughout the entire production process: I overheard him taking the
call, I sat next to him at the story meeting, I was able to record his writing process with his informed consent, conduct an interview with him
shortly afterwards and collect the source material that was emailed to
him. I did not gain access to his telephone notes. The software ran from
the moment he started writing until he filed the story for copy-editing.
If linguistic ethnography is about making sense of communicative
processes, then understanding how editorial agency is organised and
structured was a crucial step in my learning process. I now shift my
focus to how agency is practised by following how Rutger writes an
unplanned story on science policy. In keeping with the analytical tenets
of linguistic ethnography, I start from the description of agency in the
immediate situation and then work outward, i.e. from the data, and
interweave ethnographic knowledge and relevant analytical frameworks
in an attempt to relate my observations to wider issues in journalism. I
pick up the story as Rutger introduces the VIB story at the 2.00pm story
meeting.

Extract 1 is based on an audio recording of the story meeting during
which Rutger introduces the VIB story. The story meeting was attended
by nine members of staff and myself. The extract is first presented in
Dutch and then in English to increase readability.

Extract 1

DS_W16_D4_eco. Rutger introduces the VIB story 10 minutes into
the story meeting.

1	Jef:	William d'er is vandaag over gecommentarieerd
2	William:	ja? ik heb gene commentaar gezien ma k'em vanalles
3	Mitch:	en kijk ge ge praat weer voor uw beurt he
4	Jef:	't is wa da ge zegt
5	William:	wist gij het Mitch?
6	Mitch:	ja natuurlijk wist ik dat ik word daar mee wakker
7		ik luister d'er naar en dan sta ik op
8	Rutger:	ja ja om half acht ja
9	Koen:	of valt hij terug in slaap *(lacht)* al die commentaren
10	Kaat:	ik gok op dieje in slaap vallen *(lacht)*( )
11	Walter:	kheb Pieterke Pieter dan al voor z'n tekenfilms gezet
12		( ) om ( ) *(gelach)*

13 Rutger: er is ook nog euh- (*gelach*)
14 Jef: goh, gij begint daar nu al mee?
15 Koen: ja, da's ongelooflijk dat wordt een ramp die opvoeding zoiets
16 Rutger: de ondertekening van het nieuwe beheersovereenkomst
17   tussen de Vlaamse Overheid en euh het VIB en IMEC
18   die krijgen 20% meer geld
19 Koen: wat? twee maand?
20 Walter: drie
21 Koen: drie maand en hij zet hem al voor de tv (*gelach*)
22 Rutger: moet daar aandacht aan geschonken worden?
23 Mitch: 60 lijn- op 60 lijntjes op eco 4, nee?
24   als ze meer geld krijgen?
25 Rutger: ja 20 procent ( )

English translation

1 Jef: William there was a commentary on it today
2 William: yeah? i didn't see a commentary but I'm doing all sorts
3 Mitch: and look you you're speaking out of turn again see
4 Jef: you said it
5 William: did you know about it Mitch?
6 Mitch: why of course I knew that I wake up to it
7   I listen to it and then I get up
8 Rutger: yeah sure at seven thirty yeah
9 Koen: or he falls asleep again (*laughs*) all those commentaries
10 Kaat: my money is on that falling asleep (laughs)( )
11 Walter: I've got lil' Pieter Pieter in front of his cartoons
12   by then ( ) to ( ) (*laughter*)
13 Rutger: there's also ehm- (*laughter*)
14 Jef: jeez, are you already doing that now?
15 Koen: yeah, that's unbelievable that's some education right there
16 Rutger: the signing of the new management agreement
17   between the Flemish government and erm the VIB and IMEC
18   they're getting 20% more money
19 Koen: what? two months?
20 Walter: three
21 Koen: three months and he's already watching tv (*laughter*)
22 Rutger: should attention be paid to this?
23 Mitch: 60 lin- 60 lines on eco 4, no?
24   if they get more money?
25 Rutger: yeah 20 percent ( )

In line 1, Jef corrects William, who had been ranting about governmental mismanagement of an ICT project, by saying that a statement on the matter had been released (I later learned that Jef was referring to *De Ochtend* ('The Morning'), a current affairs program broadcast on national radio that reviews and previews the news). William's line 2 admits to not having 'seen' the commentary, which summons desk chief Mitch's playful reprimand in line 3: *ge praat weer voor uw beurt* ('you're speaking out of turn again'). In his defense, William asks Mitch if he was aware of any official statements (line 5), which occasions a spirited digression about the news consumption routines of desk chief Mitch. Assuming the role of consummate news professional who is always up to speed with the latest news, Mitch is 'of course' aware of the current affairs radio program that had aired the commentary, adding *ik word daar mee wakker* ('I wake up to it'). This tongue-in-cheek identity claim triggers ironic responses. Rutger takes a stab at Mitch's proclaimed news consumption zeal (line 8) while Koen calls Mitch's bluff (line 9), which Kaat seconds (line 10).

Meanwhile, William, a new father, engages in a byplay (Goffman, 1981) about his parenting practices (line 11). This byplay crosscuts Rutger's attempt at introducing the VIB story (line 13). Shifting into a formal, nominalised register typically associated with written language, Rutger's lines 16 through 18 introduce the VIB story by referring to the newly signed contract, the institutional partners involved and the budget increase. Clearly, this story pitch can only have been based on the information Rutger received (and wrote down) from the government spokesperson. Rutger received the press release electronically at 2:59pm, some 45 minutes after the story meeting had ended. Rutger's tentative line 22 ('should attention be paid to this?') is met with a question from Mitch in line 24 ('if they get more money?') which Rutger confirms (line 25 'yeah 20 percent').

This brief newsroom exchange between desk chief Mitch and reporter Rutger illustrates 'the limited discretion involved in news selection' (Golding and Elliot, [1979]1999). Amid lighthearted subordinate communication, Rutger re-entextualises the telephone conversation by appealing to the news values of prominence ('the Flemish Government') and impact ('a 20% budget increase') and by adopting a voice of neutrality: his story pitch animates just the facts. That Rutger relies on news values and facticity is squarely within the tried-and-tested parameters of journalism practice (Cotter, 2010) and allows for fast decision-making. Rutger's tentative line 23 ('should attention be paid to this') is met with an immediate decision: Mitch assigns Rutger 60 lines on page four of the business section and inquires about the newsworthiness, which Rutger confirms in line 26.

Writing the story

The screen video data show that Rutger first opens the press release in his email program, scrolls through it and sends it to the printer. Next, he opens the attached PowerPoint presentation and starts browsing the first two slides, including the text in the comments section. He then goes through the remaining four slides of the PowerPoint presentation. Asked if he knows how he is going to write the story in advance or that he first makes notes, Rutger said:

> ik heb eerst die persmedeling gelezen en die slides goed bekeken tja en dan haal je eruit wat het nieuws is namelijk dat ze meer geld krijgen. Maar euh ik heb af en toe wel euh teruggekeken in die slides om dat laatste stuk te schrijven.
>
> *I first read the press release and took a close look at the slides and then well you pull out what the news is namely that they are getting more money. But ehm every now and then I ehm looked back at the slides to write that last piece.*

To Rutger, writing news from sources is a straightforward matter. The fact that the institutes are receiving more money makes this story news-worthy. I turn now to examine how Rutger extracts 'what the news is' and how he writes 'that last piece'.

Judging from the screen video, the press release that Rutger has in front of him as he writes the article feeds him ready-made news dis-course, specifically, it provides a lead sentence and the opening sentence of his second paragraph. This demonstrates that the press release is a genre that travels remarkably well across semiotic spaces. Indeed, the 'information subsidy' (Gandy, 1982) relayed by the spokesperson makes the leap from a fleeting telephone conversation to notes scrib-bled on a notepad, survives the 2:00pm story unscathed and then re-emerges as an email attachment that finds its way onto Rutger's editing window and into his news article. Note for instance the similarity in Table 4.1 between:

Table 4.1   Similarities between texts

the opening lines of the Ministry of Science press release (original translation, not mine)	Today Flemish Minister for Science and Innovation Fientje Moerman has signed the new management agreements (2007–2011) for VIB and IMEC. The Flemish government reserves more than 400 million euro in the coming five years for research in these two top institutes. The budget of operation of both institutes increases with 20%
Rutger's story pitch in Extract 1	'there's also ehm the signing of the new management agreement between the Flemish government and erm the VIB and IMEC they're getting 20% more money'
the text produced so far (based on the writing process data):	[**lead**] The Flemish research centers VIB and Imec are getting more money from the Flemish Government. [**byline**] Policy Brussels. [**body**] The subsidy raise is included in the new management agreements that were signed yesterday in Ghent.

In each of these three texts, the signing of the contract, the institutional partners involved (the Flemish government, VIB and IMEC) and the contracted decision (a subsidy raise) are mentioned. These elements respectively account for the *how?*, the *who?* and the *what?* of this story. The *when?* and the *where?* are covered in the press release ('Today', 'UZ Gent') and in Rutger's text produced so far ('yesterday', 'Ghent'). In short, Rutger is doing what journalists are expected to do: get the facts right.

Fourteen minutes and twenty-six seconds into the writing process, Rutger writes 'Tegenover de extra middelen staan wel nieuwe eisen' (Eng. *The extra funds do come with new demands*). This text insertion is followed by more than two minutes of keyboard inactivity during which Rutger navigates to the PowerPoint presentation, reading (interpreted as keyboard inactivity and mouse scrolling) the notes of the second slide in detail. Rutger is searching for the answer to his next question: if the institutes are getting more money, what is expected in return? The answer is 'hidden' in the presentation notes and comprises three elements: the development of a corporate governance code, the realisation of a number of strategic goals and an annual evaluation based on a list of performance indicators.

Rutger copies all three demands and, in doing so, establishes journalistic balance: his article now describes the funding spike as well as the targets that both institutes have to meet. To illustrate how Rutger

0:16:47	[Movement] {2504} [Left Button] [Movement] {2393} Zo ·wo
0:16:52	rden · de · instellingen · verplicht · een · {4126}
0:16:57	individuele ·
0:17:02	corpBS BS BS ode · voor · deugdelijk
0:17:07	bedrijfsbeleid · (coproBS BS or
0:17:12	aeBS te · goeBS vernance
0:17:17	te · ontwikkelen. ·{3696}

Figure 4.2   Linear log extract

writes the corporate governance condition into his news story, I rely on a linear log file that Inputlog generates (Figure 4.2).

In this somewhat cryptic file, Inputlog reproduces the writing process in a linear fashion in five second intervals, including mouse movements (in square brackets, e.g., [Left Button] refers to a click of the left mouse button), text insertions (in lower case, e.g., ontwikkelen (Eng. *develop*) refers to the insertion of the 11 letters o-n-t-w-i-k-k-e-l-e-n), pause times in milliseconds (in curly braces, e.g., {2504} means a pause of 2.5 seconds) and backspaces (BS). The linear log shows Rutger correcting himself four letters into 'corp'(orate) governance, hitting backspace thrice and typing the somewhat more extensive Dutch alternative 'code voor deugdelijk bedrijfsbeleid' (Eng. *code of proper company management*) and parenthesising 'coporate governance' (but not correcting the typo), thereby explaining the term. On screen, the following text appears:

Zo worden de instellingen verplicht een individuele code voor deugdelijk bedrijfsbeleid (coporate [sic] governance) te ontwikkelen.

The institutions are required to develop an individual code of proper company management (coporate [sic] governance).

Finally, Rutger adds the VIB and IMEC URLs at the bottom of his article, marks up the byline and writes the headline, something he usually writes last he told me. He then revises the article, adding for instance that the management agreements were signed by 'the Minister of Science and Innovation Fientje Moerman (Open VLD)'. Finally, Rutger adds his initials, previews the text and files it for copy-editing. The entire production process takes 33 minutes and 23 seconds.

Concluding remarks

The picture that emerges is one of remarkable discursive stability across journalistic contexts. The funding increase travels from a telephone conversation across a story meeting, onto a reporter's computer screen and into the business news section. The reporter's mediating labour is, in essence, a matter of digital fact-checking and organising information for local markets. This supports the claim that newswriting is a 'reproductive process in which professionals contribute to glocalized newsflows by transforming source texts into public target texts' (Perrin, 2013). As we have seen, these glocalised newsflows coordinate and standardise the institutional activity (Smith, 2006) that the reporter engages in. The wider theoretical relevance of this sort of knowledge remains important, not only to document how journalism is changing, but also to understand what can be gained and lost from a move to a fully-fledged digital journalism.

I agree with Murphy (2011) that conducting fieldwork in a digital environment turns 'the field' [into] a considerably less concrete and empirically 'knowable' place, and that the there in 'being there', so foundational to traditional ethnography, has been fundamentally transformed in relation to media-centric issues of flow and fluidity of information within a networked society. It therefore becomes necessary to complement and augment fieldwork. The research described here employed contrastive and computer-assisted observations, a narrow research focus and key informants. Keystroke logging software was used to enhance the time spent in the field and collect data made available through developments in technology. The resulting data set allowed me to sustain a productive tension between text and social practice. More specifically, by tracking selected news stories across time and space, I was able to compare 'talk around text' (Lillis, 2008) with detailed representations of digital information practices. The added purchase is a linguistic ethnographic perspective on business news production that extends beyond the reach of linguistic and ethnographic work in journalism studies.

Acknowledgement

I am grateful to the editors for their pertinent and helpful comments on earlier versions of this chapter.

References

Barton, D. & Papen, U. (eds) 2010. *The Anthropology of Writing: Understanding Textually Mediated Worlds*, London: Continuum.

Bell, A. 1991. *The Language of News Media*, Oxford: Blackwell.

Bird, E. S. (ed.) 2010. *The Anthropology of News and Journalism: Global Perspectives*, Indiana: Indiana University Press.

Blommaert, J. 2005. *Discourse: A Critical Introduction*, Cambridge: Cambridge University Press.

Boyer, D. & Hannerz, U. 2006. Introduction: Worlds of journalism. *Ethnography*, 7, 5–17.

Briggs, C. & Bauman, R. 1992. Genre, intertextuality, and social power. *Journal of Linguistic Anthropology*, 2, 131–172.

Catenaccio, P., Cotter, C., De Smedt, M., Garzone, G., Jacobs, G., Macgilchrist, F., Lams, L., Perrin, D., Richardson, J. E., Van Hout, T. & Van Praet, E. 2011. Towards a linguistics of news production. *Journal of Pragmatics*, 43, 1843–1852.

Cotter, C. 2010. *News Talk: Investigating the Language of Journalism*, Cambridge: Cambridge University Press.

Cottle, S. 2007. Ethnography and News Production: New(s) Developments in the Field. *Sociology Compass*, 1, 1–16.

Degenhardt, M. 2006. CAMTASIA and CATMOVIE: Two Digital Tools for Observing, Documenting and Analysing Writing Processes of University Students. *In:* Van Waes, L., Leijten, M. & Neuwirth, C. M. (eds) *Writing and Digital Media*. Amsterdam: Elsevier.

Doyle, G. 2006. Financial news journalism. A post-Enron analysis of approaches towards economic and financial news production in the UK. *Journalism Studies*, 7, 433–452.

Fairclough, N. 2003. *Analysing Discourse: Textual Analysis for Social Research*, London, Routledge.

Gandy, O. H. 1982. *Beyond Agenda Setting: Information Subsidies and Public Policy*, Norwood, NJ: Ablex Publishing.

Goffman, E. 1981. *Forms of Talk*, Oxford: Blackwell.

Golding, P. & Elliot, P. [1979] 1999. Making the News. *In:* Tumber, H. (ed.) *News: A Reader*, Oxford: Oxford University Press.

Grünberg, J. & Pallas, J. 2013. Beyond the news desk – the embeddedness of business news. *Media, Culture & Society*, 35, 216–233.

Hannerz, U. 2004. *Foreign News: Exploring the World of Foreign Correspondents*, Chicago: University of Chicago Press.

Jacobs, G. 1999. *Preformulating the News: An Analysis of the Metapragmatics of Press Releases*, Amsterdam: John Benjamins.

Krzyżanowski, M. 2011. Ethnography and critical discourse analysis: towards a problem-oriented research dialogue. *Critical Discourse Studies*, 8, 231–238.

Latif, M. M. A. 2008. A state-of-the-art review of the real-time computer-aided study of the writing process. *International Journal of English Studies*, 8, 29–50.

Leijten, M. & Van Waes, L. 2006. Inputlog: New perspectives on the logging of on-line writing processes in a windows environment. *In:* Sullivan, K. & Lindgren, E. (eds) *Studies in Writing: Vol. 18. Computer Key-Stroke logging and Writing. Methods and Applications*, Oxford: Elsevier.

Lillis, T. 2008. Ethnography as method, methodology, and 'deep theorizing': Closing the gap between text and context in academic writing research. *Written Communication*, 25, 353–388.

Mellado, C., & Van Dalen, A. 2014. Between rhetoric and practice. *Journalism Studies*, 15, 859–878.

Murphy, P. D. 2011. Locating media ethnography. *In:* Nightingale, V. (ed.) *The Handbook of Media Audiences*, Oxford: Blackwell.

O'Keeffe, A. 2012. Media and discourse analysis. *In:* Gee, J. P. & Handford, M. (eds) *The Routledge Handbook of Discourse Analysis*, London: Routledge.

Paterson, C. & Domingo, D. (eds) 2008. *Making Online News: The Ethnography of New Media Production*, New York: Peter Lang.

Paterson, C. & Domingo, D. (eds) 2011. *Making Online News - Volume 2. Newsroom Ethnography in the Second Decade of Internet Journalism*, New York: Peter Lang.

Perrin, D. 2013. *The Linguistics of Newswriting*, Amsterdam: John Benjamins.

Peterson, M. A. 2003. *Anthropology & Mass Communication: Media and myth in the new millenium*, New York: Berghahn Books.

Philo, G. 2007. Can discourse analysis successfully explain the content of media and journalistic practice? *Journalism Studies*, 8, 175–196.

Rampton, B., Maybin, J. & Roberts, C. 2014. Introduction: Explorations and encounters in linguistic ethnography. *In:* Copland, F., Shaw, S. & Snell, J. (eds) *Linguistic Ethnography: Interdisciplinary Explorations*, Houndsmills: Palgrave.

Rao, U. 2010. *News as Culture: Journalistic Practices and the Remaking of Indian Leadership Traditions*, New York: Berghahn Books.

Reich, Z. & Hanitzsch, T. 2013. Determinants of journalists' professional autonomy: Individual and national level factors matter more than organizational ones. *Mass Communication and Society*, 16, 133–156.

Richardson, J. E. 2008. Language and Journalism: an expanding research agenda. *Journalism Studies*, 9.

Scollon, R. 1998. *Mediated Discourse as Social Interaction: A study of News Discourse*, London: Longman.

Small, M. L. 2009. 'How many cases do I need?': On science and the logic of case selection in field-based research. *Ethnography*, 10, 5–38.

Smith, D. E. 2006. Incorporating texts into ethnographic practice. *In:* Smith, D. E. (ed.) *Institutional Ethnography as Practice*, Lanham: Rowman & Littlefield.

Spitulnik, D. 1993. Anthropology and mass media. *Annual Review of Anthropology*, 22, 293–315.

Tuchman, G. 1972. Objectivity as strategic ritual: An examination of newsmen's notions of objectivity. *American Journal of Sociology*, 77, 660–79.

Van Dijk, T. A. 1988. *News as Discourse*, Hillsdale, NJ: Lawrence Erlbaum.

Van Hout, T. 2010. Sourcing business news: a case study of public relations uptake. *In:* Franklin, B. & Carlson, M. (eds) *Journalists, Sources, and Credibility: New Perspectives*, London: Routledge.

Van Hout, T. & Jacobs, G. 2008. News production theory and practice: fieldwork notes on power, interaction and agency. *Pragmatics*, 18, 59–84.

Van Hout, T. & Macgilchrist, F. 2010. Framing the news: an ethnographic view of financial newswriting. *Text & Talk*, 30, 147–169.

Van Hout, T., Pander Maat, H. & De Preter, W. 2011. Writing from news sources: The case of Apple TV. *Journal of Pragmatics*, 43, 1876–1889.

Van Hout, T. & Van Praet, E. 2011. Competence on display: crafting stories during newsroom editorial conferences. *In:* Pelsmaekers, K., Rollo, C., Van Hout, T. & Heynderickx, P. (eds) *Displaying Competence in Organizations: Discourse Perspectives,* Houndmills: Palgrave.

Verschueren, J. 1985. *International News Reporting: Metapragmatic Metaphors and the U-2.,* Amsterdam: John Benjamins.

Wahl-Jorgensen, K. & Hanitzsch, T. 2009. Introduction: On Why and How We Should Do Journalism Studies. *In:* Wahl-Jorgensen, K. & Hanitzsch, T. (eds) *The Handbook of Journalism Studies,* London: Routledge.

White, D. M. 1950. The gatekeeper: A case study in the selection of news. *Journalism Quarterly,* 27, 383–390.

5
How Linguistic Ethnography May Enhance Our Understanding of Electronic Patient Records in Health Care Settings

Deborah Swinglehurst

Introduction

The electronic patient record (EPR) is now widely integrated in many primary healthcare settings. Like its predecessor – the paper medical record – the EPR is a place where patients' medical notes are recorded. But it is much more. In the EPR, diagnoses, procedures and results are coded and made searchable for audit purposes; electronic templates (or forms) are completed in the chronic disease clinic; reminders and prompts urge clinicians to take specific action at specific times. Computers in the consulting room have been much studied by technology experts (in disciplines such as health informatics and systems design) and – to a lesser extent – by scholars of interpersonal communication. In the latter tradition, research efforts have tended to focus on the *impact of the computer* in what has become conceptualised as the 'triadic' consultation (clinician-patient-computer) (Booth, Kohannejad, & Robinson 2002; Margalit, Roter, Dunevant, Larson, & Reis 2006; Pearce 2007; Scott and Purves 1996; Ventres, Kooienga, & Marlin 2006).

In this chapter I describe a different approach, one which focuses on how the EPR contributes to *shaping practices*, both in the consultation and more widely. This *socio-technical* perspective assumes a dynamic interaction of people and technologies – and considers how this is enabled and constrained by local social and technical contingencies (Swinglehurst, Greenhalgh, Myall, & Russell 2010). Against this background I will describe how I used linguistic ethnography to explore the dynamic 'EPR-in-use'.

My data set arose from eight months of ethnographic observation in two UK general practices and included video-recording 54 consultations (19 clinicians) with simultaneous screen capture, recording the computer screen as the EPR was used in real time. Merging these two video streams opened the EPR to more detailed analysis than has previously been possible. Combining ethnographic observation as a way of exploring the institutional context with a micro-analysis of interaction enabled me to understand not only how the EPR contributes to constituting the interaction on a moment-by-moment basis, but also how it contributes to constituting the wider 'macro' organisational concerns of the clinic, and how these are interrelated. The EPR is a contemporary example of a 'phenomenon' which spans both time and space – that is, its meaning and influence may include past, present and future and is not constrained by its physical location.

I will begin this chapter by describing my own professional context as a GP-ethnographer and introducing the UK NHS policy context at the time of data collection. This sets out my own motivations for the research, and points to its timeliness in a climate of rapid technological change. I will then explain why I felt linguistic ethnography was a suitable research approach. After this groundwork I will introduce some short extracts of empirical data (ethnographic observations and transcripts from clinical consultations) with a view to achieving two broad aims. My first aim is methodological. I hope to paint a picture of the complexity of the EPR as a focus for research, highlighting the analytic challenges it presents and suggesting linguistic ethnography as a sophisticated approach which can handle this complexity. My second aim is to show how the EPR has become absolutely central to the accomplishment of particular concerns in the clinic. These include its role in redefining practices of chronic disease management and in meeting externally defined quality standards (Swinglehurst, Greenhalgh, & Roberts 2012). This redefinition of practice can be observed both in the 'micro' analysis of the unfolding interaction and through observation of organisational routines. The EPR can be seen to constitute the regimentation of practice, bringing new opportunities but also creating new demands and tensions.

The professional and policy context for this work

My interest in the EPR began in 2001 when, as a recently appointed general practitioner (GP), I became 'information technology lead' for my practice. Like most local practices, our clinical system had been installed about ten years earlier, but the main medical record was paper-based, with computers used primarily for appointment scheduling and prescribing. In 2000, the UK government had removed the legal obligation for paper medical records, paving the way for practices to 'go paperless'. I led the practice team in this process, enthusiastic to harness this technology to improve patient care through clinical audit. I later delivered a successful local educational programme for primary care staff on the theme of 'going paperless'.

As time went on I started to become unsettled by the ways in which the EPR was changing my work. I felt it was placing additional unanticipated demands on me in my role as personal doctor to my patients. Technically it was cumbersome, slow and unresponsive at times, and it was not always easy to find what I was looking for. Sometimes it seemed to get in the way. Colleagues expressed concern about how to keep the screen out of view from third parties in the consulting room, now we could no longer hide notes discretely on our laps. But clinical audit – which I had seen as its great potential – was indeed much easier.

Some significant changes in national policy were afoot. I will not cover these in detail, but they included the UK government's ambitious and controversial National Programme for IT (NPfIT) with its commitment to developing a fully networked electronic health record accessible from all points of care (Connecting for Health 2005). In addition, a new national GP contract was introduced (Department of Health 2003). This included a shift of responsibility for funding IT systems to Primary Care Organisations who would own the technology (instead of GPs). Computer systems had to be accredited against UK-wide standards and would become essential if practices were to meet the requirements of another key component of the new contract – the Quality and Outcomes Framework (QOF) (General Practitioners Committee 2009). QOF is an incentive scheme which rewards practices financially for demonstrating nationally approved quality standards. Clinical audit was no longer an activity undertaken in-house to examine care practices, but an opportunity for surveillance by external parties and a key instrument of performance-related pay. Although my GP colleagues were delighted we were so well placed to achieve our 'quality points' in this new climate, I began to feel ambivalent about the bigger picture, concerned that this heralded more fundamental changes at the core of general practice. I started to take a more critical view of an innovation which I had previously embraced as wholly positive. Like many 'latecomers' to linguistic ethnography (Rampton 2007) it was out of this sense of professional disquiet that my interest in researching the EPR in its social context developed.

Although the NPfIT folded in 2010 (after the election of a new government) and a fully networked electronic health record remains elusive, QOF is alive and well. The quality standards have been revised several times and QOF now constitutes approximately 30% of practice remuneration. The political zeal for gathering data to build nationally standardised comparative data sets is strong, not least because recent legislation mandated that general practitioners join Clinical Commissioning Groups (CCGs) with responsibilities for overseeing NHS budgets and commissioning care. Good data quality is seen as critical to this process (Department of Health 2010; Department of Health 2012) and there is an explicit intention to establish '*a principle of recording data once and using it in many ways*' (Department of Health 2010: 52). Although my research was conducted prior to the advent of CCGs, I mention it to draw attention to the ever-evolving wider 'macro' social structures within which the requirement for data collection at the point of care continues to gather momentum.

Why linguistic ethnography?

One of the appeals of the linguistic ethnographic approach is its scope for embracing the complexity of social life – specifically to explore the interface between the detailed nuance of evolving social interaction and the broader institutional and socio-political context within which interactions are situated. These are analytic lenses which are often kept distinct and it is not difficult to see why this is the case. For the researcher it is a considerable challenge to take on the paradox that Erickson so eloquently describes as two parallel assertions in his book *Talk and Social Theory*:

1. *The conduct of talk in local social interaction as it occurs in real time is unique, crafted by local social actors for the specific situation of its use in the moment of its uttering, and*

2. *The conduct of talk in local social interaction is profoundly influenced by processes that occur beyond the temporal and spatial horizon of the immediate occasion of interaction.*

(Erickson 2004: viii)

As I embarked on my study of the EPR I sought an approach which would allow me to explore its influence on the personal work of providing clinical care in the consultation, but which was also sensitive to the wider institutional picture which was beginning to unsettle me. A core assumption of linguistic ethnography is this profound interlinking of persons, encounters and institutions, the onus being on the researcher to explore the nature and dynamics of these linkages (Rampton 2007). In principle this is an attractive proposition, but for the novice it is also a daunting prospect, since linguistic ethnography does not encompass any specific, clearly defined method, but a number of 'sensitising concepts' (Blumer 1969). Unlike definitive concepts which *'provide prescriptions of what to see'*, sensitising concepts *'merely suggest directions along which to look'* (Blumer 1969: 148). In addition it involves gathering, and analysing different types of data, which is challenging.

In the absence of any pre-existing linguistic ethnographic work on the EPR, I built my own approach to the data from the 'bottom up' through repeated viewing of videos and a combination of fine-grained micro-analysis of interactions with broader analysis of ethnographic fieldnotes, as well as maintaining an appreciation of wider institutional and political priorities. By a deliberate process of 'slowing down' the analysis and consciously 'keeping open' possibilities I came to see (and see again – in repeated rounds of analysis) different ways of conceptualising the EPR. I drew eclectically on a range of analytic concepts to help me explore the data. In particular I built on the works of social theorist Erving Goffman (Goffman 1959; Goffman 1966; Goffman 1967; Goffman 1981; Goffman 1983) and linguistic philosopher Mikhael Bakhtin (Bakhtin 1981; Bakhtin 1986), the former offering particularly useful concepts for understanding where the EPR fits with the 'here and now' of the interaction, the latter helping me to deal more satisfactorily with the 'distributed' nature of the EPR and its role in bringing voices from 'out there' into the interaction.

An introduction to data analysis

Having sketched out the context for my work I will now introduce the first data extract (Extract 1), some ethnographic fieldnotes from my observation of a nurse in her clinic for patients with coronary heart disease (CHD). Regular review of patients with chronic diseases such as CHD has been identified as a crucial element of high quality care (Wagner, Austin, & Von Korff 1996) and the registration and recall of these patients is made easier by the EPR. Like all of the nurse-led chronic disease consultations I observed, the reviews involved the systematic completion of a computer template (electronic form) identifying tasks to be done and data fields to complete.

Extract 1. A morning in the Coronary Heart Disease (CHD) clinic

We were between patients and there was a 20 minute gap as a patient hadn't shown for his appointment. The nurse started to check some cholesterol results on the computer, referring to an in-house guideline printed on a laminated sheet. Suddenly the screen froze. The system had crashed.

She jumped from her chair and rushed out into the corridor where she was met by a secretary who had also left her desk in a panic because the usual IT person was not in today. The nurse returned and said she couldn't get on with what she wanted to do. I followed the secretary downstairs to the reception area.

The tiny office next to reception was soon full. The secretary was on the phone talking hurriedly to the IT supplier, and two of the GPs were kneeling on the floor around the server, bums in the air, fiddling with buttons, while an alarm sounded. Another GP looked on from the sidelines joking about the reliability of IT. One GP stayed in his room and didn't join this impromptu meeting round the server. The receptionists kept themselves to themselves but one of them asked me quietly 'Does this never happen in *your* place?'

I overheard the secretary saying 'One of our doctors thinks it's the UBS' only to be corrected by the doctor whispering 'not the U B S, the U *P* S.' I discovered this meant the uninterruptable power supply, which struck me as a misnomer; it was certainly causing plenty of interruption. Chaos really.

The receptionists were a bit stuck. Patients kept arriving but they didn't know who to expect and couldn't 'arrive' them (meaning mark an A next to their name on the appointments list to indicate that they were waiting). The waiting room was filling up.

After a few minutes, some lights started flashing on what may have been the UPS and there was a visible collective sigh of relief amongst the GPs. The secretary was still talking to the IT supplier but the GPs returned to their rooms to resume surgery.

I went back to the nurse's room. The screen said 'connecting' but did not appear to be connecting in any meaningful way. The nurse was flustered now and went downstairs to try to find out who her next patient was. As she followed the patient up the stairs I heard her warning the patient 'We've got a problem today 'cos the computer has crashed and isn't working.'

The patient sat down. The nurse began by saying 'I'll have to do it a little out of order because I've no computer.' She grabbed a yellow post-it note and wrote the patient's name at the top. The patient gave her a urine sample for testing. The nurse said it was fine and scribbled on the post-it note. She leaned over the corner of her desk towards the patient asking 'Do you know which medicines you are on from a cardiac point of view?' A familiar opening which I had by now come to recognise, although this time I could not help noticing that for the first time it was the patient rather than the computer screen to whom the question was directed. The patient – smartly dressed and well-spoken – put her handbag on her knee and said politely 'I'm prepared for all eventualities, my dear' as she produced a list of her repeat medications and handed it to the nurse. Reading down the list the nurse said 'So…from a cardiac point of view you're on…nicorandil, isosorbide mononitrate, atorvastatin, diltiazem. Are you on aspirin?' The patient said 'they' had stopped it because she bruises too easily, and then added that one of her medications had recently been increased during a hospital admission. The nurse handed the list back and turned to the computer, then typed a few keystrokes to see if the computer was working but it just bleeped and remained frozen. There was no further discussion about the medication or the admission.

The nurse took the patient's blood pressure, there was a brief discussion about exercise then the nurse announced 'This is <u>so</u> confusing not having the computer…uuuuuhm… (long pause)…<u>diet</u>… do you have a balanced diet?' Then 'What I think I had better do is your blood test, and just hope we are back on line after that. It just goes to show how we rely on computers.' She kept checking and rechecking the computer. Blood sample taken, she returned to her desk saying 'let's see if we have any joy (types keystrokes) OOOooh that looks encouraging.' She leaned towards the computer and said to it 'c'mon <u>you</u> can do it.' She typed in a password but nothing happened. 'Oh that looked <u>so</u> promising. Oh that is such a shame. We're so close. I'll just go downstairs and see if it is just me.' The nurse left the room and I chatted with the patient until the nurse returned about 5 minutes later.

After 25 minutes of downtime the computer came back to life. The nurse turned to it and said 'Let's see if we've got anything from your recent hospital admission' and opened up a hospital letter. She read it quietly and said to the patient 'That doesn't say anything about you increasing the medication.' The patient replied 'they did' to which the nurse responded 'I'm not disbelieving you' then turned to the computer again and sighed 'it's gone again'. The patient looked down at her repeat medication list on her lap and said that it was the nicorandil which was increased. The nurse responded 'Sadly our return to the computer was only temporary so I can't do anything at the moment. I'll go and have a chat with Dr Vaughan as the cardiologists haven't organised any follow up. So since they increased the nicorandil how much have you been using your spray?' Patient replied: 'Ooooo a <u>lot</u> less, only a third'

The nurse apologised saying 'I'm sorry it's been such a higgledy-piggledy consultation' and left the room again to speak to the patient's GP, returning with the advice that she should stay on the same dose of medication as it was the maximum dose and seemed to be helping. She made a note on her post-it note 'nicorandil ↑30mg'.

At the close of the consultation the nurse apologised again 'I'm sorry. It was a bit of a come and go consultation' to which the patient replied 'WELL DONE' then added gently '...you can go off computers.'

The nurse was running 30 minutes late by the time she was ready to see her next patient.

It may seem surprising to begin with a narrative account of one of the few occasions in my data collection when the EPR became temporarily unavailable. However, this brief experience reveals the extent to which the EPR has become embedded in practice and is a useful point of departure for highlighting some important methodological and analytic concerns.

The nurse's interaction with the patient conveys a strong sense that the cardiovascular check should be an orderly affair, and that the order of prompts and fields inscribed in the computer template is the 'right' order of conducting the clinic, warranting apology if things have to be done *'a little out of order'*. She leaves the room twice, and the consultation becomes – in her words – *'higgledy-piggledy'* and *'come and go'*. The nurse's reference in her opening question to *'the cardiac point of view'* was a common way of framing the scope of the chronic disease consultation. This, and other similar formulations (e.g. '*SO* ... *cardiac review*') establish what Goodwin refers to as 'figure' and 'ground' – what is more (and less) relevant to the professional activity taking place (Goodwin 1994). Implicit is an assumption that the discernment by patients (and nurses) of symptoms of one chronic disease from another is unproblematic; this was taken for granted even in the face of the most complex multimorbidity (Swinglehurst et al 2012).

Although I was not surprised that it was disruptive and stressful when usual routines broke down (especially with a researcher observing), this incident brought home to me the extent to which nursing care had become interwoven with technology use. The difficulty was not merely that the nurse could not access the patient's medical notes. The notes – it turned out – were less reliable than the patient's account, at least with respect to her medication. But without the template, the nurse found it difficult to 'go on' – '*Sadly our return to the computer was only temporary so I can't do anything at the moment*'. Neither does it seem likely that this senior, well qualified nurse cannot do a cardiovascular check without the prompts before her eyes. It seems much more likely that it is *because* her embodied practices have become so finely tuned to incorporate the technology that to conduct the clinic without it has become almost impossible (Swinglehurst et al 2012).

Garfinkel, in an early seminal text on medical records identified the handling of emerging local contingencies, answering the immediate question of 'what to do next?' as one of the main concerns of clinical work (Garfinkel 1967). As an observer in this clinic, my sense was that the consultation could not progress without nurse, patient and (working) template all co-present, and that it was often the template which prompted 'what to do next'.

This recursive and inextricable relationship between the EPR and contingent social practices was a significant early insight in this research project, and one which informed my decision to use a linguistic ethnographic approach. The EPR is not simply a piece of technical kit reducible to a collection of hardware and software sitting on the clinician's desk, but an example of a 'social substance' definable only in terms of the properties of a social world (Harré 2002). Whereas most previous studies of healthcare interaction either fail to incorporate the EPR at all, or 'contain' it by focusing on the 'computer' as if it were a separate entity, I was keen to develop an approach which engaged with the EPR as *integral* to interaction and social practice. If, for example, I had simply wished to consider the impact of the computer on the nurse-patient interaction, the observations detailed above may have been overlooked, as the computer was 'out of use' and the institutional context might be deemed relatively unimportant. However, by orienting to the EPR as part of a complex of interconnected social practices and institutional context, linguistic ethnography opens up richer appreciations of what is actually going on.

These ethnographic fieldnotes offer a glimpse into the organisation-wide nature of the disruption, a consequence of what Iedema has referred to as the wide 'organisational reach' of the EPR (Iedema 2003) and its inter-connectedness. As Susan Leigh Star has noted, when the server is down *'the normally invisible quality of working infrastructure becomes visible'* becoming *'the basis for a much more detailed understanding of the relational nature of infrastructure'* (Star 1999: 382). What I was witnessing was a critical incident in which the usual activities of the clinic were (largely) suspended. It led me to the uncomfortable conclusion that in extreme – and thankfully rare – situations, the EPR *becomes* the patient, at least inasmuch as attending to it and correcting its ills becomes the highest and most urgent priority amongst clinical staff.

I hope this brief account already conveys a sense of the way in which the EPR contributes to the regimentation of the clinic, and how – even in its absence – it infiltrates the discourse of the consultation. Having taken a look through what Erickson calls the 'social telescope', I will now zoom in with a 'social microscope' to look in detail at some inter-actions (Erickson 2004). Again, I will use this as a way of highlighting some of the analytic challenges presented by the EPR, as well as building on the notion of the EPR as 'regimenting' practice.

Bringing order to the asthma clinic

The next data extract is a transcript of a video-recorded interaction between a nurse and patient at the opening of an annual asthma check. It involves the completion of a template, and on this occasion this was recorded through simultaneous screen capture (Extract 2). I introduced video-recording of consultations only after spending a considerable amount of time 'lurking and soaking' as an ethnographer (Werner and Schoepfle 1989) and it was during observations of the chronic disease clinic that I had experienced the influence of the template most powerfully.

Templates are electronic forms designed to support management of individual patients ('primary use' of data) and produce aggregated data, e.g. on organisational performance ('secondary use'). Chronic disease management is the main area of incentivisation within QOF, and the relevant clinical indicators are inscribed in the template. For example, in asthma care QOF requires a record of smoking status and evidence that an asthma review has taken place. QOF guidance outlines what the review should include.

Extract 2   Opening of nurse-patient asthma

Time	N/P	Spoken word	Bodily conduct	EPR screen
01:08	N	<u>So really</u> straightforward.	N puts paper on desk	Summary screen
		(0.4)	N rotates body and gaze to face P, her hands on her lap. P looking at N	
01:09	N	Asthma assessment		
		(0.4)		
	P	Okay	P nods	
01.11	N	to see how your asthma's do:ing:	N raises both hands in front	
01.13	N	what you're doing w- with it when it's good, what you do with it when it's ba:d, (0.2) have you any problems with your ↑inhalers (0.4) .hhh	N uses fingers to count on 'good' 'bad' 'problems'	
		(0.5)	N hands open out in front of her	
01.19	N	<u>Very</u> straightforward stuff	N hands to lap	
	P	Oka[y	P nods	
	N	[all right? .hhh		
01:21	N	U:::hm	N rotates body & gaze to screen, hands on lap	
01:23	N	What I've got <u>here</u>	N gestures her open hands towards the screen	
01:24	N	Is that you're on:: (0.4) a purple inhaler?	N rotates back towards P, bringing hands together	
01:26	P	(0.2) Yeh (.) uhm (0.2)	P glances briefly towards the screen	
		seretide.		

First, some comments about my approach to transcription which is an early step in analysis. Transcription, albeit time-consuming, is an opportunity to become immersed in the data, to decide what may be relevant to transcribe and what level of detail is necessary (Bailey 2008). For me this began with repeated viewings of video data and included decisions about how to transcribe bodily conduct and details of the EPR screen. I have adapted an approach suggested by Jewitt for transcription of multimodal data, with different modes presented in adjacent columns, using time as an anchor (Jewitt 2006). I adopted Jefferson conventions for transcription of the spoken word (Atkinson and Heritage 1984) aiming to balance clarity, completeness and readability within a multimodal orientation. Readers interested in learning more about the transcription of multi-modal data may like to consult the MODE online transcription resource, to which I have contributed some of my reflections on this process (National Centre for Research Methods 2012).

Returning to this data extract, we see that the nurse frames the consultation as an assessment, setting up an evaluative tone for the meeting. First she says it is to see how '*your asthma's doing*' (an assessment of the asthma). She then reformulates this as '*what you're doing with it when it's good, what you do with it when it's bad*' (an assessment of the patient's practices). This metaphorical separation of disease ('it') from patient ('you') was common, and the use of templates across a wide range of chronic diseases appeared to encourage this disease-specific, task-oriented approach. The evaluative frame anticipates an enquiry which goes on to incorporate inhaler technique, smoking status, concordance with medication and peak flow measurements. At 1:08 and 1:19, the nurse emphasises that it is <u>really</u> or <u>very</u> straightforward. At 1:13 she counts on her fingers a three-part list, flagging the linearity of what is to follow and setting out what needs to be achieved. On the one hand this might be interpreted as reassurance, but it is a reassurance about what the patient may expect of the structure or order of the clinic, not a reassurance that his specific concerns will be addressed (Swinglehurst et al 2012). Evidence for this interpretation follows immediately after this data extract, when the nurse gestures towards the computer again as she explains '*What I've got here is some questions that I – I need to ask you ... they're fairly straightforward ones but what they tend to do with is that they will flag up whether there >actually< we have got what w- what I would call breakthrough symptoms.*' This brings an institutional imperative to the encounter ('*I need to ask you*') as she highlights once again the '*straightforward*' nature of the task, invoking the electronic template as the origin of the questions, by gesturing towards the screen. As the patient begins to show the nurse how he uses his inhaler, he coughs loudly five times, beats his chest demonstrably with his hand and announces:

Patient: 'I do suffer very badly from phlegm in the mornings ... which I presume is part and parcel of having asthma.'
Nurse: 'It can be (.) yeah which (0.4) anyway I – we'll talk about that in a minute ... we'll do the inhaler first.'

The structured inventory of questions has already become apparent in this consultation, and the patient weaves his own concerns into the assessment of 'inhaler technique' using elaborate emphatic gestures. However, the nurse quickly steers the patient's activity back to the institutional script and does not revisit the issue of the morning phlegm. She does go on, at a later stage in the consultation, to enquire specifically about asthma symptoms, but not until almost 16 minutes into the 19 minute consultation ... and when prompted by a template field reading 'night symptoms'.

The role of the EPR template in regimenting the interaction

The data which we have considered so far go some way towards showing how the practices of both nurse and patient are shaped by the institutional script within the EPR. The use of a template in chronic disease management introduces not only a new organisational regime but also a new 'interactional regime'. Blommaert uses this term to identify a set of behavioural expectations regarding physical conduct (including language) which emerge in social processes (Blommaert 2005a; Blommaert, Collins, & Slembrouck 2005). Although the original use of this term relates to language practices in a multi-lingual environment it is nevertheless a useful heuristic in this research context. This notion conveys a sense of both the emergent, situated nature of the interaction and also its 'regimentation' – a taken-for-granted dimension whereby macro-discursive systems impose constraints on what people can do and say in particular circumstances.

It was common for consultations to start and finish with the same questions. One consultation was interrupted twice by the patient standing up as if to leave, the nurse advising *'you can't go yet* (laugh) ... *we're not finished yet.'* Another ended with the nurse's announcement (facing the screen, clasping her hands together) *'Excellent. (0.8) right I've done everything yes: (0.6) you're free to go'*, the screen capture showing that it was the arrival at the final field in the template ('Asthma follow up, enter date') which identified that the nurse had 'done everything'. The patient was 'free to go' once the nurse had completed the template – her choice of words again conveying the sense of constraint within the regimentation of the clinic.

In the next section we will look closely at one more data sample (see also Swinglehurst 2014), this time a consultation between a doctor and patient within a routine surgery.

'My computer's asked me...'

Extract 3 shows a transcript of a small part of a consultation. The doctor has finished dealing with the patient's gynaecological problem and goes on to attend to an institutional requirement. The doctor is not using a template here, but responds to an EPR prompt which is displayed at the bottom right of her computer screen throughout the consultation – a 'QOF alert' showing an outstanding QOF item ('Recent Smoking Data').

At 14.32 the doctor re-orients to the screen and points to it as she announces *'now my computer's asked me whether you smoke'*. The patient looks towards the EPR and hesitates in her response. Although the QOF alert is not immediately relevant to this patient's reason for attendance, such alerts act as a constant reminder to the doctor of institutional imperatives. Here, the doctor attributes agency for her opening utterance to the EPR, suggesting that the EPR is the author of her words (Goffman 1981). This is effective in introducing some attributional distance between herself and the delicate question she asks of the patient (Clayman 1992) whilst also identifying her professional authority as somehow at issue.

As in the previous example, our ethnographic understanding of the institutional context gives meaning to the micro-analysis and helps to align our interpretation with a specific institutional imperative. The doctor is required within QOF to document whether patients aged over fifteen are 'smokers' or 'non smokers' – although even in this short extract we see that these apparently simple categorisations are often more complex in practice. The EPR not only prompts an activity – and shapes the immediate unfolding interaction – but also mediates the definition of what is important knowledge about patients, reinforcing particular definitions of 'quality' in practice. The gathering of smoking data is an example.

At 15:29 the doctor says *'so (0.2) y'know obviously °< as your doctor > I have to advise you that you shouldn't°'* She displays what Goffman calls a change in footing (Goffman 1981) namely a shift in the alignment (or

Extract 3 Extract from a doctor-patient consultation

Time	D P	Words spoken/sounds	Bodily conduct	EPR Screen
14.32	D	now my computer's asked me whether you smoke	D - > EPR. D points to screen D - > EPR, L hand to mouth; P -> EPR;	Medications screen. QOF alert showing in bottom R corner: QOF Recent Smoking Data (displays throughout consultation)
		(1.2)	D -> P; P -> EPR	
14.35	P	uhm	P -> EPR	
		(1.0)		
14.36	P	yes (.) no	P -> EPR; D -> P	
		(1.0)	P -> D	
14.38	D	he what's (that mean	D -> EPR, laughing	
	P	[I've had one in the last three days	D <-> P	
14.41	D	right (.) so (.) very occasionally	D <-> P	
14.43	P	yeah (0.2) I'm (.) I'm very much a s:ocial smoker nowadays=		
14.46	D	= so with- in a (0.2) in a week uhm how many do you get through °d'you think°		
14.49	P	well last week I think I had three		

14.52   D   right (0.4) right

          (5.0)   D turns -> EPR; P -> D.
                                             At 14.57 D turns to P again

Transcript not shown – doctor establishes that patient smoked three cigarettes last week and suggests it would be better for patient's general health if she could "ignore them", since although it is not doing "horrendous damage" it is still keeping the "receptors flapping"

15.29   D   so (0.2) y'know obviously   D -> EPR; P -> D
            °<as your doctor > 1 have to advise   D < - > P; D using highly stylised
            you that you shouldn't°   voice

          (1.6)   D nods, smiling

stance, or projected self) of participants in interaction. Firstly, she slows down her speech markedly as she says '< *as your doctor* >' reclaiming her professional authority and legitimising the anticipated advice-giving. She then uses a quiet, highly stylised voice as she seeks to influence the patient: '*I have to advise you that you shouldn't*'. This is an example of what Sarangi and Roberts call 'hybrid discourse', in that it is legitimate 'professional' advice on the one hand, but also orients to a higher 'institutional' order. Professional discourse is that which professionals routinely engage in during their practice, whereas institutional discourse concerns the way in which professionals account for their talk (Roberts, Sarangi, Southgate, Wakeford, & Wass 2000; Sarangi and Roberts 1999). Just like the nurse in the previous example ('*What I've got here is some questions that I – I need to ask you*') the institutional dimension is conveyed partly through the doctor's words '*I have to*' and partly through the stylisation in her voice which contributes to a 'new' identity as she incorporates institutional business. Goffman refers to this as the 'embedding' function of talk, meaning the way in which animators can convey words which are not their own or which reflect a different aspect of oneself (Goffman 1981).

The consultation as an opportunity for incorporating opportunistic health promotion activity (e.g. smoking advice) is not new; it has long been identified in consultation models (Stott and Davis 1979). But the use of the EPR as a prompt to this kind of talk engenders a shift from professional interaction towards an emphasis on institutional evidence and accountability and is further evidence of the regimentation of the interaction.

This extract is an illustration of the way in which clinicians now have to make new ongoing judgments about whether, when and how to attend to the institutional voice of the EPR, balancing the immediacy ('here and now') of the interaction with the more institutional ('there and then') demands of the EPR. These are 'on-the-spot' judgments about the allocation of involvement (Goffman 1966) and carry the risk that involvement in the interpersonal interaction might be disrupted (Swinglehurst et al. 2012). Attending to the voice of the EPR is not a morally neutral activity, and raises questions about whose interests are being served. Clinicians must accommodate what Blommaert refers to as different 'orders of indexicality' – that is multi-layered, stratified or 'ordered' meanings which incorporate the local and translocal, the momentary and lasting (Blommaert 2005b; Blommaert 2006; Bakhtin 1986). The new 'voices' are not necessarily timely or relevant to the 'here and now', are insensitive to the particular unfolding characteristics of the interaction and challenge very fundamentally the normative model of the consultation as a dyadic meeting of two persons which currently underpins much teaching in clinical consulting (Swinglehurst et al. 2014). In this particular example, the doctor makes the role of the EPR explicit, but in doing so she must engage in additional interaction work, and has to be creative in managing the transition between her professional self and her role as institutional representative.

Conclusion

The EPR and its complex web of socio-political and institutional relationships presents the researcher with some tricky challenges. One possible response is to render it more 'simple' (by, for example, focusing on the computer as a 'black box'), turning a blind eye to some of the inherent complexity. An alternative response is to seek out ways of embracing and investigating this complexity explicitly – linguistic ethnography offers one such approach. It has not been my intention to describe my methods, methodology and conceptual framework in full detail here. However, I hope I have succeeded in drawing attention to the nature of the analytic challenges raised by the EPR, and have made a persuasive case for considering the EPR not as 'computer' or 'data container' but as ongoing social practice which shapes care (and is shaped by it) both in the micro-detail of the interaction and more widely in general practice organisations.

References

Atkinson, J. M. & Heritage, J. (1984) 'Transcript notation,' *In Structures of Social Action: Studies in Conversation Analysis*, J. M. Atkinson & J. Heritage, eds., Cambridge: Cambridge University Press, pp. ix–xvi.

Bailey, J. (2008) First steps in qualitative data analysis: transcribing. *Family Practice*, 25, 127–131.

Bakhtin, M. (1981) 'Discourse in the Novel,' *In The Dialogic Imagination: Four Essays by M. M. Bakhtin*, M. Holquist, ed., Austin: University of Texas Press, pp. 259–422.

Bakhtin, M. (1986) *Speech Genres and Other Late Essays* Austin, University of Texas Press.

Blommaert, J. (2005a) *Discourse* Cambridge: Cambridge University Press.

Blommaert, J. (2005b) 'Language and Inequality,' *In Discourse,* Cambridge: Cambridge University Press, pp. 68–97.

Blommaert, J. (2006) 'Sociolinguistic scales,' *In Working Papers in Urban Language & Literacies, Paper 37*, Institute of Education.

Blommaert, J., Collins, J. & Slembrouck, S. (2005) Polycentricity and interactional regimes in 'global neighbourhoods' *Ethnography*, 6, 205–235.

Blumer, H. (1969) *Symbolic Interactionism* Berkeley: University of California Press.

Booth, N., Kohannejad, J. & Robinson, P. (2002) *Information in the Consulting Room – Training Package*, Sowerby Centre for Health Informatics at Newcastle.

Clayman, S. E. (1992) 'Footing in the achievement of neutrality: the case of news-interview discourse,' *In Talk at Work: Interaction in Institutional Settings*, P. Drew & J. Heritage, eds., pp. 163–198.

Connecting for Health (2005) *A Guide to the National Programme for Information Technology.* From http://www.connectingforhealth.nhs.uk/resources/archive/npfit_brochure_apr_05_final.pdf.

Department of Health (2003) *Investing in General Practice: The New General Medical Services Contract.* From http://www.dh.gov.uk/en/Publicationsandstatistics/Publications/PublicationsPolicyAndGuidance/DH_4071966.

Department of Health (2010) *Liberating the NHS: An Information Revolution.* From http://www.dh.gov.uk/en/Consultations/Liveconsultations/DH_120080.

Department of Health (2012) *Informatics: The Future – An Organisational Summary.* From https://www.wp.dh.gov.uk/publications/files/2012/07/Informatics-the-future_final.pdf.

Erickson, F. (2004) *Talk and Social Theory* Cambridge: Polity.

Garfinkel, H. (1967) ' "Good" organizational reasons for "bad" clinic records,' *In Studies in Ethnomethodology*, Engelwood Cliffs, NJ: Prentice Hall, pp. 186–207.

General Practitioners Committee (2009) *Quality and Outcomes Framework. Guidance – Updated August 2004.* From http://www.dh.gov.uk/prod_consum_dh/groups/dh_digitalassets/@dh/@en/documents/digitalasset/dh_4088693.pdf.

Goffman, E. (1959) *The Presentation of Self in Everyday Life* London: Penguin Books.

Goffman, E. (1966) 'Involvement,' *In Behavior in Public Places*, New York: The Free Press, pp. 33–42.

Goffman, E. (1967) 'On Face-work,' *In Interaction Ritual: Essays on Face-to-Face Behaviour*, New York: Pantheon Books, pp. 5–45.

Goffman, E. (1981) 'Footing,' *In Forms of Talk*, Philadelphia: University of Pennsylvania Press, pp. 124–159.

Goffman, E. (1983) The interaction order. *American Sociological Review*, 48, 1–17.

Harré, R. (2002) Material objects in social worlds. *Theory, Culture & Society*, 19, (5–6) 23–33.

Iedema, R. (2003) The medical record as organizing discourse. *Document Design*, 4, 64–84.

Jewitt, C. (2006) 'Towards a multimodal analysis,' *In Technology, Literacy and Learning: A Multimodal Approach*, Abingdon: Routledge, pp. 32–52.

Margalit, R. S., Roter, D., Dunevant, M. A., Larson, S. & Reis, S. (2006) Electronic medical record use and physician-patient communication: An observational study of Israeli primary care encounters. *Patient Education and Counseling*, 61, 134–141.

National Centre for Research Methods (2012) *MODE Online Transcription Resource.* See http://mode.ioe.ac.uk/2012/09/01/transcription-bank-deborah-swinglehurst/.

Pearce, C. (2007) *Doctors, Patients and Computers, the New Consultation. PhD Thesis.* Department of General Practice, The University of Melbourne.

Rampton, B. (2007) *Linguistic Ethnography and the Study of Identities.* Downloadable from http://www.kcl.ac.uk/innovation/groups/ldc/publications/working papers/43.pdf King's College London.

Rampton, B. (2007) Neo-Hymesian linguistic ethnography in the United Kingdom. *Journal of Sociolinguistics* 11(5): 584–607.

Roberts, C., Sarangi, S., Southgate, L., Wakeford, R. & Wass, V. (2000) Oral examination – equal opportunities, ethnicity, and fairness in the MRCGP. *BMJ*, 320, 370–375.

Sarangi, S. & Roberts, C. (1999) 'The dynamics of interactional and institutional orders in work-related settings,' *In Talk, Work and Institutional Order*, S. Sarangi & C. Roberts, eds., Berlin, New York: Mouton de Gruyter, pp. 1–57.

Scott, D. & Purves, I. (1996) Triadic relationship between doctor, computer and patient. *Interacting with Computers*, 8, 347–363.

Star, S. L (1999) The ethnography of infrastructure. *The American Behavioral Scientist*, 43, 377–391.

Stott, N. C. H. & Davis, R. H. (1979) The exceptional potential in each primary care consultation. *Journal of the Royal College of General Practitioners*, 29, 201–205.

Swinglehurst, D. (2014) Displays of authority in the clinical consultation: A linguistic ethnographic study of the electronic patient record. *Social Science and Medicine* 118: 17–26.

Swinglehurst, D., Greenhalgh, T. & Roberts, C. (2012) Computer templates in chronic disease management: ethnographic case study in general practice. *BMJ Open*, 2:e001754.doi:10.1136/bmjopen-2012-001754.

Swinglehurst, D. & Roberts, C. (2012) 'The role of the electronic patient record in the clinical consultation (in press),' *In Routledge Handbook of Language and Health Communication*, H. Hamilton & W. S. Chou, eds., Routledge.

Swinglehurst, D., Roberts, C. & Greenhalgh, T. (2011) 'Opening up the "black box" of the electronic patient record: A linguistic ethnographic study in general practice.' *Communication and Medicine*, 8, 3–15.

Swinglehurst, D., Roberts, C., Li, S., Weber, O. & Singy P. Beyond the 'dyad': a qualitative re-evaluation of the changing clinical consultation. *BMJ Open* 2014;4:e006017.doi:10.1136/bmjopen-2014-006017

Swinglehurst, D., Greenhalgh, T., Myall, M. & Russell, J. (2010) Ethnographic study of ICT-supported collaborative work routines in general practice. *BMC Health Services Research*, 10, 348.

Ventres, W., Kooienga, S. & Marlin, R. (2006) EHRs in the exam room: tips on patient-centred care. *Family Practice Management*, 13, 45–47.

Wagner, E., Austin, B. & Von Korff, M. (1996) Organising care for patients with chronic illness. *Milbank Quarterly*, 74, 511–544.

Werner, O. & Schoepfle, G. (1989) *Systematic Field Work* Newbury Park, CA: Sage.

6

Examining Talk in Post-observation Feedback Conferences: Learning to Do Linguistic Ethnography

Fiona Copland

Introduction

As this collection of work demonstrates, linguistic ethnography is a dynamic and interdisciplinary field. Yet it is also nascent, and LE researchers are exploring its boundaries through developing approaches to data collection and analysis, and uncovering, sharing and drawing on theoretical constructs from a range of disciplines including sociology, philosophy and cultural studies. Many involved in this work have come to linguistic ethnography from either ethnography or linguistics and have made a number of adjustments to the ways they conduct research; for example, ethnographers learn how to do text analysis, and linguists learn how to observe ethnographically. The questions posed by the editors of this collection to contributors (see Introduction) were designed to encourage explicit reflection on these processes and, in so doing, to demonstrate how researchers situate their work within linguistic ethnography. The questions asked are repeated here:

1. In what ways did LE enable you to get to parts of the process you study which other approaches couldn't reach?
2. In what ways has appropriating LE led to changes in your work and the methods you use?
3. How has your own discipline influenced/recontextualised the concepts and emphases within LE?

In order to answer the first two questions, I describe my background in applied linguistics research, specifically teaching English to speakers of other languages (TESOL), and show how I developed the ethnographic side of my practice while conducting research on post-observation feedback conferences in pre-service teacher training. I describe an ethnographically grounded methodological framework, which facilitated a shift in my gaze from an explicit and exclusive focus on the linguistic to a commitment to ensuring linguistic data and analyses are contextually situated. Central to the production of this shift from doing linguistic analysis to doing linguistic ethnography were two analytic questions that began increasingly to dominate my encounters with data. These were, 'What's going on?' and 'How do you know?' (see, too, Introduction). In responding to the second question in particular I realised that I needed not only to integrate ethnographic and linguistic data and analysis, but more importantly, I needed to adopt an ethnographic sensibility. In this chapter, I describe how I began to understand what this meant and how this change in sensibility led me to more nuanced and equivocal research findings than I believe a linguistic analysis alone would have produced.

I begin the chapter, however, by introducing the research traditions that have influenced TESOL research. This brief discussion will go some way to responding to question 3, which I will return to in the concluding comments.

Research in TESOL

Within the broader discipline of education, particularly in research in bilingualism/multilingualism, there is a strong and vibrant tradition of linguistic ethnographic research (see, for example, Martin-Jones and Heller, 1996; Creese, 2005; Rampton, 2006; Blackledge and Creese, 2010). However, despite sharing a strong underlying focus on how languages are learnt, taught and used, the concerns of TESOL are generally different from those of bilingualism. They centre on teaching English to those who will use it for particular purposes, such as passing examinations or doing business, rather than to those who will use English or another language in their everyday lives, particularly in the education system in a western English speaking country.

Most TESOL practitioners have learnt English as a second language and teach it in their home countries. Others are 'native' speakers of English who have travelled overseas to work in language schools or in institutions in the state sector. A smaller number teach English to overseas students in a country where English is the common language, such as England, Australia and the United States.

Many UK universities offer Master's level courses in TESOL, and these are mostly populated by overseas students, reflecting the reality that

TESOL practice is an international concern. TESOL is not generally offered as a degree subject at undergraduate level and it is no longer possible to gain qualified teacher status in TESOL in the UK through government sponsored qualifications (except in the post-compulsory sector). In many ways, therefore, TESOL is a minority interest in the UK, despite the TESOL industry being worth many billions of pounds to its economy (Graddol, 2006).

Much research in TESOL is conducted under the banner of applied linguistics. At its best, applied linguistics research has focused on using linguistic analysis to provide 'practically relevant' (Roberts, 2003: 133) solutions to real world problems. In TESOL, this has often meant measuring, explicating and classifying areas of practice, including processes of second language acquisition, (see Ellis 2009), effective classroom pedagogies (for example, Kumaravadivelu 2009), teacher and student classroom talk (for example, Walsh, 2011) and the English needed in specific contexts, such as academic English (for example, Hyland, 2009) in order to improve learning and teaching. Master's programmes in Applied Linguistics and TESOL, in the UK at least, follow this trend, providing modules on different approaches to linguistic analysis such as discourse analysis, conversation analysis, corpus analysis and systemic functional linguistics. While these programmes may also teach research methods, such as questionnaire design and action research, training in conducting ethnographic research remains relatively rare. TESOL professionals who wish to develop their research skills and professional practice, through reading in the discipline or taking a higher degree, are enculturated into a tradition of research in which linguistic analysis, and its perceived empirical rigour, is strongly endorsed.

Until I started my PhD, I classified myself as an applied linguist who specialised in TESOL. I had a background in language teaching and teacher education and an MA in Applied Linguistics. I had therefore received training in linguistic analysis but none in ethnography and I had read few studies that took an ethnographic approach. I believed linguistic analysis was sufficient to answer the questions I was interested in. Before explaining the processes which changed my view, I turn to the area of TESOL which became the focus of my study, the post-observation feedback conference in pre-service teacher training.

The post-observation feedback conference

It is common on teacher education programmes that teachers-in-training are observed by a trainer or mentor who then discusses the lesson with the teacher in a post-observation feedback conference. In most cases, feedback is given on a one-to-one basis, but on some programmes, both the teaching and the feedback can be carried out in groups. This is generally the case on the CELTA (Certificate in English Language Teaching to Adults). As explained above, there is no government sponsored teaching qualification in the UK in TESOL and so the private sector has developed its own qualifications. Commonplace in the UK TESOL context (although also popular in Australia and New Zealand), the CELTA (and other similar courses e.g. Trinity's CertTESOL) is a pre-service qualification that can be completed in one intensive month. Originally developed as a qualification to support teachers who wanted to teach English abroad, the CELTA is now taken by over 7000 teachers a year (Brandt 2006) and costs around £1,000.

A key feature of the CELTA is six hours of teaching practice which trainees must pass in order to successfully complete the course. The teaching practice is generally carried out in groups (in a two hour lesson, for example, four trainees would each teach for 30 minutes) and is observed by a trainer. After each lesson, a feedback conference is held in which the observing trainer and trainees discuss each trainee's teaching practice.

Prior to starting my doctoral research in 2005, I had worked for over ten years as a trainer on CELTA programmes in the UK and in Japan. I had become very interested in the interaction that takes place between trainers and trainees in the feedback conference. Issues of power, politeness and gatekeeping frequently arose and simultaneously concerned and fascinated me. The group feedback conference therefore became the focus of my PhD research project.

Learning to research

In the tradition of applied linguistics in TESOL, my original PhD proposal described a linguistic study in which I would analyse post-observation feedback talk by drawing on established linguistic frameworks. I had read and been impressed by a chapter by Holmes, Stubbe and Vine (1999), in which power at work was explored. The research design involved equipping research participants in a government workplace in New Zealand with recording devices. The participants were encouraged to record interactions and were also given the power to delete recordings they did not wish the researchers to hear. The researchers note that they also collected 'ethnographic data of various kinds' (1999: 356), but these data are not described.

In their section on 'Analysing the Data', the researchers provided a discourse analytic framework at three levels – speech functions, discourse strategy, and linguistic forms – which they used to show how talk in the workplace enacts power relations and the role politeness plays in this.

Given that I was also interested in themes of power and politeness and also researching talk in an institution, I decided to replicate the research methodology in my study, by giving trainers recording devices on which to record the feedback conferences, and then using a similar linguistic framework for the data analysis. As a researcher, I felt my role was to 'collect' and then 'analyse' spoken interaction to produce findings which were empirically grounded, an approach not uncommon in applied linguistics research.

My initial research design involved providing recording devices to two trainers to record a total of 64 feedback sessions with 16 trainees. However, discussions with my supervisor caused me to rethink the research design. As she explained, having worked for many years at the research site, I had completed what many believe to be 'the most difficult phase in the entire process of ethnographic research' – gaining access (Gobo, 2008: 118). Furthermore, I had, in reality, been a 'participant observer' for a number of years (see Agar, 2008: 9, for an insightful discussion of this term) and my insider perspective would affect my data collection, analysis and findings. I found these arguments persuasive and decided to redesign my study so that I could observe the feedback interactions and produce fieldnotes from these observations. In the interests of developing an emic perspective (Richards, 2003) – an appreciation of how local people, rather than researchers, make sense of the world – I also built interviews into the research design. Interviews have been described as a central data collection tool in social science research (Briggs, 1986) and are 'a growing presence in applied linguistics research' (Mann, 2010: 6). My intention was to ask participants for their opinions of the programme in general and of feedback in particular. Although my skills as an interviewer and my understanding of the interview as collaboratively constructed developed as the study progressed (see Garton and Copland, 2010 for a further discussion), the data from the interviews proved invaluable in answering my research questions and in supporting my evolving ethnographic sensibility, as will be shown.

Table 6.1 shows the data collected for the 2006 study:

Table 6.1 Data collected in 2006

Trainers and trainees	First interview	Second interview	First feedback observation	Second feedback observation	Third feedback observation	Fourth feedback observation	Group interview
Clara	24 January (A)	23 March (A)	26 January (F)(A)	2 February (F)(A)	9 February (F)(A)		
Madeleine	28 February (A)	18 May (A)	2 May (F)(A)	9 March (F)(A)	17 March (F)(A)	23 March (F)(A)	
Ned	16 January (A)	16 August (A)	6 July (F)(A)	11 July (F)(A)	12 July (F)(A)	13 July (F)(A)	
Lauren	18 July (A)	16 July (A)	18 July (F)(A)	24 July (F)(A)			
Group 1 trainees							23 March (A)
Group 2 trainees							25 July (A)

Note: Key: **(F)** = Fieldnotes **(A)** = Audio Recorded.

From day one, the value of observing interactions and writing fieldnotes was evident in a number of ways. I realised that as well as speaking, participants also remained silent for long periods of time. Participants acted and moved, made eye contact and avoided it. Their bodily movements contributed to the discussion, interactions and to the atmospheres that pervaded the conferences. I noticed that the way participants spoke to each other when the trainer was out of the room was different from the way they spoke when the trainer was in the room. And I realised how the summer's heat affected the interaction and how different the atmosphere could be on different days. These observations, which became highly consequential for my analysis, would have been missed had I relied solely on post-hoc analysis of the recordings.

Like many before me, I also realised that my presence in the room and the presence of the recording equipment had an effect on where the participants sat and how they interacted. And the importance of perspective became apparent. I formed opinions of the participants: I preferred some to others; agreed more with some than others; and came to the opinion that tensions between trainers and some of the trainees were deliberately exacerbated in some cases. In other words, I began to develop both 'reflexivity', that is, an awareness of 'the way in which the observer has an impact on what is observed, and the way in which the observation events themselves are captured in a real historical context, from which they derive meaning and salience' (Blommaert and Jie, 2010: 66); and also 'an objective view of my sub-jectivity' (ibid.), that is, a need to be circumspect about some of my interpretations because of the emotional reaction I had to the talk. Had I continued to produce a linguistic analysis using the proposed discourse analytic framework only, I may also have had an emotional reaction when listening to the recordings; however, I doubt that I would have developed reflexivity or an objective view of my subjec-tivity. These constructs proved invaluable when it came to analysing the data.

Nevertheless, by the end of the data collection process, although I was convinced of the value of ethnography and its affordances, I felt as if I had been *practising* ethnography rather than *doing* ethnography. This was because I was still becoming familiar with the way of working (observing, developing awareness, thinking, challenging my interpreta-tions, writing fieldnotes, talking to participants, making meaning from their talk and so on). Furthermore, because of my familiarity with lin-guistic data, I continued to consider the recordings and transcriptions of these the primary data set and I struggled with the fieldnotes and interviews – were these data or did they provide contextual information to support interpretation of the linguistic data?

I have described elsewhere how I resolved this dilemma (see Copland, 2015). In the following section I draw on a range of data (fieldnotes, recordings, transcriptions, interviews) to illustrate how I came to understand ethnography more fully, both as a process (through developing an ethnographically grounded analytical framework) and an epistemology; that is, a way of knowing and thinking about the world, and, specifically, about research (see Blommaert and Jie, 2010: 5, for a helpful discussion of ethnography as a 'full' intellectual programme). These two changes to my research practice were fundamental in helping me to understand the synergy created in linguistic ethnography through conjoining linguistic and ethnographic approaches to data collection and analysis.

Developing an ethnographically grounded analytical framework

As described above, the study focused on post-observation feedback in initial English language teacher training. The research questions were:

1. What are the generic features of feedback in this context?
2. Which hegemonic positions are enacted and reproduced by these trainers?
3. What strategies do these trainers and trainees use to introduce, maintain and negotiate power in their feedback sessions?
4. Are these trainers and trainees adequately prepared to take part in feedback?

The research revealed that trainers and trainees oriented to genres, that is, 'a set of conventionalised expectations that members of a social group or network use to shape and construe the communicative activity that they are engaged in' (Rampton, 2006: 128). The genres identified included: 'self-evaluation' (sections of talk where trainees provided positive and negative feedback on their own lessons); 'trainer feedback' (where trainers provided positive fend negative feedback on the trainees' lessons); and 'peer-feedback' (where trainees would provide positive and negative evaluations on the lessons taught by other trainees in their group). I focus on peer feedback in this section, because it was in the analysis and discussion of peer feedback data that the value of linguistic ethnography became clear (a fuller discussion of genre in this study and some of the following discussion can be found in Copland, 2011).

'Peer-feedback' was a feature of every feedback session and was also a theme in my fieldnotes. I consistently referred to it, noting for example, trainees' lack of engagement and undeveloped critical perspective and the effort trainers made to elicit comments from trainees. Trainees did peer feedback, but ineffectively, and trainers insisted on peer feedback, despite its superficiality. The ethnographic noticing and reflecting signalled that peer feedback was worthy of further investigation and so I conducted a linguistic analysis of peer feedback talk by identifying all instances in the data and then coding the talk according to function. This analysis showed that peer feedback generally exhibited particular features. It included a description (of what happened in the lesson) and positive feedback. If negative feedback was included, it was hedged, unelaborated and the trainee delivering the feedback linked the negative evaluation to a weakness in his/her own lesson delivery. Most of these features are present in the following example from the data: unelaborated negative feedback (italics), praise (underlined), link to weakness in own performance (bold):

Extract 1

> <u>I thought that was quite good</u>. **I wouldn't have thought of that and they** <u>really enjoyed the game at the end, didn't they, making the sentences. I thought () they seemed to really enjoy that activity of putting all the words together. I thought that was good cos that gave them the chance to use what they were learning, put it in the proper context.</u> **Um the only thing of working on, I thought, was the same as what I did last week, when somebody asks um says the wrong answer. I did the exactly the same and I said 'Ooh no!'. Um and then, like in my feedback, I think it was you suggested didn't you say to say something like 'Oh why did you think that?' or, 'Did everybody else get the same answer?'** *so to try and draw them out why they said no.* **So that stood out cos it was the same as what I did** *((laugh))*.

Both the linguistic and ethnographic analysis suggested that peer feedback was a site of unease, so I introduced it as a topic in the interviews. The trainees said they found the task of peer-feedback difficult and often face-threatening. They also said that they found giving feedback uncomfortable given their relative lack of experience. By contrast, trainers reported that peer feedback was a useful activity for trainees as it encouraged them to observe each other closely, it reduced the burden on the trainers to produce evaluative comment, and it provided opportunities for reflection. However, trainers also stated that it was often not successful because trainees were too busy focusing on their own lessons to pay attention to their peers' lessons.

The interview data confirmed my findings, from detailed analysis of fieldnotes and transcripts, that there was a mismatch between trainers' and trainees' views about the purpose, value and challenge of peer feedback. The interview data, in addition, suggested a number of reasons for this mismatch.

An ethnographically grounded analytical framework emerged organically as I worked with the different data sets, answering the questions, 'What's going on here?' and 'How do you know that?' These questions, elegant in their simplicity, are demanding. The first question required me to draw on analytical resources to interrogate first impressions and contradictory readings. The second ensured that I found supporting evidence for findings in different data sets. Both questions grounded the data (fieldnotes, recordings, interviews) in their context of use and both made me aware that my diggings and uncoverings were contingent and subjective. Developing this ethnographically grounded analytical framework involved a personal step-change, from banking on the linguistic data, with its perceived empirical rigour and validity, to developing an understanding of what the ethnographic brings in terms of accounting 'for what goes on, on the ground, in living colour' (Agar, 2008: 10). In the next section, I explain how working with this framework produced an even more fundamental shift – to embrace an ethnographic sensibility.

Developing an ethnographic sensibility

In order to explain this shift in my approach to embrace an ethnographic sensibility, I return now to examining peer feedback. As described above, most peer feedback lacked critical edge and hovered between praise and hedged negative evaluation. However, there was one sequence of peer evaluation that was 'atypical' (Erickson, 1992: 206); that is, it was unlike any other peer-evaluation talk in the data set (indeed, it was unlike any other peer-evaluation talk I had ever encountered). Its atypicality ensured that it attracted my analytic attention. In this peer-evaluation episode, trainee (S) is invited by the trainer to provide peer feedback, but flatly refuses (he said 'no'), flouting the generic conventions (i.e. a description of what happened in the lesson, positive comments, hedged negative evaluation linked to a weakness in his/her own performance). This refusal caused a degree of confusion amongst the trainer and trainees and was eventually resolved when trainee S agreed that he had some feedback to give. In my fieldnotes, I noted trainee S's refusal and its contrariness:

Extract 2

> The following interaction was very odd. He said 'No' but it wasn't clear what he meant by this. ... is he challenging the trainer, the event or something else? Is he doing it deliberately or not?

Writing the fieldnotes began the analytical process: what did trainee S mean by saying 'no'? I began to pay particular attention to trainee S in the observations. I became aware of his attitude, posture and levels of interaction when with this trainer. For example, I noted that S 'did not seem to get involved in the feedback', that he 'rarely if ever takes the floor independently' and that he 'just seems stubborn'. However, when the trainers swapped groups and trainee S had a new trainer, his behaviour changed. I noted that trainee S 'really took part' in the feedback, that he 'smiled fully' and that he 'seemed readily to accept the critique'. After one observation I wrote the following in my fieldnotes:

Extract 3:

> At the end of the card discussion, trainer 2 gave trainee S her own feedback about his lesson, which was mostly positive. ... Trainee S then asked if trainer 2 thought he had been polite or not. I guessed this was in reaction to feedback trainer 1 had given him in the last tutorial about rapport building. Trainer 2 responded, 'I thought you were very polite, in fact', which again put a smile on Trainee S's face.

Following trainee S's journey through the course, I had begun to formulate responses to the questions, what's going on and how do we know based on observations distilled in my fieldnotes, in other words, based on the ethnographic data. I then decided to conduct a linguistic analysis of the atypical interaction (extract 2) using tools of conversation analysis. Conversation analysis requires that each utterance is considered in its relationship with previous and next utterances and it suggests a set of tools for examining features such as turn-taking, organisation and repair (Richards, 2003). The extract and analysis are presented below: a trainer and four trainees, S, C, J and P (who doesn't contribute in this section) are present in the feedback conference:

Extract 4

1.	Trainer:	Um, (.) trainee S, you you've gone () a bit quiet
2.	Trainee S:	Sorry about that *((quietly))*
3.	Trainer:	Do you want to eh start off on with trainee C
		[
4.	Trainee C:	on trainee C *((laughs))*
5.	Trainer:	On trainee C
6.	Trainee S:	Umm (...) No *((falling tone))* no
7.	Trainer:	No? *((rising tone))*
8.	Trainee S:	I've I've got some thoughts sorry but I I was wasn't making
9.		notes terribly well today and I've got no real structure to them so
10		I'll I I have to generalise from them
11.	Trainer:	That's alright if they've got no real structure to them that's
12.		fine
13.	Trainee S:	Um
14.	Trainee C:	*((laughing))* You've got all the right notes but not necessarily in
15.		the right order *((laughs))*
16.	Trainee J:	*((laughs))*
17.	Trainee C:	*((inaudible comment))*
18.	Trainee 1:	The exercise at the end was really interesting fun and could
19.		have been longer and

The trainer begins the extract by suggesting that trainee S has not been contributing to the discussion ('you've gone a bit quiet'), a reasonable move given that the trainer manages who speaks in feedback (the softener 'a bit', reduces the strength of the comment) and that trainees are expected to contribute (the data going up to this section show that trainee S has not spoken for some time). Trainee S apologises, but does not provide a reason for his silence. At line 3, the trainer then invites trainee S to start his evaluation of trainee C. The trainer makes a mistake with the preposition, causing trainee C to repeat the mistake and to laugh about it (to start *on* rather than to start *with* seems to suggest that criticism will be harsher). Trainee S hesitates ('Ummm') and then pauses before uttering his refusal, 'no', in a falling tone. His turn initial filler and pause mark this as a dispreferred second pair part (Pomerantz, 1984) to the trainer's invitation in line 3 (the preferred second pair part – in this case would be to answer to the trainer's question, 'do you want to start on with trainee C?' in the usual way), while the falling tone on 'no' has a final quality – this is not a 'holding' no or a 'hesitant' no.

That the refusal is unexpected is recoverable from the trainer's questioning 'no?' at line 7. What is more, dispreferred responses require an explanation and so the questioning 'no' invites trainee S to give an account. At line 8, trainee S does so through providing a reason for his inability to provide feedback ('I wasn't making notes … I've got no real structure to them') which mitigates his 'no', perhaps as he realises he has over-stepped the generic boundaries. The trainer replies encouragingly that structure is not important, accepting the trainee's attempt to re-establish himself in the talk. Trainee C then makes a joke about S's note taking ('all the right notes but not necessarily in the right order', a joke almost universally recognised in the UK , having first been made in a classic 1970's comedy sketch in which the comedian defended his appalling performance on the piano with this remark). This 'laughable' ('a humorous utterance' which is followed by laughter, Thonus, 2008: 334) elicits the desired response from the other trainees in the room. Then, at line 18, trainee S starts to give detailed feedback on C's lesson.

In terms of answering the questions, 'What's going on here?' and 'How do we know?', the analysis is helpful. It shows that trainee S's refusal is unexpected. It also shows that the trainees at least are made uncomfortable by the refusal and that the trainer works hard to ensure that the trainee finally gives some feedback. Importantly, it shows that trainee S has a reason for not giving feedback but that this reason does not, in the end, stop him from engaging with the activity.

This ethnographically grounded analysis suggests that trainee S had a difficult relationship with the trainer and perhaps too with the trainees in the group. In the post-course focus group with the trainees, I broached this topic by asking, 'How did your experience of feedback change when you changed groups and trainers?' He responded:

Extract 5

> Through no fault of [the trainer], I really, really enjoyed the things he had to say, I was delighted to change [trainers] as we hadn't had any exchange of ideas for at least the last week of his fortnight and I thought, you know, a change of scenery would help.

This discussion later led to the following exchange:

Extract 6

> Trainee S: I felt that () we generally exchanged like compliments and stuff after the lesson after the first few () and that repeating those was in front of the trainer wasn't really worthwhile and I didn't feel that I could make any criticisms

FC: Right you didn't have any to make or you didn't want to make any

                                                              [

Trainee S: No I had them to make
             but I didn't feel I could make any
FC: Right wh why didn't you feel you could make them?
Trainee S: Just cos I didn't think they'd be received () um (..) I didn't think
             they'd be recei::ved () *((rising tone))* positively ()

When considered with the fieldnotes and interview talk, the linguistic analysis of the extract provides insights for responding to the question 'what's going on?'. When trainee S answers 'no' to the trainer's invitation to provide feedback to his peers, he unleashes his frustration with both the trainer and the other trainees. With one small word he resists the role of peer evaluator placed on him by the trainer and registers his dissatisfaction with his peers. We can make a case for 'knowing' this is so through the process of 'opening up' the linguistic analysis to ethnographic interrogation (through fieldnotes and interview data) and 'tying down' the insights gained through observing and talking to the trainees through a linguistic analysis of the unfolding talk (see Rampton et al., 2004).

However, my ethnographic sensibility was most seriously affected by what happened next. Having worked carefully with the different data sets, cross-referencing and ensuring I focused on my guiding questions, I felt fairly confident that trainee S had been deliberately provocative, and, as I have argued elsewhere (Copland, 2011), had wanted to threaten the trainer's face with his decision to say no. Given the trainer's response in the feedback conference, I was also fairly sure that he had understood the 'no' to be face threatening as I knew from corridor chats (recorded in fieldnotes) that he found trainee S 'difficult' and because I knew that refusing to take part in peer evaluation was exceptional.

Keen to explore this issue, I played extract 2 to the trainer in the interview immediately after the course. The first thing that surprised me was that the trainer said that he could not 'actually remember it', which suggests that for him the refusal was not salient as it was for me. After listening a second time, the trainer began a long reflective monologue on the extract (perhaps in answer to my original request, many turns before, to 'just comment on it'), suggesting reasons why trainee S refused to give feedback. These ranged from the refusal being intended as a joke, to suggesting and then rejecting the idea that trainee S did not know what he was being asked to do, to surmising that trainee S did not deliver feedback as he did not think that trainee C would listen to it, to suggesting that trainee S considered C's lesson so 'crap' it was not worth giving feedback on. It was a prompt from me that obliged him to consider my interpretation of the event.

Extract 7

> FC: Yeah, I I mean what I think's really interesting ... is the way he dares to say no (.) that you are the teacher in that situation (.) and what's expected is that you ask a question and people will answer the question. And he won't play ball really. He says no. You know, I'm not going to do what you're asking me to do. And, you know, your 'no' there is quite (.) I think it sounds quite surprised. Don't you do you think it does or not?
>
> T: Sure sure. That's interesting. Yeah yeah. Yep, yep. But it's interesting you're saying that cos I don't, I didn't perceive it as sort of defiant no I didn't perceive it like that when when I heard it now. I mean I can't really remember how I perceived it at that moment but I mean I didn't perceive it as that. I perceived it as oh, more of a quite, quite a low status sort of no really. Kind of well, no, I I don't know. I I can't do this. Or (...) I don't know.

The trainer's rejection of my finding was telling. If trainee S had deliberately set out to threaten the trainer's face and to cause disruption, then his efforts had been wasted on the trainer, or at least the trainer convinced me in the interview that his efforts were wasted. In terms of developing my ethnographic sensibility, however, his efforts had great impact.

As I explain above, I was convinced of the value of ethnography for ensuring context is brought into play. Indeed, in my analytical framework, ethnography became the grounding feature. However, when I realised that there was more than one reading of trainee S's 'no' I began to understand the epistemology underpinning the ethnographic endeavour and to develop my ethnographic sensibility.

As extract 7 shows, the trainer provided a different interpretation of trainee S's 'no'. In support of his interpretation is the fact that he had the epistemological high ground, being an interlocutor in the interaction under scrutiny. Furthermore, he was the one to whom the 'no' was at least interactionally aimed. In support of my original and different interpretation, that the 'no' was deliberate, I could argue that it was also partially directed at me, the observer, the lurker in the room, the person who was there to notice deviance in the interaction. (And, of course, it was aimed too at the other trainees, a daring act which they would recognise and question.) Moreover, I was party to other 'truths'.

I observed the 'no' being delivered, and even at that point, recognised it as salient. In addition, I had spoken at some length to trainee S about the intentions behind his 'no' and these intentions seemed plausible. However, threatening this interpretation is the reality that as the interviewer, I had raised the issue of the 'no' in the first place, signalling to trainee S that it was of interest to me and thereby providing him with a discoursal affordance, that is, the opportunity to speak about saying no, in terms of putting his own spin on why he said it. How does the researcher reconcile these different interpretations?

One way to achieve this is to respond to the questions, 'What's going on here?' and 'How do we know?' as they ground the analytic process, forcing the analyst to justify their interpretations. Another is to bring the analysis to the attention of participants, to tease out synergies and contradictions. Giving 'voice to the members' perspectives' (Adler and Adler, 2012: 30) through this process has the potential to reveal not only complexity but also to support the central tenet of ethnography which is to 'investigate the viewpoint of the studied' (Becker, 1996: 59). The act of sharing interpretation is what Hymes calls 'democratic: a mutual relation of interaction and adaptation' (1980: 89, cited in Blommaert and Jie, 2010: 12). In the end, the interpretation of the data will be affected by this sharing as both the researcher and the researched will undoubtedly shift their original perceptions and develop their understandings of interactions.

In terms of extract 7, the interpretation must take into account the views of the participants in the talk. If not, there is no ethnography. However, it must also reconcile the different views and findings from the data to which only the researcher has access. Blommaert and Jie (2010) argue, 'Ethnography tries to ... describe the apparently messy and complex activities that make up social action, not to reduce their complexity but to describe and explain it' (p. 12). The analysis of extract 7 reveals this complexity. I would argue that working with an ethnographic sensibility means that we take messiness for granted, seeking it out if it is not immediately apparent and being open to challenging our analyses and interpretations at all stages of the research.

Conclusion

As I now re-read the Holmes et al. (1999) chapter discussed above, it is clear that appropriating linguistic ethnography has led to changes in my work, both in the methodological framework that I use, but, more importantly in the way I view research, its purpose and its outcomes.

I now work with an analytical framework grounded in ethnography which employs detailed linguistic analysis and draws findings from the interplay between the ethnographic and linguistic data. I also understand the value of complexity and how complexity can be uncovered through, for example, asking the right questions and sharing data with participants. This ethnographic sensibility, unimaginable at the beginning of the research process, is now tangible and my research is the better for it.

At the time of writing, linguistic ethnographic approaches seem to be making little ground in the TESOL world, particularly when compared to the vitality of linguistic ethnography in research into bilingualism. Funding for TESOL research is of course an issue. Given that its concerns generally affect English speakers in overseas contexts, it is difficult to attract funding from UK research bodies (the British Council, which has recently developed a more critical perspective on the role of English, is a notable exception in this respect). There is also the issue discussed above about traditional research focuses in TESOL in which measuring and classifying areas of practice to improve learning and teaching continue to be the norm. Nevertheless, the latter at least may soon change. Currently, there is great interest within TESOL in global processes in the development of English as a lingua franca (Coleman, 2011) and the neoliberal agenda, which it has been argued, is driving this development (Block, Grey and Holborrow, 2011; Pillar and Cho, 2013). These interests dovetail nicely with current concerns in bilingual education on transcultural flows, superdiversity and ideology, which are being investigated through linguistic ethnographic approaches. In time, as these interests inevitably converge, linguistic ethnography could emerge as an attractive approach for understanding how TESOL practitioners and their students are affected by new world orders in which English has a central role.

References

Adler, P. and Adler, P. (2012) Tales from the field: reflections on four decades of ethnography. *Qualitative Sociology Review* 8/1, 10–32.

Agar, M. (2008) *The Professional Stranger (2nd edition)*. Bingley: Emerald Group Publishing Limited.

Becker, H. (1996) The Epistemology of Qualitative Research. In R. Jessor, A. Colby and R. A. Shweder (eds), *Ethnography and Human Development: Context and Meaning in Social Inquiry*. Chicago: The University of Chicago Press.

Blackledge, A. and Creese, A. (2010) *Multilingualism*. London: Continuum.

Block, D., Gray, J., and Holborow, M. (2012) *Neoliberalism and Applied Linguistics*. London: Routledge.

Blommaert, J. and Jie, D. (2011) *Ethnographic Fieldwork: A Beginner's Guide*. Bristol: Multilingual Matters.

Brandt C. (2006) *Success on Your Certificate Course in English Language Teaching: A Guide to Becoming a Teacher in ELT/TESOL*. London: Sage.

Briggs, C. (1986) *Learning How to Ask: A Sociolinguistic Appraisal of the Role of the Interview in Social Science Research*. Cambridge: Cambridge University Press.

Copland, F. (2011) Negotiating face in the feedback conference: a linguistic ethnographic approach. *Journal of Pragmatics* 43/15, 3832–3843.

Copland, F. (2015) 'Case study two: researching feedback conferences in pre-service teacher training', in F. Copland and A. Creese with F. Rock and S. Shaw (eds) *Linguistic Ethnography: Collecting, Analysing and Presenting Data*. London: Sage.

Creese, A. (2005) *Teacher Collaboration and Talk in Multilingual Classrooms*. Clevedon: Multilingual Matters.

Duff, P. and Uchida, Y. (1997) The Negotiation of Teachers' Sociocultural Identities and Practices in Postsecondary EFL Classrooms *TESOL Quarterly* 33/3: 451–486.

Ellis, R. (2009) *The Study of Second Language Acquisition*. Oxford: Oxford University Press.

Erickson, F. (1992) 'The Interface between Ethnography and Microanalysis' in M. LeCompte, M. Millroy and J. Preissle (eds) *The Handbook of Qualitative Research in Education*. London: Academic Press.

Garton, S. and Copland, F. (2010) '"I like this interview, I get cakes and cats!": The effect of prior relationships on interview talk'. *Qualitative Research* 10/5, 1–19.

Gobo, G. (2008) *Doing Ethnography*. London: Sage.

Graddol, D. (2006) *English First*. London: The British Council.

Holmes, J., Stubbe, M. and Vine, B. (1999) 'Constructing Professional Identity: 'doing power' in policy units', in S. Sarangi and C. Roberts (eds) *Talk, Work and Institutional Order Discourse in Medical, Mediation and Management Settings*. Berlin: Mouton de Gruyter, pp. 351–350.

Hyland, K. (2009) *Teaching and Researching Writing*. 2nd edition. London: Longman.

Kumaravadivelu, B. (2009) *Understanding Language Teaching: From Method to Postmethod*. London: Routledge.

Mann, S. (2011) 'A critical review of qualitative interviews in applied linguistics'. *Applied Linguistics* 32/1, 6–24.

Martin-Jones, M. and Heller, M. (1996) 'Introduction to the special issues on education in multilingual settings: discourse, identities, and power. Part 1: constructing legitimacy'. *Linguistics and Education* vol. 8, pp. 3–16.

Pillar, I. and Cho, J. (2013) 'Neoliberalism as language policy'. *Language in Society* 42, 23–44. http://dx.doi.org/10.1017/S0047404512000887.

Pomerantz, A. (1984) 'Agreeing and disagreeing with assessments: some features of preferred/dispreferred turn shapes' in J.M. Atkinson and J. Heritage (eds) *Structures of Social Action*. Cambridge: Cambridge University Press.

Rampton, B. (2006) *Language in Late Modernity: Interaction in an Urban School*. Cambridge: Cambridge University Press.

Rampton, B., Tusting, K., Maybin, J., Barwell, R., Creese, A., and Lytra, V. (2004) *Linguistic Ethnography in the UK: A Discussion Paper.* At http://www.ling-ethnog. org.uk.

Richards, K. (2003) *Qualitative Inquiry in TESOL.* Basingstoke: Palgrave.

Richards, K. (2006) *Language and Professional Identity: Aspects of Collaborative Interaction.* London: Palgrave Macmillan.

Roberts, C. (2003) 'Applied linguistics applied'. In S. Sarangi and T. van Leeuwen (eds) 70 *Applied Linguistics and Communities of Practice.* British Association for Applied Linguistics in association with Continuum, pp. 132–149.

Thonus, T. (2008) Acquaintanceship, familiarity, and coordinated laughter in writing tutorials. *Linguistics and Education* Vol. 19, 333–350.

Walsh, S. (2011) *Exploring Classroom Discourse: Language in Action.* Abingdon: Routledge.

7

Researching Health Policy and Planning: The Influence of Linguistic Ethnography

Sara Shaw and Jill Russell

Introduction

Extract 1

Well we've got a mission and the mission is to help improve policy making through better evidence. That's the mission, to help improve, ultimately, the health of people in ... the UK. So that's the bottom line and within that there's quite a lot that we can do ... to try to inject a lot more sense into the debates through evidence and through cool objective sober argument.

> Interview with senior executive at a think tank

Extract 2

I want to explore this political dimension a bit more and so I ask about people that [they] might like to influence but perhaps have not yet had much success. What emerges is what she refers to as 'a group of political people who are advisors', people that [she] describes as 'the in-crowd' and that 'are constantly flitting over the British state'. The two names she mentions are George Osbourne and Oliver Letwin*. I find this fascinating as ... this is high level political machinery that she had previously said was less important ... It seems that I am hearing two different stories here but I am unsure quite what they're telling me and why.

> Journal entry, 1 February 2012

*At the time of the study George Osbourne was Chancellor of the Exchequer for the UK Coalition Government, and Oliver Letwin was Minister for Government Policy in the Cabinet Office.

These data extracts are drawn from an interview and a research diary that form part of the data set for a study on the role of think tanks in shaping health policy and planning. Think tanks are civil society organisations that specialise in producing and disseminating knowledge that is relevant to public policy (Medvetz, 2008; Pautz, 2011). These 'two different stories' relate to different accounts of the planning process that were present in think tanks' work: one focusing on the production and use of evidence to feed into policy and the other on political work involving people, values, ideas and interactions in shaping policy. Such stories (or narratives) work to shape policy problems and practices (Yanow, 1996; Rydin and Ockwell, 2005; Hajer, 2006). Identifying and unpacking them (for instance, examining who is involved, and the main arguments in play) proved vital to our analysis and understanding of think tanks' role in shaping health policy. Our findings revealed how think tanks publicly ('front-stage') present a storyline to position themselves as 'independent research organisations', drawing on the language of technocratic health planning to define their role as producing evidence and feeding this into policy. This confers legitimacy in the eyes of decision-makers and the public. Away from public view ('back-stage'), the storyline shifts with think tanks talking about how they link with particular actors and interests (e.g. via private dinners with decision-makers) as they seek to influence health policy and healthcare delivery. We found that employing these two stories enabled think tanks to present themselves as neutral, value-free advisors on NHS reform, offering a 'view from nowhere' (Nagel 1989), whilst simultaneously trying to promote and maintain particular interests, gain political power and, ultimately, shape the policy agenda.

Behind these two narratives of think tank work lie two different representations of health policy and planning processes. Most analysts and researchers interested in health policy align with a positivist conception of healthcare planning and conceive it as a formal, rational process that can be planned in advance. Others adopt an interpretive approach, describing policy as 'a set of shifting, diverse, and contradictory responses to a spectrum of political interests' (Edelman, 1988:16), focusing on how meaning is constructed through policy and examining, for instance, the argumentative structures and practices involved (Rydin and Ockwell, 2005; Hajer, 2006). We align with this latter approach.

In this chapter, we describe how and why we have come to study healthcare planning from this interpretive approach, and the contribution of linguistic ethnography to our work on think tanks. In the first section we locate ourselves working in a medical school environment in the 1990s. We recount how and why we came to explore how policies get produced and reworked through language and social interaction, why we developed an interest in an interpretive approach to policy analysis, and what this meant for our work. In the second section we draw on our research examining how think tanks shape health policy. We demonstrate how linguistic ethnography has guided this work, exploring (and demonstrating) the relationship between theory and data. We conclude by reflecting on how bringing linguistic ethnography to interpretive policy analysis enriched our work on think tanks.

At the heart of this chapter lies a dialogue between linguistic ethnography and an interpretive approach to studying health policy and planning. In foregrounding this dialogue, we have only been able to give limited detail of our overall research design and methodology. Readers can find a more detailed account of the study theory, methodology, findings and ethical issues in Shaw, Russell, Korica and Greenhalgh (2014); Shaw (2015); and Shaw, Russell, Parsons and Greenhalgh (2015).

Locating our research

For over 20 years we have worked as qualitative researchers in health-care, gaining much of our research experience working in medical schools. Over the years we have undertaken research and evaluation projects about various aspects of health policy and practice, using interviews, focus groups and occasionally some observation. As is the norm in the medical school environment (where controlled trials, systematic reviews and surveys dominate), these qualitative methods were under-pinned by an implicitly neo-positivist view of language and meaning. Like many qualitative researchers in medical schools, we were trained as analysts to look for 'themes' in our data. We treated language as a transparent medium, a lens through which we could unproblematically examine and understand the real nature of events and people's views and experiences (Gubrium and Holstein, 2003; Hammersley, 2007). Our exploration of meaning was limited to identifying and documenting respondents' intentional, stated meanings (Wagenaar, 2011).

We then came across a body of work in policy studies that proved to be a turning point in our thinking. This work not only recognised the empiricist emphasis (grounded in instrumental rationality as a means of explaining human action) as naïve, but also regarded policy analysis and policy outcomes as 'infused with sticky problems of politics and social values' (Fischer, 2003, 11). We engaged with writers such as Frank

Fischer, Carol Bacchi, Murray Edelman, Dvora Yanow, Deborah Stone, Maarten Hajer and Henk Wagenaar who opened our eyes to the emerging field of Interpretive Policy Analysis. The work of these writers differs in many respects (indeed, some may not regard their work as being grounded in interpretive policy analysis). However, what ties them together is the way that they understand policy and policy analysis as involving dialogue, argument and interaction and their analytic focus on meaning-making. They see policymaking not simply as a means for finding acceptable solutions for preconceived problems, but as the dominant way in which social conflicts are regulated. They connect policy and planning with politics and encourage us to focus, not only on *what* a policy means, but also on the role of language in constructing and enacting policy and social life more widely, and thus *how* a policy means (Yanow, 1996; Wagenaar, 2011). Through the lens of interpretive policy analysis, policymaking is no longer a value-free, technical project, but is essentially argumentative. The stories that we referred to at the start of the chapter capture a condensed form of narrative in which particular arguments are employed by people as shorthand in discussions about policy. The argumentative character of policy plays an important role in positioning actors (Rydin and Ockwell, 2005), as they are drawn to particular stories that represent common interests and form 'discourse coalitions' around them (Hajer, 2006).

Through this body of work, language and social interaction increasingly became focal points of our work. However, lacking any background in linguistic analysis, we were uncertain how to incorporate this into our research practice. A course in *Key Concepts and Methods in Ethnography, Language and Communication* provided immersion in micro-level data analysis sessions, allowing us to learn through practical engagement what it means to undertake an analysis based on the study of language-in-use (Shaw, Copland and Snell, this volume). It encouraged us to combine our existing interests in ethnography with our emerging interests in language, and to employ an eclectic mix of methodological strategies in our research, an approach often referred to as 'bricolage' (Kincheloe 2001), which made more sense to us than the narrow, compartmentalised focus on specific 'schools of thought' we had previously encountered in learning about discourse analysis.

The majority of UK health research remains firmly wedded to the positivist conception of healthcare planning described above. There is, however; a growing community of researchers who are bringing interpretive approaches to bear on issues of health policy and health service delivery (see, for instance, chapters by Jeff Bezemer and Sarah Collins in this collection). We locate ourselves within this community, adopting linguistically sensitive approaches to healthcare planning. Our recent research exploring how think tanks shape health policy provided us with an opportunity to examine the role of language and interaction in the context of evolving health policy.

Studying think tanks' role in shaping health policy and planning

Health policy and planning as the focus of our study

In recent decades, think tanks have emerged as a significant part of the global knowledge economy. The growth of think tanks has been described as 'nothing less than explosive' (McGann, 2013: 14), with an estimated 6600 operating across 180 countries (ibid.). This growth has emerged out of social and political changes occurring since the 1980s (see Shaw, Russell, Korica and Greenhalgh 2014). It has enabled think tanks to increase not only in number, but also in the scope of their work, with greater input into policymaking across a range of areas. Whilst they vary in terms of their focus, activities and funding, think tanks are increasingly visible participants in health policy.

The starting point for our study was health policy. This is different from much of the existing work in linguistic ethnography, which has strong roots in education and literacy studies and has drawn researchers to focus on, for instance, language practice and classroom interaction (Rampton, 2007; Tusting and Maybin, 2007; Lefstein and Snell, 2011). Whilst policy and planning are clearly relevant (for instance, in considering how policy initiatives such as the national curriculum are enacted in the classroom [Lefstein, 2008]), it is not the prime focus for much linguistic ethnography. Hence, in order to examine the relationship between think tanks and health policy our initial orientation was not only to micro-level interaction but also to interpretive theory that could help us to define the analytic problem of studying policy (Wagenaar, 2011).

Interpretive policy analysis situates policy as something broader than tangible pieces of legislation and regulation administered by government. Rather, the idea of 'public policy' indicates an area of social life that is simultaneously distributed (through multiple and dispersed policy practices) and held in common (via overarching policy narratives that make sense of events and guide political action), involving 'a never ending series of communications and strategic moves by which various policy actors in loosely coupled forums of public deliberation construct intersubjective meanings' (Hoppe, 1993: 77). These meanings are continually translated into collective narratives, projects and plans through a range of activities, actions, interactions, organisations and actors (including think tanks). Our focus on policy therefore meant that there was no single 'policy space' similar to a classroom into which we could walk, observe 'health policy' and collect naturally occurring data of interaction. This is because the practices that make up 'policy and planning' are dispersed and do not sit neatly in a single, accessible, naturally occurring space. And think tanks do not engage with policy and planning via a single route but occupy different social spaces allied to a range of political, media, knowledge production and business activities (Medvetz, 2012, 2008).

Defining our case

Interpretive policy analysis provided a clear starting point for our study, privileging policy and politics as 'the object of study' (Tusting and Maybin, 2007), and guiding us to focus initially on the dispersed policy spaces and practices that make up health policy and planning. The distributed and fragmented character of policy meant that, in order to unravel the narratives allied to think tanks (and the individuals allied to them) and their role in shaping health policy, we needed to explore the work of think tanks via various sources and genres of data.

We undertook a collective case study (Simons, 2009) of think tanks' role in shaping health policy. We began by developing a typology of UK think tanks that have health and healthcare as part of their programme and, from this, selected four think tanks, ensuring a range of activities, histories and funding sources. The four think tanks (all referred to anonymously here, and elsewhere, as Think Tanks A, B, C and D) together provided an opportunity to study policymaking from a range of perspectives. However, we needed a concrete instance of health policy and planning on which to focus. At the time of the study, the Coalition Government had set out a substantial programme of reforms to the NHS in England, including general practitioners taking on a substantial role commissioning healthcare and a new economic regulator overseeing extended competition amongst (public and private) healthcare providers. We focused on this programme of reforms in order to have a tangible example of health policy and planning on which to focus data collection and analysis, and to explore how think tanks engaged with it. All four think tanks in our sample were engaged in work relating to this programme of reforms either directly (in three cases) or tangentially (in one case).

Collecting and analysing data

Our study emerged from one author's (SS) experience of working in Think Tank B, an organisation based in central London who describe themselves as 'an authoritative and independent source of evidence-based research and policy analysis for improving health care in the UK' (mission statement 2013). The focus of their work is the provision of 'evidence for better health care', emphasising a technocratic process where the think tank role is to produce evidence, feed this into policy and so improve healthcare. SS worked at Think Tank B for two years, from February 2009 to March 2011, during which time she kept a journal reflecting on her role. Originally a personal project, this journal was resituated as an auto-ethnographic account as the study was conceived and SS, once again, took up an academic position. This process raised a number of ethical questions, in particular about the nature of consent and the accountability of the research – a detailed account can be found in Shaw (2015).

Think tanks remain largely hidden in existing analyses of health policy and planning. The reason for this stems, in part, from difficulties negotiating access to such dispersed policy practices. Through auto-ethnography, we were able to examine and retell events and activities related to health policymaking – in this case related to a substantial programme of reforms to the NHS in England (DH 2010), and the context in which think tanks' activities unfold. Take the following extract in which SS is trying to make sense of her working environment after close to a year in post:

Extract 3

> I have been struck by the formality of some of the emails … They often bring with them the sense of a 'formal managerial request' where I am required to act in some way, my response should also be formal and thought through and this will be recorded and filed somewhere for future reference or 'good record keeping'.
>
> This approach to managing, decision-making and communicating all has a rather strange effect on me … It makes me feel that research is dictated from 'on high' and that my role is simply to undertake and deliver rather than investigate and explore.
>
> Journal, 5 January 2010

Such journal entries enabled us to move from personal experience of specific activities ('some of the emails', 'formal managerial request', 'requiring me to act in some way') to connect with particular cultural practices and approaches to planning that are grounded in an accepted way of doing things ('approach to managing', 'dictated from on high'). Hence what began as a personal project documenting experience of working within a think tank provided ethnographic insight into organisational practices and activities.

This auto-ethnographic account provided a useful, preliminary insight into the activities of think tanks. To examine the activities, artefacts, interactions, spaces, values and ideas (Yanow, 1996; Hajer, 2006; Wagenaar, 2011) allied to think tanks' work, we supplemented this account with documents and interview data drawn from across the think tanks in our sample.

Documents

Documents are important for those seeking to understand the meaning of policy (Freeman and Maybin 2011), in that they represent shared narratives amongst coalitions of actors (including decision-makers, think tank executives, practitioners and publics).

We included 30 documents drawn from across the four think tanks, allowing us to examine formal accounts and presentations of work, the content of arguments and discursive strategies (for instance, via formal publications and policy briefings) within our sample, and the interrelationship with emerging health policy. Take the following example from a document published by one of the think tanks in our sample outlining their work priorities at the time of the study:

Extract 4

Competition

The Health and Social Care Bill paves the way for an extension of competition and market mechanisms in the NHS in England.

We are contributing to the evidence base by taking forward a number of projects that will establish [Think Tank B] as an important source of independent information and analysis on the use of competition and market mechanisms in health care.

Project highlights include:

- The Health Care Markets programme – a strategic partnership with the Institute for Fiscal Studies to undertake empirical research on the use of market mechanisms in health care
- a project to assess how payment mechanisms can best be developed in future

- playing a prominent role in helping to influence the development of regulatory policy by the Department of Health and Monitor.

This extract focuses specifically on 'Competition' and situates this as a priority area of work. The extract explicitly references the governments' reforms ('The Health and Social Care Bill', 'the development of regulatory policy') and gives voice to proposed mechanisms for change outlined by the government ('an extension of competition and market mechanisms', 'the use of competition and market mechanisms in health care', 'how payment mechanisms can best be developed'). Such talk entails courses of action, seeking to guide health policy and health service delivery in particular ways and not others. This is achieved by, in this instance, foregrounding particular values allied to a market-oriented approach to designing and delivering healthcare services (for instance, via 'The Health Care Markets Programme'). The language used references formal government proposals (see, for instance, DH 2010), and situates Think Tank B as a legitimate contributor to the development and delivery of such proposals ('as an important source of independent information and analysis', 'playing a prominent role', 'helping to influence').

Such talk was most visible in the formal publications of think tanks in our sample. In theory these were publicly accessible documents (available via think tank websites) aimed at a 'universal' audience (Perelman and Olbrechts-Tyteca, 1971). In practice they used technical language that limited their accessibility and suggested that they were targeted at an 'ideal' audience of healthcare planners and decision-makers. For instance, echoing the content of proposed NHS reforms, they emphasised: 'reduced costs through integration and competition', 'improving productivity in the areas set out in the Operating Framework', and how 'Monitor and the supporting regulations for NHS procurement need to promote both competition and collaboration'. This highlights the interplay between documents and actors, with powerful individuals potentially able to provide legitimacy to policy and either establishing or reinforcing discourse coalitions (where actors come together around narratives that represent shared interests [Hajer, 2006]).

Think tanks in our sample did not overtly support government proposals: notable challenges included the likely negative impact of price competition on the quality of health services. Direct challenges were the exception rather than the rule. All appeared to use policy talk in an effort to address and engage decision-makers by emphasising shared beliefs (e.g. 'moves to increasing competition are right'); using similar terms and phrases (e.g. 'the Nicolson Challenge', a mandate from the NHS Chief Executive to find 'efficiency savings' of

£20 billion); presenting briefing papers and publications in the same genre as government documents; and citing many of the same sources (e.g. publications from other think tanks). This rhetorical work is key in providing legitimacy to publications (through authorship and referencing of policy talk) and in directing readers to particular policy narratives.

Interviews with think tank representatives

Although useful in providing a snapshot of particular values and intentions, documents alone fail to account for think tanks' actions that precede or follow as part of the health policy and planning process (Shaw, 2010). We therefore undertook a series of narrative interviews with think tank representatives (four informal and ten in-depth, see Shaw, 2015) allowing us to examine interviewees' accounts of the health policy and planning process.

We had already begun to examine the language that think tanks use in their work, informed by our theoretical interest in rhetoric and argument (Shaw, 2010; Russell and Greenhalgh, 2011). Interviews allowed us to extend this work, examining the language and arguments that think tank actors employ to account for the work they do.

Initial examination of documents and our auto-ethnographic account highlighted how think tank actors tend to use particular language to emphasise the work that they do and how they do it (for instance, Extract 4). We were particularly struck by think tanks' use of the terms 'independent' and 'independence' which think tanks cited in publicly accessible documents (such as strategic plans, mission statements, annual reports, website pages and research publications), situating themselves as, for instance, 'an independent, charitable, non-party think tank whose mission is to set out a better way to deliver public services and economic prosperity'.

We used interviews as an opportunity to explore with think tank actors how and why they use such terms. We found that all four think tanks (to varying degrees) undertook a range of neutralising work as a way of situating their work as value-free. For instance, think tank actors situated themselves as politically neutral by using spatial metaphors ('bang in the centre', 'there's no overt line', 'the centre of expertise', 'even handed', 'doing the middle path') drawing attention away from contentious areas of policy talk such as competition to more neutral and disinterested areas ('like data, like the right kind of leadership, the right kind of regulation'). This served to situate think tanks as working in a neutral and independent space, free from political agendas, financial interests, and values, and therefore making them well-placed to improve health and healthcare.

When we asked interviewees to describe their work to us in interviews, they frequently reverted to describing what they were *not* as a means of situating themselves in an unclassified and neutral space. Take the following extract from an interview with a senior executive at one think tank discussing what independence means:

Extract 5

> So one of the things that's ... sort of positive, but actually quite challenging is – we are independent, we therefore don't have a constituency, therefore we don't have a particular voice to represent and we don't have an obvious position to take on things. You know, actually if you're representing an interest group, you often have probably quite a strong basis for taking a position because it's what's in the interests of the group that you're representing. So the way in which [we] come to a position, we don't, it's not dictated by any interest, has to be, in my view, much more based on a reasonable assessment where possible, of the evidence.

This senior executive avoids framing their organisation in specific terms and instead describes the organisation as not having 'a constituency', 'a particular voice' or 'an obvious position to take'. In doing so he reinforces his organisation's position as value-free ('we are independent', 'it's not dictated by any interest'). Whilst values do enter the conversation ('[we] come to a position'), this interviewee defends their own intellectual ground by emphasising that any position is grounded in objectivity ('based on reasonable assessment ... of the evidence'). This position was reflected throughout our interviews with think tank actors, with an emphasis on instrumental approaches to policy and planning that foregrounded neutrality through rigorous analysis and production of objective, independent evidence (see extracts 1, 4 and 5).

Social theory and data analysis

Our focus on different sources of data provided a rich picture of the context, people, activities, artefacts, ideas and values that make up think tanks' work in relation to health policy and planning. Our early analysis revealed how different ideas and values appeared to be talked about in different ways in different contexts (e.g. formal publications, actors' accounts of their work), and that this process needed to be managed via a range of neutralising strategies. To make sense of our emerging analysis, we introduced two 'sensitising concepts' to our work as a means of extending analysis and 'suggest[ing] directions along which to look' (Blumer, 1954:8). Having engaged with wider theory about the context in which policy and planning take place, we introduced concepts of 'front-stage' and 'back-stage' healthcare planning (Degeling, 1996, following Goffman, 1959) and 'sacred' and 'profane' language (Degeling, 1996, following Durkheim, 1964). These concepts drew us to examine the more public and private settings in which health policy and planning take place; and to distinguish the theory of policymaking – with its claimed values of objectivity and rationality (see above) – from accounts of how things work in practice. Take the following extract, from an interview with a senior executive at one of the participating think tanks, discussing what has enabled them to influence evolving NHS reforms:

Extract 6

I have come to realise that writing it down actually does matter a great deal, oddly.

Why do you think that is?

So, I think it gives you the authority. And in a lot of the process, well, people either want something to go, you know, in a lot of these processes they want something to go back to – 'why are you doing this?', 'in response to ...' – and with a kind of, a kind of audit trail ... There's a sort of seemliness to that process. So I think, I think it's very difficult actually to influence without the sort of, without having the written analysis to underpin it, which you have published. And actually, of course, in the parliamentary discussions where our work was quoted, they don't quote a conversation they've had with you, they quote what you've written ... And that discourse is a very important part of this. Now what is really helpful is combining that writing with the explaining personally. And also the warming people up to the fact that you're going to write, and in many cases I had prior conversations with people about how I was going to word this – sought their advice on [discussion about specific reforms]. And I changed some of the wording too, having reflected on their advice.

Okay, almost framing of what you were going to say?

Yes. So I iterated. So I did, I didn't, I didn't do things quite so sequentially ... I guess the engagement with people was a two-way process where I was trying to influence them, but I was also taking their advice. So that what we would say was capable of being more influential.

Okay. And you felt that process worked very well with what came out at the end of it?

Yes. Because I mean I think what we recommended then was things that, you know, and that is a classic Civil Service, you know, kind of: 'So if I change that word here, will you sign up to that? Right, I'll check that with that person there'. And 'if we do that, can you live with that?' 'Yes, check that back.'

This interviewee emphasises the importance of formal written accounts in providing legitimacy and weight to think tanks arguments ('writing it down actually does matter a great deal', 'it gives you the authority') and a citable source of ideas ('they quote what you've written', 'a kind of audit trail', 'having the written analysis to underpin it') that decision-makers are able to draw on ('in the parliamentary discussions', 'classic Civil Service'). The production of formal front-stage accounts involved an interactive process ('a two-way process', 'combining that writing with the explaining personally', 'warming people up'), establishing common ground between think tank actors and decision-makers ('changed some of the wording', 'reflected on their advice') and working together 'back-stage' to co-produce accounts of NHS reforms ('So if I change that word here, will you sign up to that?'). This production of written accounts was visible in the activities of each of the four think tanks to varying degrees (dependent on their capacity and resources).

Think tanks' formal accounts of their work linked with 'sacred language' of policy and planning (Degeling, 1996), drawing on modernist conceptions of health policy that describe the policy process as an exercise in informed problem-solving (Parsons, 2002), and in which a problem is identified, data collected and analysed, and evidence provided to policymakers on which they can then base decisions. In their 'front-stage' accounts think tanks emphasised a set of technical skills and activities (for instance, 'experimental intervention', 'innovative quantitative analysis'), which informed precise 'research and policy analysis', which then fed into 'the administrative machinery' of government. This was underpinned by an emphasis on evidence-based research and policy, with all four think tanks emphasising standards of rigour underpinned by instrumental rationality.

By employing such 'sacred' planning discourse front-stage, think tanks publicly deferred to values such as rationality, objectivity and due process and established a sense of commonality with healthcare planners and decision-makers. This reinforced think tanks' self-presentation as independent organisations, and situated them as legitimate advisors on the problems – and potential solutions – of NHS reform.

To return to the two narratives that we described at the start of our chapter, on the one hand think tanks' deference to 'sacred' planning discourse signalled to decision-makers that they knew about and adhered to the rules of the game 'front-stage'. On the other, this enabled think tanks to identify and interact with decision-makers 'back stage', and to speak about and practise planning in ways that gave more explicit recognition to its political dimensions.

Studying policy and politics: bringing linguistic ethnography to interpretive policy analysis

Interpretive policy analysis and linguistic ethnography have both added important dimensions to our work. Rather than attributing different aspects of our work to different approaches (which tends to dichotomise rather than synthesise), we conclude by describing how our own dialogue across interpretive policy analysis and linguistic ethnography has enabled us to better understand and analyse the dispersed, micro-level practices that make-up health policy and planning, and the role of think tanks in shaping these.

This dialogue between linguistic ethnography and interpretive policy analysis is best illustrated with a concrete example. The work of Goffman is frequently drawn on by those adopting linguistic ethnography (see Rampton, Maybin and Roberts, this volume). It was an area of work that we engaged with on the *Key Concepts* course, encouraging us to connect with dramaturgical theory (specifically performance and impression management, Goffman, 1959). Whilst this work is highly relevant to our own research, it tends to focus on specific instances of interaction in single, defined spaces (e.g. classroom, police interview room) rather than multiple and dispersed micro-level policy practices. Engagement with interpretive policy analysis enabled us to foreground policy and planning as the object of our study, theorise them and then, building on Goffman's work (1959, see also Degeling, 1996), connect with relevant sensitising concepts (front-stage and back-stage) to guide our analysis. In this way, we connected the concepts and methods of linguistic ethnography with the policy-oriented approach of interpretive policy analysis.

The social theory allied to interpretative policy analysis has been important in guiding our conceptualisation of policy as a series of dispersed, micro-level practices (Yanow, 1996; Bacchi, 2000; Stone,

2001; Hajer and Wagenaar, 2003; Hajer, 2005; Wagenaar, 2011). This has guided data collection to ensure (as far as possible) that a range of actors, settings, interactions, artefacts and arguments allied to policy and planning were included within our study. We have at times been frustrated by a limited attention to data and close analysis of language within interpretive policy analysis (see, for instance, an article examining the development of alcohol policy, which employs 'rhetorical frame analysis' but then holds back from detailed analysis of language or rhetoric [Hawkins and Holden, 2013]). For us, this is where linguistic ethnography comes to the fore: the dialogue between language and context is one of the qualities of linguistic ethnography that we valued most and, guided by social and political theory, has led us to explore both 'front-stage' and 'back-stage' contexts of think tanks' work, along with the different linguistic resources employed in each; and to undertake close analysis of think tank language and arguments.

There is a clear commitment in linguistic ethnography to making analytic claims accountable to evidence (Rampton, Maybin and Roberts, this volume). We described above how policy is simultaneously distributed via multiple and dispersed policy practices, and at the same time held in common via overarching policy narratives that make sense of events and guide action. This presents particular challenges for us in 'making analytic claims accountable' (ibid.). Whereas many linguistic ethnography studies are able to demonstrate the key analytic point in a small strip of talk or a few exchanges, analysis of health policy and planning narratives often stretches over multiple and extended documents and/or exchanges and cannot easily be captured in a specific segment of data. Whilst this does not detract from close analysis, it does make it difficult to present 'evidence' of analytic claims in the conventional way. This is an irresolvable characteristic of our work. However, the dialogue between linguistic ethnography and interpretive policy analysis has been helpful in simultaneously encouraging us to undertake close analysis of policy practices (in ways that are unusual for linguistic ethnography) and pushing us to evidence our analysis (in ways not traditionally undertaken within interpretive policy analysis).

It has been argued that linguistic ethnography brings 'a formal, abstract discipline and tried and tested, finely-tuned methods for analysing text together with more open, reflexive social orientation of ethnographic methods, which offer analytic purchase on the related social practices and structures' (Tusting and Maybin, 2007: 576). This dual focus encourages rigorous linguistic work that also addresses social practice. However, it can lead to methodological tensions between the more 'closed' focus on linguistic text and a more 'open' sensitivity to context (ibid.). These tensions are characterised by on-going discussions about if and how language ties ethnography down and ethnography opens linguistics up (Rampton, 2007). In our work on think tanks, we regard this process as a balancing act, negotiating ethnography and language throughout the study so as to enable a conversation about text and context and expand understanding of the ways in which think tanks work to shape health policy.

Methodological tensions also raise interesting questions about the analytic gaze and what counts as data. We have drawn attention to the specific focus on policy as the object of our study and described the ways in which different data sources have, together, helped us to understand the work that think tanks do in shaping NHS reforms. It was interpretive policy analysis that provided a focus on policy, guided consideration of text and context, and enabled us to answer the 'what is data' question. Rather than asking 'what is going on here and how do we know it?' as we were encouraged to do on the *Key Concepts* course (Shaw, Copland and Snell, this volume), interpretive policy analysis encouraged us to ask 'how does a policy mean?' (Yanow, 1996), and 'how do we know it?'. This guided us to collect different sources and genres of data (documents, interviews) that, together, could provide insight into the overarching architecture of health policy and the narratives, coalitions and arguments allied to it.

Our study of think tanks' role in shaping health policy has illustrated the benefits that can be gained from a dialogue between linguistic ethnography and interpretive policy analysis. Linking language, context and social practice has been particularly valuable. This, of course, is characteristic of other work in the social sciences (Hammersley, 2007; Tusting and Maybin, 2007), with researchers having long been interested in the intimate relationship between policy, political language and political acts (see, for instance, Edelman, 1988; Degeling, 1996; Yanow, 1996; Bacchi, 2000; Fischer, 2003). History aside, it seems that linguistic ethnography has provided us with what Rampton (2007) calls 'a site of encounter': an opportunity to engage with and reflect on 'established lines of inquiry' (for instance, sociolinguistics), to introduce new foci for linguistic ethnography research (for instance, policy and planning), blend linguistic ethnography with relevant social theory and methodology (for instance, through the lens of interpretive policy analysis) and actively engage with an interdisciplinary community of like-minded scholars.

Acknowledgements

Thanks to all four think tanks for their enthusiasm and openness in participating in the study; to Trish Greenhalgh, Wayne Parsons and Maya Korica for their contributions in shaping the study; and to Fiona Copland, Jo Maybin and Julia Snell for their valuable comments that have helped to shape this chapter. The views expressed in this chapter are those of the authors and do not necessarily reflect the perspective either of the individuals interviewed or the organisations in the sample.

References

Anderson, L. (2006) 'Analytic autoethnography', *Journal of Contemporary Ethnography*, 35(4): 373–395.

Bacchi, C. L. (2000) 'Policy as discourse: what does it mean? where does it get us?', *Discourse Studies in the Cultural Politics of Education*, 21(1): 45–57.

Blumer, H. (1954) 'What is wrong with social theory', *American Sociological Review*, 18: 3–10.

Degeling, P. (1996) 'Health planning as context-dependent language play', *International Journal of Health Planning and Management*, 11: 101–117.

Durkheim, E. (1964) *The Elementary Forms of the Religious Life*, (1912, English translation by Joseph Swain, 1915), George Allen & Unwin, London.

Edelman, M. (1988) *Constructing the Political Spectacle*. Chicago University Press, Chicago, Ill.

Fischer, F. (2003) *Reframing Public Policy: Discursive Politics and Deliberative Practices*. Oxford University Press, Oxford.

Fischer, J. and Forester, J. (eds) (1993) *The Argumentative Tin Policy Analysis and Planning*. Duke University Press, Durham NC.

Goffman, E. (1959) *The Presentation of Self in Everyday Life*. Double Day Anchor Books, New York.

Gubrium, J. F. and Holstein, J. A. (2003) *Postmodern Interviewing*. Sage, London.

Hajer, M. (2005) 'Setting the stage: a dramaturgy of policy deliberation', *Administration & Society*, 36(6): 624–647.

Hajer, M. A. (2006) Doing discourse analysis: coalitions, practices, meanings. In van den Brink, M. and Metze, T. (eds) *Words Matter in Policy and Planning*, pp. 65–76. Koninklijk Nederlands Aardrijkskundig Genootschap.

Hajer, M. and Wagenaar, H. (2003) *Deliberative Policy Analysis: Understanding Governance in the Network Society*. Cambridge University Press, Cambridge.

Hammersley, M. (2007) 'Reflections on linguistic ethnography', *Journal of Sociolinguistics*, 11(5): 689–695.

Hawkins, B. and Holden, C. (2013) 'Framing the alcohol policy debate: industry actors and the regulation of the UK beverage alcohol market', *Critical Policy Studies*, 7(1): 53–71.

Hoppe, R. (1993) Political judgement and the policy cycle: the case of ethnicity policy arguments in the Netherlands, in Fischer and Forester (eds).

Kincheloe, J. L. (2001) 'Describing the bricolage: conceptualizing a new rigor in qualitative research', *Qualitative Inquiry*, 7: 679–692.

Lefstein, A. (2008) 'Changing classroom practice through the English national literacy strategy: a micro-interactional perspective, *American Educational Research Journal*, 45(3): 701–3.

Lefstein, A. and Snell, J. (2011a) 'Promises and problems of teaching with popular culture: a linguistic ethnographic analysis of discourse genre mixing', *Reading Research Quarterly*, 46(1): 40–69.

Medvetz, T. (2012) *Think Tanks in America*. University of Chicago Press, Chicago, IL.

Medvetz, T. (2008) *Think Tanks as an Emergent Field*. The Social Science Research Council, New York.

Nagel, T. (1989) *The View from Nowhere*. Oxford University Press, Oxford.

Parsons, W. (2002) 'From muddling through to muddling up. Evidence based policy-making and the modernisation of British Government', *Public Policy and Administration*, 17(3): 43–60.

Pautz, H. (2011) 'Revisiting the think tank phenomenon', *Public Policy & Administration*, 26(4): 419–435.

Perelman, C. and Olbrechts-Tyteca, L. (1071) *The New Rhetoric: A Treatise on Argumentation*. Notre Dame, IN: University of Notre DamePress.

Rampton, B., Tusting, K., Maybin, J., et al. (2004) 'UK Linguistic Ethnography: A discussion paper'. Available from: http://www.ling-ethnog.org.uk/documents/papers/ramptonetal2004.pdf.

Russell, J. and Greenhalgh, T. (2011) Rhetoric, evidence and policymaking: a case study of priority setting in primary care. In Dawid, P., Twining, W., & Vasilaki, M. (eds) *Evidence, Inference and Enquiry*. British Academy, London (distributed by Oxford University Press).

Shaw, S. E. (2015) Ethnography, language and healthcare planning. In Copland, F. and Creese, A. (eds) *Linguistic Ethnography: Collecting, Analysing and Presenting Data*. Sage Publications, London.

Shaw, S.E. (2010) 'Reaching the parts that other theories and methods can't reach? How and why a policy-as-discourse approach can inform health-related policy', *Health*, 14(2): 196–212.

Shaw, S.E., Russell, J., Korica, M. and Greenhalgh, T. (2014) 'Thinking about think tanks: a call for a new research agenda', *Sociology of Health & Illness*, 36(3): 447–461.

Shaw, S.E., Russell, J., Parsons, W. and Greenhalgh, T. (2015) 'The view from nowhere? How think tanks work to shape health policy', *Critical Policy Studies*, 9(1): 58–77, DOI:10.1080/19460171.2014.964278

Simons, H. (2009) *Case Study Research in Practice*. Sage Publications, London.

Stone, D. (2001) *Policy Paradox: The Art of Political Decision Making* [3rd edition] WW Norton.

Tusting, K. and Maybin, J. (2007) 'Linguistic ethnography and interdisciplinarity: opening the discussion', *Journal of Sociolinguistics*, 11(5): 575–583.

Wagenaar, H. (2011) *Meaning in Action: Interpretation and Dialogue in Policy Analysis*. M.E. Sharpe, Armonk, N.Y.

Yanow, D. (1996) *How Does a Policy Mean? Interpreting Policy and Organizational Actions*. Georgetown University Press, Washington, D.C.

8
Bursting the Bonds: Policing Linguistic Ethnography

Frances Rock

Introduction

Malinowski suggested a need to 'burst the bonds of mere linguistics' (1949: 306) through attention to context. He recognised that 'a statement, spoken in real life, is never detached from the situation in which it has been uttered' (1949: 307) and, accordingly, an utterance's 'context of situation' determines its meaning (1949: 306). Context shapes understanding of Malinowski's words, themselves. The contemporary scholar might read 'mere' as a slight which characterises linguistics as 'small or insignificant' by analogy with collocations like 'mere mortals' which have this attributive usage (Oxford Dictionaries Online 2014). Yet we can instead take 'mere' as a descriptive adjective meaning 'pure, unmixed, unalloyed; undiluted, unadulterated' or an intensive adjective, meaning 'absolute, sheer' (Oxford English Dictionary 2014). Thus Malinowski's words are usefully understood as a call to complement 'pure' linguistics rather than denigrate 'insignificant' linguistics. This appeal to 'burst the bonds' of linguistics has been heeded by scholars in Linguistic Ethnography (LE) driven by its enticement to move beyond the textual. Indeed this phrase has become something of a rallying cry in LE (for example Jacobs and Slembrouck 2010: 236; Tusting and Maybin 2007: 577; Lillis and Curry 2010: 19). In this chapter, I describe my response in view of opportunities and challenges I have encountered in undertaking linguistic ethnographic research on policing.

Language in legal settings is often presented as being troublesome for relations between lay people and institutions. Academics (for example Patry and Penrod 2013), media sources (for example Guardian Newspaper 2013) and government agencies (for example Thomas 2010) frequently attribute this trouble, simply, to 'comprehension difficulties'. Cognitive and psychological perspectives tend to objectify these 'difficulties' as part of a mono-dimensional mental process operating outside the social. My work is part of a tradition which instead views comprehension as socially situated and integrated into interaction (for example Bremer and Roberts 2013 [1996]). Closely examining naturally-occurring interactions as well as forms of data less traditionally seen as (socio)linguistic (such as observation, qualitative interviews, photographs and fieldnotes) has allowed me to recognise the complexity, conflicting demands and varied experiences of communication in routine policing.

After briefly describing my research and situating it in relation to LE, this chapter examines two main questions:

> (1) What can an LE perspective contribute to investigating the notion of 'face' (Goffman 1967: 41), which has been studied predominantly as a linguistic phenomenon?
> (2) Can we adapt the analytic reach of 'crosstalk' (Gumperz, Jupp and Roberts 1975), a phenomenon which has been central to LE, by extending its application to new forms of data?

In exploring these two themes, I consider the affordances and restrictions of using LE to research legal settings.

LE: Bursting the bonds

LE scholarship bursts the bonds of linguistics in three important ways. I outline each below, indicating their relevance here.

Firstly, LE is not a discipline which rigorously enforces procedures or methods (see Rampton, Maybin and Roberts, this volume: 32–36). Instead it provides space to draw-in relevant theories and concepts – guided by the commitment to understanding interaction in context. In my case, I took a social practices approach, recognising activities like reading and writing within institutional relations (for example Barton and Hamilton 1998). This enabled me to consider writing, reading and speaking as part of law's social structures and to examine how those activities influence people's construal and appropriation of language resources including spoken, heard, written and read forms (for example Rock 2005). Incorporating LE involved not simply adopting a 'method' (for example part of an apparatus for collecting data), but encouraged a particular way of being in and knowing through research (Blommaert 2009: 260–261), as this chapter will show.

Secondly, LE is not concerned with viewing itemised units of language in exterior, dualist 'context' (Blommaert 2006: 6), but with recognising language as truly situated. This encourages making connections, not only across interactions (through talk, writing and other media), but also with the consequences of making meaning for issues which researchers label, for instance, power, function and community. Recognising these connections helped me to take a more holistic perspective, connecting data and theory. LE is valuable for research on language in legal settings, where the situatedness of language becomes particularly salient (for participants) and particularly observable (for researchers). However, certain aspects of legal communication might be inaccessible to the researcher, as I will discuss.

Thirdly, and for me, the most compelling aspect of LE, distinguishing it from other approaches, is the particular way that it values the insider's view (Pike 1990: 28). LE is not the only framework within linguistics which considers language users' perspectives (cf. Integrational Linguistics, for example Harris 2003). Yet this aspect of the LE paradigm distinctively combines three elements. First, participant observation as a means to gather information; secondly, close work on observational data, combined with other sources, in order to give voice to emic perspectives. These are mediated, throughout the research process, by the third and final element, reflexivity about the researcher's position in order to recognise others' stances (Maybin and Tusting, 2011; Rampton *et al.*, 2004; Tusting and Maybin, 2007). By combining these three elements, LE reimagines data through 'ego effacement', 'fellow feeling' and ultimately communion (Geertz 1974: 45). This attention to lived experience wrapping around language, and vice versa, creates distinctive analytic possibilities (Tusting 2013: 2–3) being not simply about asking people what they do with and through language but really entering practice by combining asking, watching, seeing, hearing, listening, even doing, reflexively.

Situating my work

I became interested in researching legal sites after having been involved in the legal system as a witness to a crime. This process gave me a particular view of the collection and status of legal evidence in a police investigation, courtroom trial and criminal appeal. This was combined with a vocational imperative to apply linguistics. I became interested in LE when I encountered New Literacy Studies during my MA at Lancaster University, UK. This interest developed as I felt a need to recognise the complexity of situated language use in legal sites beyond the bonds of 'mere' linguistics. I sought to build on work combining linguistic and ethnographic/anthropological elements to examine policing (for example Caldeira 2002) and law (for example Black and Metzger, 1965; Walter, 1988; Berk-Seligson 1990; Conley and O'Barr 1990; Hale 1997; Mertz 2007).

In this chapter, I recruit two sets of data. The first was collected in the police custody setting, as part of my doctoral research. The second data set is from my current research on texts and procedures of police complaints. Both projects are underpinned by related research questions about (i) how successive texts are connected through inter-textuality and recontextualisation – forming into chains (Bakhtin 1986: 93) and (ii) how individual texts contain the contributions of various speakers and writers – becoming mosaics (Kristeva 1986: 37). In addition to these theoretical questions, I have been concerned with applied research questions about how versions of texts function in practice.

Working in legal settings brings a challenge: identifying something called 'legal settings' or 'law' or even 'policing' or 'crime' is potentially divisive (see Rampton, Maybin and Roberts, discussions on 'race', this volume: 22 and 41) and contrary to the ethnographic imperative to avoid essentialising. Declaring an interest in 'the legal', or in a particular location, classroom or 'language', one implies these can be cleaved from other areas of human experience and activity. Yet for LE to be meaningful and practical it must be 'about' something. My response has been to turn situatedness into an analytic advantage. I have used a particular text (such as the police caution), procedure (such as that for handling police complaints) or interaction (such as telephoning for police assistance) to trigger and structure research. In short, the situatedness of linguistic artefacts and practices has provided coordinates through which to navigate the surrounding people, spaces and activities. In custody, for example, I started with two texts and traced their trajectories through networks of interactions and instances (Rock, Heffer and Conley 2013). This included talk during police interviews and throughout custody as well as in the wider policing world of offices, streets, canteens and parties. The two focal texts also pointed to written intertextual connections to legislation, appeal court judgements, policing guidelines, training materials, law manuals, police notebooks, cartoons, jokes and more.

Having briefly outlined my approach to LE and to my research, two worked examples show how LE has developed my understanding of policing.

LE in practice: managing 'face' in custody

Police officers interviewing suspects in custody must deliver information about the right to silence by reciting and, if necessary, explaining an official wording, the police caution (Pace Codes of Practice, Code C, Note 10d, 2013). The caution must be delivered irrespective of whether the suspect claims to know its content. One might expect that a wording so common and obligatory might be delivered with little personal attention. However, in this section I show that pragmatic concerns, in this instance around face, figure prominently and demonstrate the value of linguistic and ethnographic insights on this, following Copland (2011).

The concept of face, or the 'positive social value' that we claim for ourselves through our 'line' in interactions, was introduced by Goffman who advanced a 'rule of self-respect' indicating speakers' attempts to develop their social value and a 'rule of considerateness' indicating that they do the same for others (1955: 323). Brown and Levinson added two dimensions to this valuing or 'attention to face': positive face (desires to be liked and approved of) and negative face (desires to be unimpeded) (1987: 13). In the intervening years, face has received extensive attention (for example Haugh and Bargiela-Chiappini 2010). Some recent discussions explore the place of an emic, insider perspective (for example Arundale 2013), which is considered below.

My data collection around the police caution illustrates my shift towards the ethnographic. I began the research by seeking naturally-occurring talk – examples of police officers delivering and explaining the caution in investigative police interviews. I gradually moved towards the emic by conducting research interviews with officers and suspects about their experiences of cautioning and detention. Ultimately I undertook various forms of observation and shadowing in custody, producing fieldnotes and photographic records. The discussion below reproduces this layering.

I begin with naturally-occurring data from police interviews. Excerpt 1 shows the official wording of the police caution and its typical delivery. All names are pseudonyms:

Excerpt 1: The police caution

```
1  Phil   you do not have to say anything (.) but it may harm
2          your defence if you do not mention (.) when
3          questioned (.) something which you later rely on in
4          court anything you do say may be given in evidence
5          do you fully understand that caution?
6  Steve  I do yes
```

The caution (lines 1–4) is followed by a question, about the suspect's self-assessed comprehension (line 5), and an affirmation (line 6). Despite the claim of the suspect (Steve) to understand, the officer (Phil) immediately goes on:

```
7  Phil   I'm gonna ask you some questions (.) it's up to you
8          whether you answer some or all of them the ones
9          that you do answer are recorded ...
```

This turn (lines 7–9) might be somewhat perplexing to Steve who, having just stated that he understands the wording, is treated to an explanation anyway. The explanation is not preceded by any orientation to its presence, rather the officer just begins. Without this introduction, Steve may not realise that the officer is reiterating the caution. If he does realise, he might feel somewhat offended because Phil has failed to address Steve's face needs, suggesting, by explaining, that Steve does not understand or cannot assess his own understanding (threatening positive face) and impinging on him with explanation (threatening negative face).

Even if officers do orient their addressees to an impending explanation, they may still ignore face, like the officer cited below also speaking after a suspect has claimed understanding:

I'll just explain it to you anyway (.) it mean– the first bit means that if you don't want to say anything you don't have to ...

Here, the suspect's claim to understand is greeted with the *non sequitur* 'I'll just explain it to you anyway' which simultaneously dismisses and distrusts his claim. To use Brown and Levinson's terminology, these are bald-on-record explanations (1987: 94), ignoring, or perhaps playing on, the suspect's face needs.

These two officers could have framed their explanations differently, as Paul, a different officer shows in an equivalent turn:

Excerpt 2: I don't want to insult your intelligence

1	Paul	I'll just give you a brief explanation of that caution (.)
2		I don't want to insult your intelligence
3		but it keeps uh (.) lawyers fully employed sorting out
4		uh words like that (.) okay (.)
5		so I'll tell you what I understand by it (.)
6		'cos it is important (.) that you do understand it

Paul spends considerable time introducing his upcoming explanation of the caution by mitigating face-threat (lines 2–6) (Goldsmith and MacGeorge 2000: 235). He begins by acknowledging the potential of explanations to offend (line 2) and implying that the suspect is intelligent enough to need no explanation, attending to positive face. Nonetheless Paul is clearly intent on explaining and throughout lines 3–6 he pursues two mitigating themes. First, that the wording is complex, even to trained specialists ('it keeps lawyers fully employed sorting out ... that') and thus misunderstanding does not index stupidity. This complimentary talk minimises threat to positive face. Secondly, that the wording 'is important' which justifies any potential imposition or negative face-threat (after Brown and Levinson, 1987: 66). He also hedges around the likely quality of his own explanation casting it as being merely 'what I understand' (line 5) rather than definitive. This subtly addresses positive face by uniting him and the suspect in potential incomprehension. Compared to the first two officers, his mitigation is exhaustive.

Officers present diverse grounds for mitigation when cautioning (Rock 2007: 210–214). One factor employed repeatedly is the suspect's level of familiarity with detention. Suspects who are new to detention, in particular, are told that they will hear an explanation 'because you've never been ... interviewed ... before' or because 'it's the first time that you've been brought into custody'. Naturally-occurring data can tell us that mitigation happens and can indicate how and when. Yet without ethnographic data, we cannot get much further. Paul might just be a very nice chap who wants to avoid offending someone already in a difficult situation. On the other hand, legal commentators attribute such mitigation to sham concern underpinned by a desire to downplay the importance of rights information and thus of invoking rights (for example Leo 1998: 216). An LE approach enables us to go beyond simply noting attention to face, or hypothesising about its causes, by using more data in richer ways.

For Malinowski, an ethnographic stance permits examination not merely of 'how human life submits to rules' but also how 'rules become adapted to life' (Malinowski 1926: 127). In analysing legal settings, a tight focus on language can make rules appear overly influential. Ethnography permits a view of life's fit around law's rules. In cautioning, the 'rule' is that the caution must be stated and delivered. Life submits to rules in that officers caution and explain. However, rules become adapted to life when officers add things which are not provided for in the rules, in the case of the officers just discussed, attending to face through mitigation.

Copland (2011, and this collection) has shown how LE enriched her examination of face. She interviewed the very speakers who had engaged in potentially face-threatening interactions soon after those interactions. This approach was not possible for me. I had collected naturally-occurring talk from 800 authentic police interviews but did not have access to follow-up with any of those speakers, a restriction of the legal setting. However, as cautioning is standardised, I saw value in combining the naturally-occurring data from police interviews with research interviews with different officers, not featured in the naturally-occurring material. This meant that making connections between the data from police interviews and research interviews was not something to accomplish during research interviews (cf. Copland 2011: 3840) but rather when analysing the two sets of data – it became an analytic rather than data-collection activity. The disconnection of the naturally-occurring and elicited interviews turned out to be methodologically useful. It allowed officers to give their perspectives on their language use, rather than only their responses to specific data that I had selected and allowed me to recognise links between matters which I identified as important in naturally-occurring data and matters which officers flagged, independently, in research interview data. One of these was face, as I now show by illustrating how research interviews provide perspective on naturally-occurring data.

In research interviews, officers claimed that they found explaining the caution interpersonally problematic. This is important because it suggests that what looks like attention to face by officers during police interviews like those cited above. Police officers in research interviews appeared aware of the potential for face-threat. For example, Tom noted "I'll explain it to suspects but without trying to be patronising'.

Maggie, another officer, asserted 'I think [explanation] just humanises it a little bit more'. We cannot know whether these officers are sincere; genuinely intending to reassure without demeaning suspects or whether they are merely performing thoughtfulness as an in-interview identity. However, this is not what ethnographic research seeks to discover. Rather these speakers' words show that police officers at least recognise the potential for the interpersonal in moments of total regulation.

Excerpt 3 is from a research interview in which an officer, Pat, describes making decisions about explaining the caution. He presents explaining as a potential threat to positive face in that it might imply negative evaluation of one's interlocutor:

Excerpt 3: Almost on first name terms

```
1   Pat   the next question after [cautioning] is 'do you
2         understand' now if he's a regular and you're
3         almost on first name terms sort of thing I find it
4         sufficient to say 'do you understand' because if
5         he says 'yes' and if I then decide to describe the
6         caution to him I'm insulting his intelligence
7         because I've done it before
```

The notions of 'insulting' suspects' 'intelligence' (line 6) and attending to suspects familiarity with detention (line 2) both feature here as they did in the naturally-occurring data presented above. Pat suggests that these factors influence his decisions about whether to explain and how explanation impacts on face. Thus, in the naturally-occurring data, we saw officers selecting between various forms of mitigation and bald-on-record strategies and in the research interview data, we see officers exploring those selections. Even these few, short interview fragments show connections between forms of data, providing questions to pursue across data sets.

Some officers embrace opportunities to engage with suspects through cautioning, such as one who told me that explaining in her own words was to her 'not something that the job allows me to do (.) I choose to do it' (Caroline). For others, stating and explaining the caution was a miserable experience, like Nathan who told me that he did not understand the caution because 'nobody's ever said to me this is actually what it means it's been left to me sort of thing' (Nathan) and therefore rarely explained it. He interpreted procedure in the context of his potential loss of positive face through explaining poorly. Through such comments in research interviews, we come to see cautioning as not merely a bit of procedure, but something that officers take positions on and take into their practice, internalising or rejecting, doing or avoiding, with face as part of their considerations.

The naturally-occurring data and research interviews were augmented through six months of observation in one police custody unit and 20 'go-alongs' (Kusenbach 2003) with police officers to arrests and interviews. These generated fieldnotes, photographs and unexpected insights. For example, one officer revealed that he kept copies of past versions of the caution in his locker like a stamp-collector (cf. Cameron and Kulick 2003: 102). These data enhanced my understanding of cautioning as socially situated practice. Figure 8.1, showing the suspect's seat in one police interview room, illustrates how the artefactual impacts on face.

The arrangement in Figure 8.1 was typical of interview rooms when I conducted fieldwork. Ostensibly the coloured carpet was provided to indicate the correct placement of the suspect's chair for visibility on video. Video-recorded interviewing was not compulsory at the time yet the chair was always positioned this way. Suspects were put 'on the

Figure 8.1   On the spot

spot', as one suspect put it (Fieldnote 10). This positioning creates a spatial form of negative face-threat, imposing on the suspect by separating her visually from others in interview, including any of 'her' personnel such as a solicitor, and pinpointing her for attention. Some suspects would apparently note this negative face-threat and seek redress by edging out of the square, a minor act of defiance, which attracted comment during my research. Through combining forms of data, we begin to see cautioning contributing to multimodal institutional control of talk and movements. We also see attention to face involving not only talk but also artefacts and space.

In examining custody, I accessed rich data in wide-ranging formats which worked collectively to burst the bonds of linguistics, as I have briefly exemplified in relation to face. Following the custody research my work moved onto different aspects of police procedure and to data that might be considered less rich; so much so that I began to wonder whether LE was still part of my work. In the next section of this chapter, I present some of this material. I examine how, even if data is less diverse, an LE 'perspective' (as described by Blommaert 2009: 261) can still figure. He explains that this 'perspective' comes from adopting LE's theoretical direction by (i) recognising language as 'deeply and inextricably' situated in social life and (ii) taking an LE stance towards what we can know about language (ontology) and how we can find it out (epistemology) (2009: 263). My approach, when facing data access restrictions, common in legal settings, has not been to disregard LE but to consider these two aspects. In the example below, I describe how a concept which is central to LE, crosstalk, provides insight despite the dearth of data, bursting bonds in a different sense.

LE in practice: analysing crosstalk in speakers' accounts

Position pieces on LE frequently identify Gumperz's work as foundational and catalytic to the LE enterprise (for example Rampton et al. 2004: 9–10; Rampton et al. this volume). One theme often noted is that of interactional differences between speakers from different cultures (for example Creese 2008: 231). Gumperz et al use the label 'crosstalk' to describe communicative breakdowns when speakers' 'unconscious linguistic conventions' differ (1979: 5). Gumperz unites such conventions under the label 'contextualisation cues' saying that these cues, when functioning smoothly, enable speakers to signal, and listeners to interpret, what activity they are engaged in, how semantic meaning should be understood and how text relates to context (1982: 57). Gumperz himself examined crosstalk and contextualisation cues in police-lay interaction (2001).

The notion of crosstalk is generally applied to interactions between speakers lacking a common language background. Yet as the lines between languages are problematised (for example Creese and Blackledge 2010: 106), we also recognise the difficulty of identifying commonalities amongst those who believe they speak 'the same language' (Gumperz 1999: 453). In view of police officers' shared ideologies (McElhinney 2003), institutionality (D'hondt 2009) and Communities of Practice (Rock 2005), and linguistic heterogeneity amongst the public, interactions between police and lay people can become sites of crosstalk not unlike some intercultural interactions. Understanding contextualization cues is not solely a matter of culture, in any case, but also situational and societal structures (Gumperz 1992; Sarangi 1994). Indeed, as well as afflicting 'intercultural interactions' Jacquemet notes crosstalk in 'asymmetrical encounters' where 'one side seeks help and provides personal information and the other listens and adjudicates' (2011: 493), like the police-lay encounters discussed here.

The data below are from an ongoing study of complaints against the police. This work initially centred on static written texts; standardised complaint response letters from the police. However, I was able to augment these data through research conversations with complaints staff about their writing practices and interviews with complainants. The police service's categorisations of complaint topics includes a category entitled 'incivility, impoliteness or intolerance' which captures almost a fifth of all complaints according to most recent figures (IPCC 2012: 5). Incidents in this category frequently involve miscommunication. Without directly observing complained-about events, which would be impossible except by chance, we can only examine 'incivility, impoliteness or intolerance', as represented by participants. Participants' accounting indicates their take on such communicative breakdowns. This section exemplifies the productiveness of the notion of contextualisation cues when applied to speakers' accounts rather than naturally-occurring talk.

In Excerpt 4, from a research interview, a complainant, Debbie, presents the background to her situation (lines 1–3) and the reasons she made a complaint (lines 4–20).

Excerpt 4: Two police turn up at my door

```
 1    Debbie    I phoned  up  the  police  and  said 'look
 2              y'know (.) events have been going on for
 3              three years it needs to come to a stop' um

 4              and then I had a .h uh- two police turn up at
 5              my door um very late at night um

 6              (.) I didn't know what um what was going
 7              on what the situation was um

 8              basically threatened me um that I would be
 9              arrested taken to X Police Station I'd have
10              a um y'know (.) a- a- a blot on my sort of
11              y'know ((copy book)) sort of thing um

12              very threatening they didn't introduce
13              themselves um they made me feel really
14              intimidated

15              at the end of the day I'd gone to the police
16              for help um because of what was going on

17              and that is really what I made the complaint
18              about was the fact that I had these two
19              police officers turn up at my door .h
20              unannounced (.) threatening me basically
```

Debbie explains, in lines 1–3, that she had been seeking police action about her neighbours' behaviour for three years. This timespan might, itself, appear to be grounds for a complaint. She had, earlier in the interview, recounted feeling ignored by police and cornered by technicalities which prevented police action. Yet this, it turns out, was not the basis of her complaint. Having endured, as she saw it, three years of torment from her neighbours which she felt the police had brushed aside, the matter about which she complained, in the end, was one single interaction with officers who visited her house which she describes (lines 4–14) and evaluates (lines 15–20).

A view of contextualisaton cues helps us to examine Debbie's report using Blommaert's 'LE perspective'. An elemental step is to recognise Debbie's account as a version, not necessarily her only version and certainly not a definitive version, but the version selected for this particular occasion. The next step is to recognise the quantity and range of themes raised, the richness of her talk and the way that it shows positioning. The final stage is to consider how this relates to theoretical ideas, in this instance, crosstalk and contextualisation cues.

Debbie describes the officers' arrival in lines 4 and 5. She could have positioned this positively, indicating that their response, given the time of day, suggested that they realised matters had become urgent. However, instead she uses the expressions 'turn up' (line 4) and 'very late at night' (line 5) which collectively represents the attendance as unexpected and the timing as undesirable. She notes that the officers came to her home – which could again have been construed as a sign of personalised, attentive policing – through 'turn up at my door' (lines 4–5), the semantic prosody of which implies intrusion. She also notes that two officers visited. Again, this could have been cast positively as evidence that police were taking things seriously, but she seemingly cites this number to indicate heavy-handedness.

Debbie then moves into describing the 'incivility, impoliteness or intolerance' that she claims occurred (lines 4–14). Contextualisation cues 'may have a number of ... linguistic realisations', as I mentioned in introducing them. One area of potential trouble is the conversational opening, the way that an interaction begins (Gumperz, 1982: 131). Openings have been identified as influential in other policing settings (for example Cromdal et al. 2012). Debbie's account certainly presents the opening as a time when contextualisation was at issue. She suggests that the officers 'didn't introduce themselves' (line 12) and thus opened in a way that failed to make sense of the encounter for Debbie. Indeed she introduces the account itself with the words 'I didn't know what was going on what the situation was' (lines 6–7). Her earlier characterisation of the officers 'turn[ing] up', suggests that pre-opening, advance-notice of their arrival, was omitted, implying an encounter founded on imposition and surprise. Apparently unsure of the purpose of the speech event, Debbie construed pragmatic aspects of the officers' talk negatively. Specifically, her paraphrase of their illocutionary intent (intended meaning (Austin 1962: 101)) was 'threat'. Her repetition on this is striking as she recounts '[they] threatened me' (line 8), '[it was/they were] very threatening' (line 12); '[they were] threatening me' (line 20). She also recounts a specific threat, in lines 8–11, which was both immediate, involving arrest and removal to a police station (lines 8–9), and had longer-term consequences through a 'blot' on Debbie's 'copy book' (lines10–11). These general and specific suggestions of threat had a perlocutionary effect (force or outcome on the hearer (Austin 1962: 101)) which she describes, saying, 'they made me feel <u>really</u> intimidated' (lines 13–14). Debbie's response is not surprising. As Gumperz explains, when a listener misinterprets a cue or its function 'it tends to be seen in attitudinal terms. A speaker is said to be unfriendly, impertinent, rude, uncooperative or to fail to understand' (1982: 132). Debbie's account constructs missed contextualisation cues as creating negative evaluations.

Debbie concludes by encapsulating her position. The transition into summary is marked by the phrase 'at the end of the day' (Antaki 2007: 539). The first element of the summary (lines 15–16) is an assertion of Debbie's position as an innocent person who had 'gone to the police for help'. This positions her treatment as particularly outrageous. The final part of her summary (lines 17–20) revisits the event identifying it unambiguously as '<u>really</u> what I made the complaint about'. Emphasis on 'really' implies her reasonableness in not complaining about the previous three years of delays (lines 17–18). She casts her account as 'fact' (line 18). In this final summary, Debbie rehearses the elements which made the event so unpalatable: the presence of 'two ... officers' (heavy-handedness) (lines 18–19, echoing line 4); the officers having 'turn[ed] up' (line 19, echoing line 4) 'unannounced' (entailing neither pre-opening nor opening) (line 20, echoing line 4); the encounter infringing Debbie's territory 'at my door' (line 19 echoing lines 4–5) and that they were 'threatening' (line 20 echoing lines 8–12). The use of present continuous tense in lines 4–5 and 18–20 contributes to the impact of Debbie's account by making it appear temporally local to the present.

Whilst we cannot directly observe this incident, Debbie represents it as one in which contextualisation cues were missed and thus conversational inferences perhaps misfired (cf. Gumperz 2001: 35). Jacquemet casts crosstalk not as resulting from 'different' cultural assumptions, ways of structuring information, and ways of speaking, as Gumperz (1979: 4–5) did, but instead coming from 'unexpected' assumptions (2011: 493). This adjustment fits well with Debbie's positioning of the officers' behaviour not as totally incomprehensible but as open to being read as socially unacceptable. Whether Debbie genuinely did not know 'what was going on' and 'what the situation was' (lines 6–7), or genuinely experienced the negative emotions described, even whether the officers were really threatening, is not our concern. What is analytically interesting is how she reads-off meaning from the situation and recontextualises the officers' talk and actions. The concept of crosstalk illuminates this.

My data access woes in the complaints arena were less striking than those experienced by other researchers (for example van Praet 2001: 216). Yet like van Praet I have sought to turn them to the advantage of the research. She did this by examining the very barriers to research access, coming to see them as reflecting 'values and assumptions' of those studied (2010: 231). I have done so by conceptualising the data I have in LE terms. Returning to Blommaert helps to explain this. He is critical of those who view LE as just a method 'for collecting particular forms of data'; for separating context from talk or for facilitating description. In this section, discussion of one short excerpt indicates the productiveness of keeping LE concepts in play even when not obviously invoked.

Close

In legal settings, being able to make decisions, take actions and be heard shapes practical outcomes, ultimately verdicts and sentences. Meaning-making determines justice. With this in mind, I have taken up Malinowski's challenge to 'burst the bonds of mere linguistics', by incorporating LE, collecting and analysing multiplex data, even in data-constrained research sites, taking a reflexive stance on theory and a disposition which listens and observes. I have demonstrated this approach through two case studies: the first examining mitigation of face-threat alongside understanding of face by interactants to show linguistic notions re-visited; and the second demonstrating how the LE notion of 'crosstalk' can adapt to unlikely data.

At the beginning of this piece, I noted three key features of LE which make it distinctive. I now consider how these have been evidenced in this chapter. First, I noted that LE does not have an inflexible arsenal of methods or procedures. Instead, the analyst draws-in relevant data and theory and can consider social situatedness as the guiding principle when facing methodological and theoretical questions. In my first case study I showed how data collection evolved as my understanding developed driven by the data itself; naturally-occurring data triggered interest in interview data which triggered interest in seeing and experiencing contexts both physical and intertextual. The theoretical lens, face, was selected on the basis of the data too. In the second case study, crosstalk provided ways to learn from an account by recognising the value of the account in itself and working-up a conception of it as data.

The second feature I noted in an LE approach was the need to avoid compartmentalising 'language' and 'context' and instead recognising their intimate, complete connection. In the first case study, I showed how particular forms of context were informative, particularly speakers' own perspectives and the physicality of the interview room. Likewise, in the second study, context and language were not disentangled but seen as a complex which influenced Debbie's account and made it meaningful despite separation from the event reported.

Finally I noted the importance of the emic perspective in LE. I used interview data which, whilst it presents an 'insider' perspective of sorts, can seem rather blunt in relying on self-report and accounting. In both case studies, I recognised the restrictions of this but also its affordances. In some analyses, researchers enter into speculation about speakers' motives and intentions. Instead, by sensitively incorporating voices, data can layer to support observations about socially situated language use. In my first case study, I showed how viewing face as meaningful to participants made it possible to say more than by examining only its trace in naturally-occurring talk. This recognised the theoretical notion of face as embedded across forms of data. In the second case study reconceiving of the emic took the form of examining an account as a recontextualisation of an instance of crosstalk.

In conclusion, I have sought to complement linguistics using LE. Whist this chapter has provided two simple examples, LE in my wider work has enabled me to better understand the work of police officers as situated social practice. I have come to understand some ways in which lay people bring knowledge of other social settings to law. I encourage others who feel the bonds of traditional disciplinary approaches and perspectives to take up LE and, in doing so, gain new understandings of institutions.

References

Antaki, C. (2007) '"Mental-Health Practitioners" Use of Idiomatic Expressions in Summarising Clients' Accounts' *Journal of Pragmatics,* 39(3), 527–541.

Austin, J. (1962) *How to do things with words,* 2nd Edition, ed. J.O. Urmson and M. Sbisá. Cambridge, MA: Harvard University Press.

Bakhtin, M. (1986) *Speech genres and other late essays* Trans.: McGee, W. Ed.: Emerson, C. and Holquist, M. Texas: University of Texas Press.

Barton, D. and Hamilton, M. (1998) *Local literacies: Reading and writing in one community* Routledge: London.

Berk-Seligson, S. (1990) *The bilingual courtroom: Court interpreters in the judicial process* Chicago: The University of Chicago Press.

Black, M. and Metzger, D. (1965) 'Ethnographic Description and the Study of Law' *American Anthropologist* 67(6), 141–165.

Blommaert, J. (2006) 'Ethnography as counter-hegemony: Remarks on epistemology and method' *Working Papers in Urban Language and Literacies* (Paper 34) 1–8.

Blommaert, J. (2009) 'Ethnography and democracy: Hymes's political theory of language' *Text and Talk* 29(3), 257–276.

Bremer, K. and Roberts, C. (2013 [1996]) *Achieving understanding* Oxford: Routledge.

Brown, P. and Levinson, S. (1987) *Politeness: Some universals in language usage* Cambridge: Cambridge University Press.

Caldeira, T. (2002) 'The Paradox of Police Violence in Democratic Brazil' *Ethnography* 3(3), 235–263.

Cameron, D. and Kulick, D. (2003) *Language and sexuality* Cambridge: Cambridge University Press.

Conley, J. and O'Barr, W. (1990) *Rules versus relationships: The ethnography of legal discourse* Chicago: University of Chicago Press.

Copland, F. (2011). 'Negotiating Face in Feedback Conferences: A Linguistic Ethnographic Analysis' *Journal of Pragmatics* 43(15), 3832–3843.

Creese, A. (2008). 'Linguistic ethnography' In: King, K. and N. Hornberger (eds), *Encyclopaedia of Language and Education, Volume 10: Research Methods in Language and Education*, 2nd Edition. 229–241.

Creese, A. and Blackledge, A. (2010) 'Translanguaging in the Bilingual Classroom: A Pedagogy for Learning' *The Modern Language Journal* 94(1), 103–115.

Cromdal, J. Landqvist, H. Persson-Thunqvist, D. and Osvaldsson, K. (2012) 'Finding out what's happened: Two procedures for opening emergency calls' *Discourse Studies* 14(4), 371–397.

D'hondt, S. (2009) 'Good Cops, Bad Cops: Intertextuality, Agency, and Structure in Criminal Trial Discourse' *Research on Language and Social Interaction* 42(3), 249–275.

Geertz, C. (1974) '"From the Native's Point of View": On the Nature of Anthropological Understanding' *Bulletin of the American Academy of Arts and Sciences* 28(1), 26–45.

Goldsmith, D. and MacGeorge, E. (2000) 'The Impact of Politeness and Relationship on Perceived Quality of Advice about a Problem' *Human Communication Research* 26(2), 234–263.

Guardian Newspaper (2013) 'The Pryce of a jury's failure' http://www.theguardian.com/law/2013/feb/21/vicky-pryce-case-jury-failure Last accessed: 30/08/13.

Gumperz, J. (1982) *Discourse strategies* Cambridge: Cambridge University Press.

Gumperz, J. (1992) 'Contextualisation revisited' In: Auer, P. and A. Di Luzio (eds) *The contextualization of language* Amsterdam: John Benjamins 39–54.

Gumperz, J. (1999) 'On interactional sociolinguistic method' In Sarangi, S. and C. Roberts (eds) *Talk, work and institutional order: Discourse in medical, mediation and management settings* Berlin: Mouton de Gruyter 453–471.

Gumperz, J. (2001) 'Contextualisation and ideology in intercultural communication' In: Di Luzio A., S. Günthner and F. Orletti (eds) *Culture in communication: Analyses of intercultural situations* Amsterdam: Benjamins 35–53.

Gumperz, J., Jupp, T. and Roberts, C. (1979) *Crosstalk* Southall: NCIIT.

Hale, S. (1997) 'The Treatment of Register Variation in Court Interpreting' *The Translator* 3(1), 39–54.

Harris, R. (2003) 'On redefining linguistics' In: Davis, H. and Taylor, T. (eds) *Rethinking linguistics*. London: Routledge Curzon 17–68.

Jacobs, G. and Slembrouck, S. (2010) 'Notes on Linguistic Ethnography as a Liminal Activity' *Text and Talk* 30(2), 235–244.

Jacquemet, M. (1994) 'T-Offenses and Metapragmatic Attacks: Strategies of Interactional Dominance' *Discourse and Society* 5(3), 297–319.

Leo, R. (1998) 'The impact of *Miranda* revisited' In: Leo, R. and Thomas, G. (eds) *The Miranda Debate: Law, Justice, and Policing* (1998) 208–221.

Lillis, T. and Curry, M. (2010) *Academic writing in a global context* London: Routledge.

Malinowski, B. (1926) *Crime and custom in savage society* London: Routledge.

Malinowski, B. (1949) 'Supplement I' In: Ogden, C. and I. Richards (eds) *The meaning of meaning* London: Routledge and Kegan Paul.

Maybin, J., and Tusting, K. (2011) 'Linguistic ethnography' In: Simpson, J. (ed.), *Routledge Handbook of Applied Linguistics* London: Routledge 229–241.

McElhinny, B. (2003) 'Fearful, Forceful Agents of the Law: Ideologies about Language and Gender in Police Officers' Narratives about the Use of Physical Force' *Pragmatics* 13(2), 253–284.

Mertz, E. (2007) *The language of law school: Learning to 'Think Like a Lawyer'* Oxford: Oxford University Press.

PACE Code of Practice, Code C (2013) London: The Stationery Office.

Patry, M. and Penrod, S. (2013) 'Death Penalty Decisions: Instruction Comprehension, Attitudes, and Decision Mediators' *Journal of Forensic Psychology Practice* 13(3), 204–244.

Pike, K. (1990) 'On the emics and etics of Pike and Harris' In: Headland, T., K. Pike and M. Harris (eds) *Emics and etics: The insider/outsider debate* London: Sage 28–47.

Rampton, B. (2007) 'Neo-Hymesian Linguistic Ethnography in the United Kingdom', *Journal of Sociolinguistics* 11(5), 584–607.

Rampton, B., Tusting, K., Maybin, J., Barwell, R., Creese, A., and Lytra, V. (2004) UK linguistic ethnography: A discussion paper. http://www.ling-ethnog.org.uk/ documents/discussion_paper_jan_05.pdf Last accessed: 30/08/13.

Rock, F. (2005) '"Sometimes you pinch stuff": Communities of practice in an institutional setting' In: Barton, D. and K. Tusting (eds) *Beyond communities of practice* Cambridge: Cambridge University Press 77–104.

Rock, F. (2007) *Communicating rights: The language of arrest and detention* Basingstoke: Palgrave.

Rock, F., Heffer, C. and Conley, J. (2013) Introduction In: Heffer, C., F. Rock and J. Conley (eds) *Legal-lay communication: Textual travels in the law* Oxford: Oxford University Press 3–32.

Sarangi, S. (1994) 'Intercultural or Not? Beyond Elaboration of Cultural Differences in Miscommunication' *Pragmatics* 4(3), 409–427.

Thomas, C. (2010) *Are juries fair?* Ministry of Justice Research Series 1/10 London: Ministry of Justice Available at: http://www.justice.gov.uk/downloads/publications/research-and-analysis/moj-research/are-juries-fair-research.pdf Last accessed: 30/08/13.

Tusting, K. and Maybin, J. (2007) 'Linguistic Ethnography and Interdisciplinarity: Opening the Discussion' *Journal of Sociolinguistics* 11(5), 575–583.

van Praet, E. (2010) 'The Dual Voice of Domination: Ritual and Power in a British Embassy' *Talk and Text* 30(2), 213–233.

Walter, B. (1988) *The jury summation as speech genre: An ethnographic study of what it means to those who use it* Amsterdam: John Benjamins.

9
The Geography of Communication and the Expression of Patients' Concerns

Sarah Collins

Introduction

This chapter aims to demonstrate the value of a linguistic ethnographic approach in understanding patients' and health professionals' experiences of health care. Specifically, it explores the interrelationship between details of interaction and broader issues that play a formative part in patient-professional consultations: namely, environmental features shaping the expression of patients' concerns. Linguistic ethnography enables consideration of how language is deployed within, and shaped by, the social and cultural context in which it occurs – here, the head and neck cancer outpatients' clinic. Linguistic ethnography offers a means by which respective contributions of the clinic setting and interaction in the consultation can be understood and combined, to give a more comprehensive, nuanced picture of patients' expression of concerns. In the present study, combining linguistics with ethnographic data expands (Tusting and Maybin, 2007: 581) the view of communication in the clinic, bringing to attention how its geography is navigated by patients and health care professionals to allow different forms of interactional encounter, and how, by the same token, various clinic spaces shape the expression of patients' concerns moment-by-moment in interaction.

Health care communication encounters have been studied using distinct methodological approaches: detailed linguistic analyses of interaction in consultations; ethnographies of health care clinics; interview studies of patients' and health professionals' motivations and experiences. Ethnographic studies have explored structures of health care organisations and peoples' movements within these to illuminate principles in social interaction, including ethnographies of health care organisation (Sudnow, 1967; Allen, 2001); patients' autobiographical accounts (Piff, 1985; Diamond, 1998); studies of spatial and temporal dimensions of institutions (Roth, 1963; Rushing, 1964; Zerubavel, 1979). Linguistic features have been documented through conversation analysis: see, for example, Heritage and Robinson (2006) on how the design of physicians' opening questions provides an interactional space for patients to express their concerns.

This chapter illustrates an attempt to broaden our understanding of patients' concerns, while maintaining a focus on the details of interaction. The aim is to understand how, where and why patients' concerns are presented, and the forms of expression they take. I argue that, to achieve this, ethnographic exploration of the illness context and individuals' circumstances is required alongside detailed analyses of interaction. The way participants in a setting understand and handle the reason for being there – the giving or receiving of health care – is grounded in the environment in which they are operating. To inform analyses of health care interaction, and to make findings relevant to professional practice and patient experience, attention must focus not only on the language used, but also on the organisational, spatial and temporal contexts in which talk is produced.

Linguistic ethnographic descriptions of how consultations are enacted within particular environments provide a more comprehensive picture of patients' concerns than research on details of the interaction alone. A patient's voiced concern is shaped by *what* a patient says in a health professional-patient encounter, *how* it is said, *where* it is said (in the corridor, in the main consulting room), and by the professional's invitation and response to the concern, according to their role. Linguistic ethnography offers a means of accommodating spatial, temporal and other dimensions, alongside analyses of consultations, such that – as Backhouse and Drew (1992: 573) write about space – each of these environmental constituents can be understood to be: 'an "active" or at least a participating, component of any activity taking place within it'.

Drawing on analyses of recorded consultations, ethnographic observations, and qualitative research interviews collected in the multidisciplinary health care setting of a head and neck cancer outpatients' clinic, this chapter seeks to illustrate how different sets of data and analyses may be innovatively and profitably combined; how interactions and comparisons between different forms of data and analyses can enhance understanding of patients' and health care professionals' experiences, interpretations and management of their communication encounters; and, from a methodological standpoint, to consider how this combined approach might contribute to the development of linguistic ethnography, and how linguistic ethnography might illuminate the complexities and nuances of patients' expression of concerns.

Background to this study

The present study comes from a research project on patient participation in decision-making funded by the Department of Health, involving five clinical settings (Entwistle et al., 2002). We identified, among other findings, how different health professional approaches in the consultation offered more or less opportunity for patient involvement in decision-making (Collins et al., 2005); and, in a follow-up study funded by the Economic and Social Research Council, explored the combined effectiveness of different health professionals' consultations with patients in multidisciplinary care (Collins, 2005).

One of the settings was the head and neck cancer outpatients' clinic. I regularly visited one clinic, over a period of five months, observing and recording consultations and interviews with patients and the multidisciplinary team: surgeons, oncologists, radiologists, specialist nurses, clinic nurses, a dietician and a speech and language therapist. I spent one day in another clinic in a different region, observing consultations and talking with individuals from the multidisciplinary team. I collected 61 consultation recordings and conducted 39 semi-structured qualitative interviews, involving 31 patients and eight health professionals. Analyses focused on patient participation in decisions about treatment and care. I conducted interviews prior to and following the consultation, with each participant, to discuss the communication in the consultation and their views and experiences of patient involvement. Consultations were transcribed in detail for conversation analysis, which began with detailed notes on sequences from the recordings to identify interactional features, such as: the ways patients voiced and phrased concerns, and the design of professionals' turns in which they presented diagnoses or treatment. Each data set was treated separately in the first instance. For all data, I employed an inductive analytic technique, constantly revisiting the data to identify categories, noting emerging themes and where these recurred, and recording variations (such as different forms of expression of patients' concerns).

From a very early stage, my observations (recorded in fieldnotes) during initial visits to the clinics and conversations with prospective participants, highlighted the importance of geography and the use of different spaces in the clinic. For example, I began with an assumption that the surgeon's consultations in the main consulting room would be the ones to record; but it soon became apparent that many other forms of patient-professional encounter also played a part in enacting, and shaping, opportunities for patients' involvement in decisions about their care. These included spontaneous, conversation-like encounters between patients and professionals (particularly the nurses, the speech and language therapist and the dietician) in the corridor, and reflective, open-ended consultations with the specialist nurse following the delivery of a cancer diagnosis by the surgeon in the main consulting room. Following discussion with the multidisciplinary team, I was given consent to include these other forms of patient-professional interaction. I continued to make detailed ethnographic observations of the spatial layout of the clinic and its effects on communication. I kept notes on relationships between observed features of interactions between patients and health professionals in the clinic, and the space in which the interaction took place: for example, I noted the informal, spontaneous way that topics and concerns were raised in the corridor, with patients taking opportunities provided by conversation to mention something worrying them; whereas in the consulting room, those same concerns were presented in response to an invitation from the doctor.

Using an ethnographic linguistic approach to understand the health care consultation

For the purposes of this chapter, I am revisiting my observations of the geography of communication in the clinic to explore the potential of the relationship between ethnography and linguistics, and to seek to answer the following questions. How can 'the consultation' be defined and understood, given its shifting forms and locations in the clinic? How does space and the physical configuration of the clinic shape the language used in consultations? How is the clinic geography, with its various forms of patient-professional encounter, managed by patients and professionals to promote patients' participation? In seeking to provide answers to these questions, I will focus on patients' concerns regarding their understanding of their cancer diagnosis and prognosis and its treatment and management.

Findings

Early conversations with participants revealed that the way concerns were expressed (outside the consultation; invited by the professional; opportunistically in a lapse or interval in the spoken activity; as an extension of an answer to another question; deferred to a consultation at another time) was shaped by the clinic environment. Through observations, interviews with patients and health care professionals, and review of the consultation recordings, I became increasingly attuned to the need to pay attention to the physical layout of the clinic, and health professionals' and patients' use of clinic space, in order to locate and understand the opportunities for patients to express their concerns.

Spatial dimensions in the clinic

In interviews, and as recorded in my fieldnotes from conversations with the multidisciplinary team, professionals constantly referred to 'environment' when talking about how they co-ordinated care for patients, how they communicated with them and how they involved them in decisions. That this was such a discussion point is testimony to the challenges the environment presented. Communication took place everywhere, and despite the challenges and apparent chaos, the ways space was used enabled different forms of expression of patients' concerns, involving different members of the multidisciplinary health care team. For patients, the clinic's geography furnished their experiences of illness and of their care. Through it they gleaned information and insights into the nature of their cancer and the treatment options available, and, in voicing their concerns in interviews with myself, and explaining whether or not they would express these to the doctor, they made reference to this geography. In both clinics, the three main arenas in which consultations took place were the consulting room, the 'quiet room' and the area comprising the corridor and waiting room (Figure 9.1).

The consulting room housed formal presentation of diagnoses and medical treatment options. The corridor and waiting room created opportunities for chance meetings and picking up on patients' concerns that remained unvoiced, or partially expressed, in the consulting room. The quiet room provided uninterrupted space for reflection and consolidation of the prior, more formal surgeon consultation.

The consulting room

Patients' consultations with surgeons in the main consulting room were highly public, and regularly involved the whole multidisciplinary team. The door was opening and shutting throughout, which allowed other professionals to move between the different areas in the clinic – to 'float about', as the dietician put it. There was always talk and movement in the background. The lack of privacy in this central consultation reflected a real dilemma. Having the team gathered together allowed for

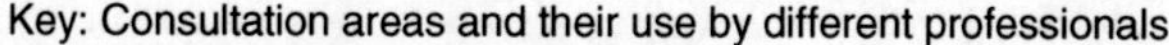

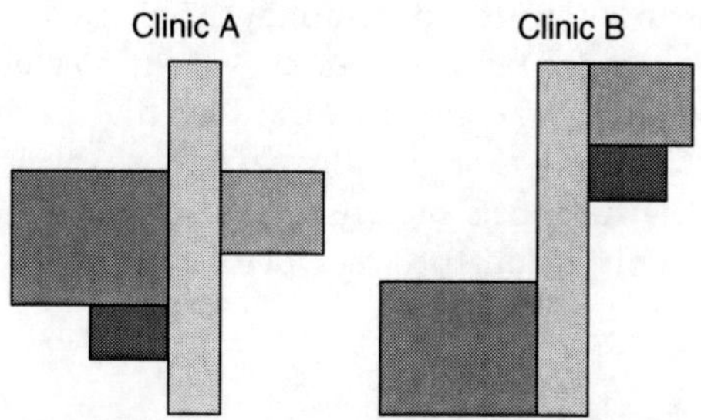

Figure 9.1 The layout of the head and neck cancer clinics
Note: Key: Consultation areas and their use by different professionals.

multidisciplinary discussions to take place and decisions to be jointly made; and yet, at the same time, created a situation in which assurance of comfort or confidentiality for the patient became practically impossible. Patients felt deterred from asking questions in the main consulting room, as illustrated here, where this patient describes how different doctors gathered to observe the unusualness of her case (see also Extract 6):

Extract 1

When you find out you've got cancer, and when you go to see [lead surgeon], and he's telling you what's happening, and there's a whole team of people around him ... you're just confronted by a load of men ... and that can be very off-putting. It can be very difficult to ask questions – because they're all looking at you.

(Patient with facial cancer, Interview, A-310)

Recordings of the various interactional encounters showed that patients would reserve their questions for the follow-up consultation with the nurse (see Extract 5), or ask those questions in the corridor, during informal encounters with the nurse, speech and language therapist or dietician (see Extracts 7 and 8).

Because the doctor's input and expertise were confined to the main consulting room, these consultations (with the head and neck cancer surgeon and other clinicians such as the radiologist and the plastic surgeon) contained all the topics within the surgeon's remit (i.e. decisions about surgery, and descriptions of what the surgery would involve). In the case of newly diagnosed patients, this meant that these consultations proceeded immediately from the delivery of the cancer diagnosis to discussion of treatment. This gave priority to the treatment to be provided, and to a certain extent precluded reflection or discussion of patients' concerns regarding the diagnosis and the treatment. The following example illustrates how the surgeon begins by confirming the diagnosis of tonsil cancer, and in the next turn resumes a discussion begun the week before with the patient about possible treatment:

Extract 2a

```
1   Dr:   ... there's no doubt in my mind that you've got a tumour in your tonsil,
2         (0.3)
3   Dr:   Okay? .hhh and as I said to you last week I think that there are .hh two
4         ways of
5   Pt:   Doin' it
6   Dr:   Doing that ...
```

(Consultation, B-348–102)

This sequence illustrates a pattern identified in surgeons' consultations in this study: proceeding from presenting the diagnosis (line 1) to talking about treatment (lines 3–4) either in the same turn, or in two consecutive turns, with no intervening contribution from the patient (see Collins et al., 2005).

The surgeon continues by describing the operation and the possibility of radiotherapy afterwards, and this presentation of treatment concludes with the surgeon recommending the operation as opposed to doing nothing (lines 7–8):

Extract 2b

```
1   Dr:   ... having the operation will be (0.3) not the most pleasant experience
2         b't I-I you know I wouldn't suggest it if I didn't think it (.) was an
3         appropriate course of action,
```

4   (0.4)
5   Dr: An I do::,
6   (0.4)
7   Dr: An I think that (.) yee- as <u>you</u> say, h the other alternative to do nothing, is::
8   (.) you know, (.) just (0.5) a hundred percent gonna <u>fai:</u>l,
9   (0.4)
10 Pt: That's right.
11   (0.3)
12 Dr: .h So uh
13   (0.2)
14 Pt: I don't think I have a choice:.
15 Dr: No:. not really,
16   (0.2)
17 Dr: Not really, =
18 Pt: =uh: in that f- in that re- respect.
19   (0.7)
20 Dr: SO, I was planning on doing this a week next Tuesday.

(Consultation, B-348–102)

The patient expresses agreement ('That's right' line 10; 'don't think I have a choice', line 14), and the surgeon presents the upshot ('SO ... ') of his treatment proposal by stating his plan for when the operation will be done (line 20).

In the main consulting room, in addition to how the structure and pace of the head and neck cancer surgeon's presentation of diagnosis and treatment limited early opportunities for patients to express concerns, there are constraints on how much information can be covered, given the multiple inputs from different doctors, and the necessity of talking about several areas of treatment in quick succession:

Extract 3

I often feel when I'm called in to see the patient, they've already seen enough doctors and are having a job coming to terms with the fact that they're gonna have to come into hospital very soon for a very serious operation ... which will result in that they might never be able to speak or eat normally again. And that they're gonna perhaps look quite deformed. And they've had to take that on board within a space of twenty minutes or even less.

(Interview, Plastic Surgeon, A-104)

Surgeons' talk in the main consulting room carried statements of intent and action couched as forms of reassurance, and (as professionals reported in interviews) came at the cost of progressing patients' understanding of their condition and its treatment:

Extract 4

> I tell them they've got cancer and I try to deliver it 'the bad news is you've got cancer; the good news is that we can give you good treatment and you stand a very good chance ...' even if that means that initially, I will gloss or put a very good spin on the outcome.
>
> (Interview, ENT surgeon, A-133)

The quiet room

The 'quiet room' was used to follow up cancer diagnoses given in the surgeon's consultation. This was common knowledge to everyone in the waiting room. The specialist nurse observed that leading people to the quiet room was like 'putting up a signpost to say "bad news-giving this way"'.

Once inside, the degree of privacy stood in stark contrast to the main consulting room. There were few interruptions (the nurse bringing tea; a surgeon confirming a biopsy result); any interruption constituted an intrusion, and apologies were always made. The specialist nurse would begin the consultation in the quiet room with an invitation to the patient to reflect on what they had heard: sometimes verbally, for example, 'What do you think to that then?'; sometimes simply through offering a cup of tea, or emitting a sigh. Patients would regularly express, in response, concerns unvoiced in the main consulting room. The patient in Extract 2, who presented as in agreement with the surgeon's recommendation to have the operation, expressed a rather different view in his consultation with the specialist nurse, which opens as follows:

Extract 5a

> N: hhhhhhhhhhhh
> Pt: I don't like the sound of all that
> N: Don't you ...
>
> (Consultation, B-348–134)

This opening, when compared with Example 2 above, illustrates how the quiet room afforded space and priority to patients' expression of their concerns and reactions to the news and treatment decision presented in the main consulting room.

From this opening, the consultation proceeds with the patient listing several concerns, regarding radiotherapy, having to spend a long time in hospital, and a worry that his teeth won't fit so he'll 'look a right idiot'. At a later point, the patient returns to the question of radiotherapy, saying that he had expected the surgeon to mention something else like this:

Extract 5b

```
 1   Pt:   well let's get the operation over first. (0.3) .hh then hit me with something
 2         else.
 3         (.)
 4   N:    Right.
 5         (1.3)
 6   Pt:   Mmm.=
 7   N:    =Mmm
 8         (1.2)
 9   Pt:   Another question is how long do I want to stay alive.
10         (3.9)
11   N:    And how long do you want to stay alive.
12         (2.8)
13   Pt:   Not that long actually,
14         (0.7)
15   N:    °Ri[ght°
16   Pt:      [I'm seventy-six (now). (2.1) I'm not (0.3) crowing about me age. (.)
17         but I'm ( ) surprised I've reached that age,
18         (0.8)
19   N:    Yeah.
20         (0.4)
21   Pt:   [Right well what kind of a life does it leave me at the end=
22   N:    [Mm hm
23   Pt:   = of it.
24         (0.5)
25   N:    Right.
26         (1.2)
27   Pt:   I've no desire to be a vegetable. sitting in a (0.7) nursing home.
```

(Consultation, B-348–134)

The space for reflection afforded by the quiet room leads to the patient voicing feelings and concerns about the unexpected mention of radiotherapy (lines 1–2), whether he wants to live much longer (line 9), the potentially disfiguring and disabling treatment (line 21), and about the quality of life after an operation (line 27). As mentioned previously (see Extracts 1 and 2), patients' restricted forms of contribution in the main consulting room compared to the quiet room demonstrate how space constrains or opens up patients' expression of their concerns. Extract 5 shows the patient is in the position of determining the topics and questions for his consultation with the nurse, through his expressed concerns, which the nurse, in turn, pursues ('and how long do you want to stay alive?', line 11).

The corridor and waiting area

The corridor and waiting area provided most opportunity for the nurse, speech and language therapist and dietician to make contact with patients. The dietician commented that the layout made a significant difference to her communication:

Extract 6

> In [a previous clinic] I was right at the end of a corridor, and I wouldn't necessarily see all the patients coming through ... Whereas you're right in the heart of this clinic, you see a lot of people you know just to say hello to, find out how they're getting on ... And you can feel free to go in with any of the consultants.
>
> (Dietician, Interview, Clinic A)

Conversations in the corridor, immediately before and after the surgeon's consultation, provided opportunities for patients to rehearse a concern, clarify their understanding, ask a question, or revisit a decision. Here, communication was more open and fluid. The fieldnotes, consultation recordings, and interviews showed how conversations in the corridor were generally brief and spontaneous, and served a variety of purposes: a patient's rehearsal of a concern before mentioning it to a surgeon; a professional's opportunity to catch up with a patient's progress; clarification of a treatment issue the surgeon had raised in the main consultation. I observed that, for patients on return visits to the clinic, it was as possible for them to approach professionals spending time in the corridor as it was for those professionals to approach them: passing one another, or being visible, in the corridor, allowed conversations to take place. This lent these consultations symmetry and informality, marking them out from those in the main consulting room. The following extract, from an impromptu conversation in the corridor between a patient who has had a laryngectomy and the speech and language therapist, prior to the patient's consultation with the surgeon, is a case in point. Sitting in the waiting room, the patient saw the speech and language therapist, and sought her out. They both moved to the other side of the corridor, where an unused space and the wall they leaned against provided some privacy, and the patient began to outline his current concerns, as a means of preparing for his consultation with the surgeon. The extract opens with the speech and language therapist reinvoking a topic, 'swallowing', mentioned first by the patient, and the speech and language therapist's apology for interrupting suggests a symmetry about each other's respective contributions to the interaction. The patient responds to this invitation by specifying his concern, 'little bit harder to swallow', and reflecting on possible reasons for this. He continues to list a number of topics he wishes to raise with the surgeon in the main consulting room, to which the speech and language therapist responds with minimal acknowledgements and agreements that endorse what the patient is saying:

Extract 7

```
 1   SLT:   .hhh Yes (.) sorry (.) I interrupted you (.) your swallowing
 2   Pt:    Yeah (0.3) (it's just) about the last two weeks [it's been a=
 3   SLT:                                                   [mhmm
 4   Pt:    =little bit 'arder tuh swallow
 5          (0.4)
 6   Pt:    .hh an ahh don't know if it's my oesophagus is getting a little bit swollen
 7          (.) or my saliva is a bit thicker or what I don't kno[w I'll ask th- =
 8   SLT:                                                        [Right
 9   Pt:    =professor t'day
10   SLT:   Ye:s ye:s
11          (.)
12   Pt:    A couple of other little things to ask him as well
13   SLT:   Ri[ght
14   Pt:      [Er:m (.) basically do I 'ave to 'ave anymore tests to make sure that it's
15          gone
16   SLT:   Right
17   Pt:    Er: yuh know for example a scan o[r ] whatever I don't kno[w
18   SLT:                                    [yeh]                    [yeh (.)°yeh°
```

```
19   Pt:    An' also the after effects of the radiotherapy's still there
20   SLT:   ?Yeah[:
21   Pt:           [an I've stopped me drink...
```

(Consultation, B-103–306)

In this sequence, the patient expresses, among other concerns, a desire to know whether the cancer has gone or not 'do I have to have anymore tests to make sure that it's gone' (lines 14–15). Working through this list with the speech and language therapist in the corridor provides a form of rehearsal and a means of legitimising concerns the patient wishes to express to the surgeon.

Another example, taken from my fieldnotes, illustrates how the corridor provided an opportunity for patients to revisit concerns not fully addressed in the main consulting room.

Extract 8

In the main consulting room, the patient asked the surgeon a question about the frequency of the radiotherapy treatment that was being proposed. 'We work two weeks on you see' the patient added, by way of explanation. This second explanatory part was not picked up on by the doctor, who answered the question in terms of the radiotherapy schedule in general, but not in a way that addressed the patient's concern (how would the radiotherapy fit around his work – would it affect it?). The patient didn't pursue his reason for asking. Later I heard the patient put the same question to the speech and language therapist, outside the consulting room door. The speech and language therapist heard both the question and the concern underpinning it, and relayed the whole back to the surgeon, to have it answered for the patient.

(Fieldnotes, Clinic B)

In the waiting area, the visibility of people's illness, in close proximity, signified cancer, and forewarned of treatment. This might be considered expedient: noticing others' conditions gave patients a way of gauging their own progress. The waiting room also provided a measure of how busy the clinic was that day. Patients tailored what they said to the surgeon accordingly, saving questions for another time:

Extract 9

I find if you go early in the day ... you're in and out pretty quickly and everything's okay ... if you're later he tends to be running late by then, and also he looks very tired ... so ... I really wouldn't want to start asking questions to him then – sometimes I've gone in and he looks exhausted.

(Interview, Patient with facial cancer, C-310)

Patients developed an awareness that different treatments signified different degrees of severity. From sitting in the waiting room, they compared themselves with others to measure their own progress; often, to reassure themselves about their own state. For example, patients expressed their relief (on hearing they did not need surgery) in terms that presented themselves as better off than others around them:

Extract 10

I'm only glad I hadn't to ... talk like a dalek. I know it's awful for these people that do but I would never have spoken again.

(Interview, Patient with throat cancer, C-357)

Patients also related how they drew on others' experiences, sitting in the waiting room, to prepare themselves for what lay ahead:

Extract 11

There was a young chap just before [my partner] ... He was our little rock if you like. We could see all his stages – that's the next one, then that's the next one ... It was follow my leader sort of thing.

(Interview, Partner of a man with laryngeal cancer, D-349)

Movement between different spaces in the clinic

By virtue of a patient's movement between different areas, coupled with professionals' use of these, connections between different forms of encounter were made. Certain complements (between spontaneous versus pre-arranged encounters; one-to-one versus multidisciplinary consultations; meetings of more fixed or more variable duration) came into play. This interdependence and complementarity allowed more comprehensive coverage of patients' concerns, in their health care, than could be managed within the main consulting room alone: for example, concerns about whether the cancer had gone or not (Extract 7), or about time off work for treatment (Extract 8).

But it also created tensions and limitations on what could be spoken about where, sometimes leading to mixed messages, or leaving gaps to be filled by another professional that remained unaddressed. Side-effects are a case in point. Because situations were generally presented most positively at the outset, patients often did not discover consequences of treatment until these had come into play. Side-effects of post-operative radiotherapy were not always mentioned in the main consulting room. If they were, they were only partially revealed, and professionals' descriptions tended to downplay their most negative aspects, as in the following example from a consultation I observed:

Extract 12

> The patient asked: 'What after effects will I get from radiotherapy?' The doctor's reply was hedged, and qualified by minimisers and understatements: 'as treatment builds up ... as the dose builds up ... you <u>might</u> not want to have salt ... it's really <u>just</u> a sore throat ... croaky voice ... skin gets a <u>bit pink</u>.' The patient's question suggested he'd assumed there would be more effects – the impression left by the doctor's response was that these did not really amount to 'effects'.
>
> (Fieldnotes, Clinic B)

Extract 13 below, from an interview with a patient and his wife, shows how patients gathered information from different professionals and patients, which varied according to where this was talked about in the clinic. From patients in the waiting room, he had heard that radiotherapy makes your throat so sore it affects your eating and swallowing. He understood the effects were likely to be greater than professionals described in the main consulting room (as the speech and language therapist had conveyed to him in the corridor), and took it as given that professionals were unlikely to tell that level of detail ('they aren't going to say it's going to do that ...'). The absence of any explicit discussion, and the conflicting information he had received, made it difficult for him to voice any concern he might have about radiotherapy treatment:

Extract 13

> Pt: Well, I have heard [from other patients], it does affect your eating.
> W: You mean to eat normally?
> Pt: Because your throat's that sore, you can't eat, or swallow properly.
> SC: Right. And would that be a reason why you might choose not to do it, if it was going to be like that?
> Pt: Oh aye. But they aren't going to say it's going to do that, are they?

SC: Well I don't know. I mean ... is it not your choice at all?
W: Well they have told you that your throat will be sore. [The speech and language therapist] told you that.
Pt: But [the radiologist] said, 'it won't'.
W: But then again different people have different reactions to it.
P = patient, W = patient's wife, SC = interviewer

(Interview, D1-347)

The main consulting room was the first port of call for patients attending the clinic: co-ordination between different health professionals' consultations depended on the centrality of the surgeon's consultations. Everything else was assigned boundaries in relation to it, and consultations there overlapped with every other patient-professional encounter. In a nurse consultation following the surgeon's, topics covered were gone over in more depth, but the surgeon's consultation would have mapped these out in the first instance. In a preceding consultation with the speech and language therapist, a patient rehearsed a concern before telling it to the surgeon.

In the corridor, waiting room and quiet room, patients could expand their understanding of topics and treatment options presented by doctors in the main consulting room. New understandings arose in points of connection and overlap between different encounters, for example in revisiting a treatment decision made elsewhere and discussing its implications in detail.

Strategic use of space in the clinic

The co-existence of different 'spaces' allowed patients to express different aspects of their concerns. Through their concerted use – for example talking about a patient's concern about treatment in the corridor, and then addressing this concern more formally in the consulting room – professionals could create a variety of forms of communication. By meeting the boundary, or providing overlap between, a consultation in one space in the clinic with another, patients' concerns found fuller expression.

It was possible for professionals to orchestrate meetings with patients and other members of the multidisciplinary team: by 'floating around' in the corridor, or by being 'seen' in the consulting room. For the specialist nurse, dietician, and speech and language therapist, this reliance on movement meant not only that the clinic's geography played a significant part in their ability to make contact with their patients; but also that they were able, through movement, to overcome some of the challenges presented by the physical layout (such as the boundaries between more public and private spaces) for *all* professionals' and patients' communication with each other. (See also Rushing's (1964) study of occupational therapists' work in a psychiatric hospital, and Allen's (2001) observations of nurses' movements in hospital as 'institutional glue'.)

The bounded nature of the surgeon's consultation in the main consulting room meant that problems that might come later tended not to be raised at all. Certain treatment topics, if not mentioned in the main consulting room were later raised in passing, as if already spoken about. For example, loss of sensation from nerve damage during surgery, effects on teeth, problems in everyday stoma management: these patients generally discovered for themselves. This led some patients to speculate, in interviews, as to whether, had they known these long-term effects, they would choose those forms of treatment. Autobiographical accounts provide similar reports of casual references to side-effects: a first mention of dental treatment (Diamond, 1998: 83), or hair loss (Piff, 1985: 23).

Summary

In the present study, initial observations in the head and neck cancer outpatients' clinic led me to my decision to combine an ethnographic approach with linguistic analysis, to understand the ways patients and professionals navigated the clinic's geography. Had my data only been recordings of consultations, or only interviews with the research participants, I would have missed crucial parts of the process through which patients' concerns are expressed. Furthermore, combining both approaches invites re-appraisal of interpretations and analyses from the respective sets of data. The clinic brought its own constraints to bear on the consultation; its environment was in many respects at odds with patients' care, and could exacerbate the patient's feeling of being 'mind-boggled'. At the same time, patients and professionals relied on the environment to interpret the significance of an event, or to prepare for the consultation. Patients' experiences of the clinic environment gave them insights into the progression of illness and the effects of treatment. Patients would modify their own communication with professionals accordingly, voicing concerns and questions in the corridor. Sitting in the waiting room presented patients with new concerns and experiences of others' illness and treatment. There they would see the progression of disease and recovery, and share experiences with others; and when the waiting room was busy, or at the end of the day, they would edit their talk with the doctor accordingly.

Discussion

As a researcher investigating patient participation in decisions about treatment for head or neck cancer, the geography of communication in the clinic presented itself as pivotal to understanding patients' experiences of and involvement in their care. This then required that attention be paid to linguistic and ethnographic aspects of patient-professional encounters.

In conversation analyses of patients' concerns, the focus has been the expression of these concerns within particular phases of the doctor-patient consultation. Heritage and Robinson (2006: 89) write:

> Problem presentation is the only phase of medical visits in which patients are systematically given institutional license to describe their illness in their own terms and in pursuit of their own agendas.

A linguistic ethnographic approach, however, extends our understanding of 'the medical visit', highlighting, as in the present study, how much of the consultation takes place without the doctor, and how patients may express their concerns in other, apparently casual or chance encounters, with different professionals. These encounters all complement the formal doctor-patient consultation. This suggests other forms of institutional license and constraint at work – such as the geography of the clinic – in addition to the structures and phases of the consultation.

A broader definition of the consultation, informed by ethnographic observations of the geography of the clinic, therefore leads to more comprehensive understanding of patients' concerns. For example, in the main consulting room, if a patient is not provided with, or chooses not to take, an opportunity to voice their concern, then linguistic analysis of this consultation recording alone will be insufficient to detect the concern, or to account for why it is not presented.

Taking the geography of the clinic into account renders visible, and accessible to the researcher, other forms of 'consultation', and illustrates how different physical spaces in the clinic shape the language used: expansive, reflective talk in the quiet room; corridor conversations indexing concerns in anticipation of the meeting with the surgeon; surgeon-led presentations of diagnosis and treatment in the main consulting room; exchanges in the waiting room through which patients evaluate different treatments and their side-effects, provide one another with encouragements and with information regarding stages of treatment and recovery. This raises the question of how we define the consultation in multidisciplinary health care: not, perhaps, a discrete encounter, but a series of interconnected, overlapping, encounters, which, when taken together, provide the sum of patients' experience of consultations in the clinic and a variety of opportunities for patients' expression of concerns. Goffman's (1959) study of the movements between the kitchen of a hotel and its other, more public, spaces shows how different forms of talk are employed across these to achieve particular goals and maintain certain relationships between workers and guests. Lewin and Reeves (2011) made similar observations about team communication: the ways professionals in health care teams on hospital wards navigate between what they term 'planned, "front-stage" encounters' and ' "backstage", opportunistic encounters' to manage team-working in an acute care setting. With regard to the present study, approaching consultation research with consideration for use and ownership of different clinic spaces invites consideration of multiple forms of participation for patients. For example, limited forms of participation in the main consulting room are augmented by extended opportunities in the quiet room.

Combining linguistics and ethnography, then, challenges dominant medical thinking about how care is provided, where and by whom. By the same token, linguistic ethnography challenges assumptions in health care communication research. By taking the broader environment into account, health care, and the research approach taken in studying it, can be understood as a system of complements. Recognition of spatial dimensions in health care encounters extends the view of the consultation beyond the patient's appointment with the surgeon, and shows how patients' concerns are concealed and disclosed in a variety of locations within the clinic, with different professionals.

Linguistic ethnography affords a wider context – the view that greets the patient in the waiting room, the various contexts in which consultations happen, a longitudinal perspective – for understanding the nature and expression of patients' concerns. This transforms the research: from a study of doctor-patient interaction to one more comprehensive and representative of patients' and professionals' experience. From a researcher's perspective, a more holistic view of patients' concerns can be provided by considering examples from different consultations, research interviews and clinic observations. In future research, questions concerning clinic geography could be extended. For example, though Clinics A and B were similar in configuration, at Clinic B the radiotherapy department was on the floor below in the same hospital, whereas at Clinic A the radiotherapy department was in another hospital three miles away; and this influenced the way in which radiotherapy was presented (at Clinic B, radiotherapy was a more immediate, relevant option, often presented side-by-side with surgery).

In the present study, the combination of linguistics and ethnography broadened the starting points and avenues for discussion regarding the relevance of the research for everyday clinical practice. By providing examples of uses of space, and highlighting the geographical dimensions and constraints at play in the general running of the clinic and in encounters with patients, as well as examples of linguistic features in consultations, the findings became more concrete and accessible to discussion with participating patients and health professionals. We discussed ways existing clinic space could be employed more strategically and with greater awareness of its communication potential: for example, making use of escorting patients to and from the consulting room by engaging in conversation; and at Clinic B, where the main consulting room had a sliding door so that it could adjoin to a neighbouring room, we discussed ways this might facilitate more free-flowing consultations.

Detailed observational studies of different settings using linguistic ethnography have real potential. They can enable further exploration of environmental influences on communication, allow findings to be generalised, and serve a comparative purpose in identifying shared and distinctive features of how different spaces promote, or inhibit, patients' expression of concerns.

Linguistic ethnography offers a route into understanding the relationship between space and interaction: a means to stimulate thinking about these dimensions of institutional communication as they are played out in practice. Above all, the head and neck cancer clinic itself – its environment, the multidisciplinary team, the narratives of its patients, advances in diagnosis and treatment, social contexts of illness – offers a rich fabric of social, linguistic and cultural dimensions for research grounded in everyday experience. The challenge for linguistic ethnography is to remain alive (as discussed in Creese, 2008) to the interplay of these different dimensions, and to maintain its inherent reflexivity, constantly sounding out linguistic observations with ethnographic ones, through constant comparison and dialogue between different sets of data. Thus linguistic ethnography can make a significant and novel contribution to our understanding (in research and practice) of patients' experience of health care.

Acknowledgements

I am most grateful to all the patients, health care professionals and administrators who took part and made this research possible. The data were collected in a study 'Exploring patient participation in decision-making', led by V. Entwistle and I. Watt, and funded by the Department of Health: Health in Partnership Programme (reference 3700514).

References

Allen, D. (2001) *The Changing Shape of Nursing Practice: The Role of Nurses in the Hospital Division of Labour.* Routledge, New York.

Backhouse, A. and Drew, P. (1992) The design implications of social interaction in a workplace setting. *Environment and Planning B: Planning and Design*: 573–584.

Collins, S. (2005) Explanations in consultations: the combined effectiveness of doctors' and nurses' communication with patients. *Medical Education* 39: 785–796.

Collins, S., Drew, P., Watt, I. and Entwistle, V. (2005) 'Unilateral' and 'bilateral' practitioner approaches in decision-making about treatment. *Social Science and Medicine* 61: 2611–2627.

Creese, A (2008) Linguistic Ethnography. In *Encyclopedia of Language and Education*, (2nd Edition, 10, 229–241). King K.A., Hornberger N.H. (eds), Springer Science.

Diamond, J. (1998) *C: Because Cowards Get Cancer Too.* Vermilion, London.

Goffman, E. (1959) *The Presentation of Self in Everyday Life.* Penguin, Harmondsworth.

Entwistle, V., Watt, I., Bugge, C., Collins, S., Drew, P., Gilhooly, K., and Walker, A. (2002) *Exploring Patient Participation in Decision-making: Report to the Department of Health on Project HS010 RGC0771.* Health Services Research Unit, University of Aberdeen.

Heritage, J. and Robinson, J.D. (2006) The structure of patients' presenting concerns: physician's opening questions. *Health Communication* 19(2): 89–102.

National Cancer Alliance (2002) *Head and Neck Cancers: Patients' Views and Experiences.* NCA Report no. 3, January 2002, Oxford.

Lewin, S. and Reeves, S. (2011) Enacting 'team' and 'teamwork': using Goffman's theory of impression management to illuminate interprofessional practice on hospital wards. *Social Science & Medicine* 72: 1595–1602.

Piff, C. (1985) *Let's Face It.* Victor Gollancz, London.

Roth, J.A. (1963) *Timetables: Structuring the Passage of Time in Hospital Treatment and Other Careers.* Bobbs-Merril, New York.

Rushing, W. (1964) *The Psychiatric Professions: Power, Conflict and Adaptation in a Psychiatric Hospital Staff.* The University of North Carolina Press, Chapel Hill.

Sudnow, D. (1967) *Passing On: The Social Organisation of Dying.* Prentice-Hall, New Jersey.

Tusting, K. and Maybin, J. (2007) Linguistic ethnography and interdisciplinarity: Opening the discussion. *Journal of Sociolinguistics* 11/5, 2007: 575–583.

Zerubavel, E. (1979) *Patterns of Time in Hospital Life.* University of Chicago Press, Chicago.

10

Applying Linguistic Ethnography to Educational Practice: Notes on the Interaction of Academic Research and Professional Sensibilities

Adam Lefstein and Mirit Israeli

Academic concepts, methods and research knowledge are often criticised as irrelevant or useless for addressing problems of educational practice. Liat, a full-time Science teacher and part-time Masters student, expressed this sentiment in a recent seminar on 'Discourse, Teaching and Learning': 'I'm four years into this degree [programme] and the academic world is truly irrelevant to that of the educational system. It's all bullshit: research, research, research. Nothing at all relevant to schools, nothing.' (We have translated this and all other quotations from the workshops from Hebrew; the original transcripts are available upon request.) This chapter is about our attempt to address this challenge by introducing educational practitioners to linguistic ethnographic research of classroom practice.

We came to linguistic ethnography from educational work with teachers and students in schools, and it is upon the realm of professional practice that we seek to bring linguistic ethnographic insights to bear. This move is less straightforward than it may seem. Linguistic ethnographic methods are not ideal for addressing central questions that occupy educational practitioners, such as what students are learning or how effective the teaching is. Moreover, practitioners' professional sensibilities are generally different from ethnographers' analytic dispositions. Nevertheless, linguistic ethnography has broadened our understanding of pedagogy and classroom practice, and we are convinced that linguistic ethnographic perspectives can potentially benefit practitioners. Indeed, we spend a lot of our time trying to communicate these perspectives to teachers. In this chapter we use that experience as an opportunity to examine the differences between linguistic ethnographic and pedagogic perspectives, to explore their interaction in teacher development workshops we have conducted, and to reflect upon the advantages and limitations of linguistic ethnography as a tool for teachers, and how it might be adapted. We highlight fundamental divergences between how we and the teachers look at classroom practice, and describe how and why we often talk past each other.

Some relevant contexts

Empirically, our discussion builds on a number of different encounters with teachers and other educational practitioners in which we studied together video and audio recordings of classroom practice. These encounters include:

- A series of workshops for teachers participating in a research study in an East London Primary School in the 2008–2009 school year (see Lefstein & Snell, 2011a, 2014; most of the ideas in this chapter are the development and elaboration of themes that initially emerged in collaboration with Julia Snell).
- Master's degree courses at the University of London Institute of Education between 2007–2010 and at the Ben-Gurion University of the Negev (Israel) between 2010–2013.
- Numerous presentations and workshops for teachers, principals and inspectors in Israel over the past three years.

All these activities have informed our thinking about the interaction of pedagogic and linguistic ethnographic perspectives. In this chapter we focus in particular on the data analysis sessions in the 'Discourse, Teaching and Learning' M.A. seminar at Ben-Gurion University of the Negev, which Lefstein taught and Israeli audited in the 2012–2013 academic year. Almost all of the M.A. and PhD students participating in this year-long course are practising or former teachers. Our ideas in this chapter were developed and honed through examination of the course data analysis sessions, in which students brought in recordings of their own or colleagues' classroom practice.

Theoretically, our discussion builds upon Goodwin's (1994) concept of professional vision, defined as 'socially organized ways of seeing and understanding events that are answerable to the distinctive interests of a particular social group' (p. 606). Professional vision brings together *gaze*, ways of attending to and perceiving phenomena; *discourse*, ways of talking about the phenomena being viewed; and *thinking*, ways of interpreting and conceptualising the phenomena under consideration.

According to Goodwin, professions initiate their members into unique ways of seeing and understanding phenomena in their area of expertise. These systems of perception and reasoning are developed through practices of *coding*, the use of established categories and codes to describe and construct the object of inquiry (e.g., in archaeology, which is Goodwin's primary example, colour schemes for classifying shades of dirt); *highlighting*, 'methods used to divide a domain of scrutiny into a figure and a ground, so that events relevant to the activity of the moment stand out' (p. 610) (e.g., drawing on the ground with a trowel to demarcate changes in colouration); and *producing material representations* (e.g., a map of the excavation).

Professional vision not only organises practitioners' gaze, discourse and thinking, it also constructs their particular ways of seeing and understanding as superior to those of lay people. For example, Goodwin shows how an expert police witness used practices of coding, highlighting and constructing material representations to help the jury see a case of apparent police brutality from the standpoint of the suspected police officers rather than from their victim's perspective. Through this example, Goodwin shows how vision is politically contested, and how different ways of organising vision can serve the interests of different social groups.

Professional vision is relevant to our chapter in a number of ways: first, we look at the differing visions that we and the teachers bring to the viewing and analysing of video-recordings of classroom practice – respectively, linguistic ethnographic and pedagogic visions. Second, we look at the different practices of seeing, organising vision and discussing the viewed phenomena that we and the teachers engage in. Third, we situate the differences between our respective professional visions within the field of power relations and competing interests served by our different visions.

While we find professional vision to be a useful concept for studying these events, we should also clarify some of the gaps between our case and the archetypical cases that Goodwin examined. First, teachers typically lack the sort of focused, collaborative practices for the development of vision that are employed, for example, by archaeologists. The actual work of teaching is almost always carried out alone, without many opportunities to consult with colleagues about what is happening and how to make sense of it. Even when a more experienced peer is present – for example, during lesson observations in initial teacher training or in the (very rare) practice of joint teaching or peer observation and feedback – teachers do not have the luxury of stopping the action to consult in real time. Viewing a video-recording of classroom practice is not the same as observing in the classroom, nor is a teacher's gaze while observing the same as her gaze while teaching.

Second, neither the teachers' nor our own professional visions are monolithic. We are both also teachers, and many of the participants in the events we analyse are also novice or experienced researchers – and current and former students, parents, women, men, amateur film critics and more. Nevertheless, the division between two dominant ways of seeing and talking about the lessons is analytically convenient, and fits well with most of what we have observed and experienced.

Contrasting pedagogical and linguistic ethnographic perspectives

In this section we discuss the central differences between the two visions that have emerged from our reflection on the various workshops conducted with teachers. We analyse differences on multiple dimensions, including key questions, assumptions, common methods, forms of reasoning and problems (summarised in Table 10.1; note that due to space limitations not all the rows on the table are discussed explicitly in the chapter).

It is not by chance that the two perspectives appear here as diametrically opposed. Our analytic strategy involves comparing the two perspectives, such that each serves as the backdrop against which aspects of the other stand out. No doubt, other important aspects of teacher professional vision have gone unnoticed by us, since they accord with our own perspective. Moreover, each perspective has emerged in interaction with the other. Hence, what we present here is not necessarily how teachers think about and gaze upon video-recordings *in general*, but rather how they have responded when discussing the materials with us, i.e. when pressed to consider our linguistic ethnographic perspective. Likewise, our particular take on linguistic ethnography is partially the product of our work with teachers: we emphasise certain aspects of linguistic ethnography in our teaching specifically as a response to perceived problems with how teachers respond to video. Hence, the professional visions discussed here are not necessarily inherent, independent or general.

We illustrate the two professional visions with an example taken from a data analysis session in the 'Discourse, Teaching and Learning' M.A. seminar at Ben-Gurion University of the Negev in May 2013. Most of the 14 students attending the course were practising teachers who returned to University part-time to study for an M.A. degree in Curriculum and Instruction (other students were in the doctoral programme or studying educational counselling). The course aims to introduce participants to central approaches in the study of classroom interaction, discourse, teaching and learning, and to give them opportunities to critically examine practice in their own or another's classrooms. The hope is that some of the students will go on to conduct research in classrooms, taking advantage of the concepts and methods studied, and that all of the participants will find the perspectives encountered helpful in reflecting on their own pedagogical beliefs and practice.

The seminar is organised into two semesters. In the first semester students are introduced to key concepts and methods in the study of discourse and interaction, and to central issues and seminal studies in classroom discourse research. In the second semester, the seminar functions as a data analysis workshop for investigating video- and/or audio-recorded materials chosen by the students.

The example we focus on here occurred in one of the data analysis workshops. Tomer, a Computing teacher at an Experimental School in affluent north Tel-Aviv, brought to the session a video recording of two segments from a 7th grade history lesson. Tomer selected these segments as relatively good examples of an innovative educational programme, for which he acts as school coordinator, called Identity Exploration. In explaining this programme, Tomer quoted from Flum & Kaplan (2006), who suggest that 'the primary focus of students' engagement in schoolwork should be to intentionally and consciously examine, investigate, and evaluate the relevance and meaning of content and action to their sense of who they are and who they want to be' (p. 102). Tomer sought to examine in the course data analysis session the extent to which the students actually engaged in such identity exploration. He was concerned about this question for professional reasons – as programme coordinator it is his job to help teachers facilitate pupils' identity exploration – and also as he intended to focus on this issue in his seminar research paper.

Table 10.1   Contrasting pedagogical and linguistic ethnographic perspectives

	Pedagogical perspective	Linguistic ethnographic perspective
Key questions	*Focus of analysis*: Evaluation of professional practice • Is the teaching good? • Are the students learning? • How could the practice be improved? • What does it say about *me* and/or *her* as a teacher?	*Focus of analysis*: Description of interaction • What is going on here? • What kind of discourse genre is this? • In what ways is the episode an interesting or unusual case of this discourse genre? • What structures, ideologies and identities are being enacted and/or resisted?
Key assumptions	• The main thing that happens in classrooms is teaching and learning. • The teacher is in charge / controls the activity. • The key categories for understanding pupil participation and success are levels of cognitive ability.	• Classrooms are sites of multiple activities and concerns, such as social identification, negotiating interpersonal and power relations, and 'doing school'. Academic learning is often marginal to both pupils and teacher. • Often pupils constrain teacher activity just as much as teachers constrain pupils; control is jointly constructed. • 'Ability' is at least partially a social construction, context-dependent. • Teachers and pupils act rationally; the analyst's challenge is to understand what makes seemingly irrational action rational within the given context.
Key concepts (examples)	Learning, understanding, engagement, interest, motivation, discipline, ability, specific teaching strategies.	Discourse genre, footing, repair, participation framework, preference organisation, procedural display, social identification.

Common methods	*Logic of inquiry*: projection of pedagogical preferences onto the event 1) What should we expect from good teaching? 2) Is it evident in the episode? i.e. is this good teaching? 3a) What should the teacher be doing differently? OR 3b) Are there mitigating circumstances?	*Logic of inquiry*: micro-analysis of interesting or surprising events 1) Interrogation of context. 2) Selection of moment for micro-analysis. 3) Line-by-line brainstorm. 4) Weighing emergent interpretations. 5) Generalising beyond the event.
Common forms of reasoning	• General, holistic / impressionistic. • Own experience as a key source of authority and basis for claims. • Attributing actions to type of pupil or teacher.	• Specific, pointing at line numbers, words. • Research literature on classroom discourse (and generally on interaction) as a key source of authority and basis for claims. • Attributing behaviour to situation.
Common material representations and highlighting systems	Lesson plans, worksheets, pupil work, examinations, report cards; *Occasionally*: teacher evaluation (e.g. RAMA tool).	Audio- and/or video-recordings, transcripts, fieldnotes, pupil work; *Sometimes*: lesson plan, curricular materials.
Chief limitation	Focuses on what is missing rather than what is present.	Privileges (a) the 'here and now' (recorded data) over longer time scales, and (b) social dynamics over cognitive interests, thereby marginalising learning.

In the workshop we investigated this and other issues through a process that included the following stages (this was the basic structure for all the data analysis workshops, though the divisions were often less neat than outlined here):

(a) Presentation by Tomer of the background to the school, segment and his research;
(b) Watching the segments and attending to the transcript provided by Tomer;
(c) Posing clarification questions;
(d) Watching the segments for a second time;
(e) Relatively free-flowing discussion in which students comment upon what they noticed or found significant or interesting, and address Tomer's question about whether pupils engage in identity exploration in the segments. During this segment the course lecturer is relatively silent.
(f) Focused micro-analytic investigation of select events, led by the course lecturer.
(g) Conclusion, in which we reflect back upon the workshop and what, if anything, we learned.

We now use this and similar sessions (where appropriate) to illustrate the differences between pedagogic and linguistic ethnographic professional visions.

Key questions

The focus in the pedagogical perspective is on the quality of the teaching practice. Practitioners ask 'Is this good teaching?' and look for evidence of that in teacher actions and student responses (i.e. Are they learning?). The question Tomer posed for the workshop – 'Are there manifestations of pupil individual [identity] clarification within the context of the material studied?' – is of course a good example of this.

Practitioners often relate personally to these questions, with their own practice, and their own identities as teachers, in the background of the discussion. Bearing in mind that teachers rarely have opportunities to observe one another's practice, the examples of classroom practice discussed in the course often functioned as a mirror onto their own practice, raising questions about how *I* would have taught this topic or responded to that situation, and what does the comparison with the video-recorded segment say about *me* as a teacher?

Coming from a linguistic ethnographic perspective, these normative questions about the quality of the teaching seem premature if not altogether misguided. As ethnographers, we have been taught to try to understand a culture on its own terms, non-judgmentally. Moreover, even if ultimately we want to discuss the quality of the teaching, we must first understand what is going on. Description and analysis are logically prior to evaluation. Linguistic ethnographers tend to ask questions about the event as situated interaction. For example, with regard to the segment that Tomer brought to the course, we tried to make sense of what we viewed as unusual student contributions to the class discussion, in which they recounted personal stories about prejudices and how they had learned to not think stereotypically about others (the class were studying the history of relations between Jews and the Church in medieval Europe). We wondered what discourse genres the students and teacher were drawing upon? What were the criteria for 'successful' participation in this discourse activity? And what identities and ideologies were being enacted by the students?

Key assumptions

What we see is shaped by what we expect to see, i.e. what we assume to be happening in classrooms. Such expectations and assumptions are not typically explicated by teachers or researchers, but we can infer them from what participants notice and how they talk about it. The key point of difference between the two perspectives is that teachers generally assume that most classroom activity is about learning, while linguistic ethnographers tend to be suspicious that displays of formal learning often reflect other, non-academic issues and concerns. Consider, for example, the following contribution to the event that Tomer brought to the data analysis workshop. Following a discussion of the stereotypes used to describe Jews in medieval Europe, one of the pupils, Noa, recounts how she learned to stop using the term 'blonde' as a stereotypical description of unintelligent girls (as in 'ditzy blonde'):

All my best friends are blondes. So on many occasions I've said to them, 'What a "blonde" thing to say', meaning like ditzy. Actually sometimes – once my friend told me that it is really not nice that I say this to her and that I'm actually making a generalisation and she's actually pretty smart and gets good grades. So I've stopped doing it because I also realised it was a generalisation which is not very nice of me. So basically I think they didn't under—. They

> generalised about all Jews and said that all of them are dishonest, all
> of them are this. When actually they're people who may be amazing.

A few of the teachers participating in the discussion pointed to this
contribution as an ideal example of identity exploration. Noa, after all,
appears to be relating the historical material being studied to her own
life, and using the curricular contents as an opportunity to explore who
she is: a person without prejudice, who doesn't make judgments on the
basis of friends' hair colour.

As linguistic ethnographers, we interpreted Noa's contribution differently. The seminar lecturer noted, first, that part of what Noa was doing
was to identify herself and friends publicly, in addition to commenting
on the historical material. Second, he wondered to what extent she has
actually learned something from the history lesson, and to what extent
she is performing the role of the ideal 'identity explorer'. He pointed out
what a well-crafted conversion narrative she has presented, and how it
conforms to teacherly expectations for denouncing prejudice, being sensitive to others and learning from mistakes. The differences between the
teachers' and our interpretations were shaped in part by divergences in
our assumptions and expectations. Rather than assuming that students
are by definition engaged in learning, we assume that much of what
happens in classrooms is related to managing one's identity and social
relations, and performing school-appropriate roles (without necessarily
engaging in learning; see, e.g., Bloome, Puro & Theodorou, 1989).

A second key difference between the assumptions underlying the two
perspectives relates to the presumed distribution of agency and responsibility. While the pedagogical perspective tends to attribute almost all
responsibility for classroom activity to the teacher, who is assumed to
be generally in control of the classroom, in the linguistic ethnographic
perspective power relations are co-constructed by teachers and students,
with the latter often constraining the former no less than the former
influence the latter. So, for example, in many of our video clips the
teachers talk most of the time. Teachers viewing these clips interpret
the situation as one in which the teacher has 'dominated' classroom discourse, has occupied all available space and thereby crowded out pupil
voices. When we look at these clips, we often see the teacher offering
pupils opportunities to participate, for example, by posing questions to
them, but the latter have not cooperated – they 'coerce' the teacher to
talk through their own silence.

A third difference relates to assumptions about pupils' ability and
how central it is for understanding what happens in classrooms.

Teachers often use 'high' and 'low ability' as key factors for predicting or explaining student classroom participation and academic success. Ability is often assumed to be innate, and inherited (either genetically or socially) and therefore for the most part beyond the control of the school. Thus, for example, in Tomer's lesson, the participating teachers explained the pupils' good behaviour and relative articulateness as a function of the school's location in affluent north Tel-Aviv. For linguistic ethnographers, low and high ability are viewed as social constructions, the context-dependent product of pupils' interaction with their environment rather than some innate quality that moves with them from place to place. Schooling is organised such that some pupils appear 'bright' and others 'slow', and part of the analyst's task involves uncovering these processes (see Varenne & McDermott, 1998, on the way that schooling constructs social categories of relative ability, and Snell & Lefstein, 2012, on how teachers' interpretations of classroom events are shaped by their assessments of pupil ability).

Common methods

We now turn to differences between the two perspectives with regard to their logics and methods of inquiry. For linguistic ethnography, we have a relatively robust tradition of methodological reflection to build upon; for pedagogical inquiry, we have sought to reconstruct the implicit methods of inquiry from our interactions with the teachers in our workshops. As such, the comparison is rather problematic: on the one hand, a carefully thought through and debated set of research methods; on the other hand, a set of intuitive, *ad hoc* moves practitioners make when confronted with unfamiliar representations of classroom practice. But our point is not to argue for the relative merits of one or the other system, rather to highlight the differences in order to find ways of coping with them better.

The primary issue in the pedagogical perspective – i.e., Is the teaching good? – leads to three central analytic moves:

1. *Identification of relevant standards for good teaching.* Since the question of what constitutes good teaching is highly contested in Israel, very often analysis begins with claims about what is important in teaching this particular subject or that particular age group. For example, participants in the discussion of Tomer's data drew attention to a range of various indicators of teaching quality, among them student behaviour (on task, attentive, not disruptive), student interest, depth and accuracy of historical investigation, relevance to

students (and their identities), quality of the teacher responses to student contributions, the extent to which students responded to one another, and the 'feel' of the classroom climate. In some cases, the standards were made explicit; in most cases they can be inferred from what was said.

2. *Evaluation of the episode according to those standards.* Depending upon course participants' values and priorities, the episode that Tomer presented (from the identity exploration / history lesson) was deemed to be excellent or problematic teaching. For example, the initial responses of a number of students was to compliment the teacher on the orderly and respectful classroom learning environment. One commented, 'The students are so exceptional – first of all there's something respectful about them. It really shows that time isn't wasted on discipline problems, no stopping the flow [of the lesson].' Another affirmed, 'Yes, they're so well-behaved.' Other students favourably evaluated the lesson because the students appeared to be so involved, and related the topic of discussion to their own lives and selves. On the contrary, two other students contended, students' discussions of their own experiences marginalised and even distorted the historical knowledge that should be the focus of a history lesson. This issue – personal relevance vs disciplinary knowledge – was a central topic of group discussion. However, since the main point of contention is normative – What should be our educational priorities? – the episode itself provided little assistance in developing our ideas, and indeed was quickly abandoned in favour of more general claims about what knowledge is worth knowing and how people learn.

3. *Drawing conclusions about how practice should be improved and/or what the recorded practice says about the observed teacher.* After assessing the quality of the teaching observed, participants often offer suggestions of what the teacher should be doing differently. For example, in the discussion of Tomer's data one of participants suggested that the teacher should have challenged students' problematic historical analogies, and most of the participants agreed that Tomer needs to work with the teacher on summarising and extending pupils' ideas (rather than moving on to the next pupil without offering substantive feedback). Another teacher explained that in such a situation as the observed teacher found himself she would split the students into more intimate, small discussion groups, or pursue the personal issues raised in one-on-one consultations. Evaluations – both negative and positive – often give rise to explanations, which are usually

rooted in the unique circumstances of the lesson (e.g., 'it's because he's a supply teacher that they treat him this way') or student background. In the case of Tomer's data, for example, teachers commented on the students' relatively affluent background as a 'mitigating' factor in the teacher's success: the implication being that if he were to teach that way with 'normal' students he would have a much harder time achieving such a positive classroom climate and good student behaviour.

Our specific approach to linguistic ethnographic analysis of classroom discourse and interaction has been elaborated elsewhere (Lefstein & Snell, 2011b, 2014); here we briefly touch upon the main analytic processes we engage in when conducting micro-analysis of interesting or surprising events. After having received explanation of background, watched and/or heard the recording twice, and studied the transcript, we engage in the following:

1. *Interrogation of context.* We try to make sense of the event more globally before delving into specifics. This typically involves asking questions about the context (the school, participants and the lesson) and the type of event or discourse genre(s) participants are engaged in.
2. *Selection of moment(s) for micro-analysis.* We often collect initial comments in which each participant notes something that caught their attention. This first round of comments usually draws attention to particular moments that warrant further investigation, because they are not well understood, because participants have offered conflicting interpretations of them, and/or because something interesting or unexpected is happening in them.
3. *Line-by-line micro-analytic brainstorm of select moments.* We then proceed line-by-line, brainstorming about 'Why that now?' 'What else could have happened, but didn't?' 'How does this turn relate to the preceding one?' (see Rampton, 2006).
4. *Weighing emergent interpretations.* We pursue the different possibilities, testing out ideas on the basis of the available evidence, or discussing how interpretations could be further elaborated through investigation of the rest of the corpus or further data collection, for example.
5. *Generalising beyond the event.* Finally – and we often don't manage to get to this stage in the time available in the seminar – we speculate about the possible patterns or meanings that extend beyond the

event and address larger social issues and/or theoretical ideas. Such generalisation is speculative at this stage, and part of the discussion is methodological: what else would we want to investigate in order to test and/or extend these theoretical ideas further?

So, for example, in the discussion of Tomer's data, we selected for further analysis the event in which Noa talked about how she learned to stop referring stereotypically to her 'blonde' friends. We asked about what kind of event Noa was engaged in, looked in detail at the way she constructed her utterance, and how it related to the previous and subsequent turns. Among other issues, the micro-analytic brainstorm raised questions about what is being expected of students in such a lesson, i.e., what are the rules of the identity exploration game? This line of analysis gave way to speculation about the emergence of what Ecclestone and Hayes (2009) call 'therapeutic education', and how the rise of this educational ideology might be affecting classroom order, power relations and the teaching of disciplinary content.

Common material representations and highlighting systems

As we noted above, teachers do not engage in the sort of collaborative gazing activities that Goodwin observed among archeologists, or indeed, that linguistic ethnographers engage in. Moreover, while the archeologist can hold her object of observation steady while she examines it – for example, spraying a sample of dirt with water in order to accurately gauge its colour – the objects of teachers' gazes are dynamic, and talk back. Teachers' professional visions are formed for the most part while interacting with pupils – alone, without professional colleagues. Teachers do collaboratively look at representations of practice, but most of these are relatively indirect artefacts of teaching and learning such as lesson plans, worksheets, pupil work and examinations, or bureaucratic artefacts such as report cards and official documents in which schools provide accounts of policy compliance and/or pupil progress. We see these two phenomena – that teachers' professional visions for the most part emerge and are developed outside of collaboration and discussion with colleagues, and that when teachers do collaboratively discuss artefacts of practice, these tend to be relatively indirect representations of what actually happens in the classroom – as critical factors shaping the lack of a shared language for precise description of classroom activity.

Linguistic ethnographic analyses, in contrast, are largely based upon – and therefore better adapted to – audio- and video-recordings of classroom practice (and accompanying transcripts). Linguistic ethnographers also collect data from supplementary sources, such as fieldnotes, pupil work, lesson plans and curricular materials, but these are typically viewed as secondary, useful for contextualising the event but not worthy of the same level of attention as the core, recorded data, certainly in this context. (See Roberts [2001] and Agar [1986] on the distinction between core and contextual data. The status of non-recorded data is a point of contention among linguistic ethnographers; see Snell & Lefstein, 2015, for a discussion of some of the institutional pressures that privilege analysis of recorded data sets.)

Recordings are a partial representation. They capture a certain point of view – i.e. where the camera and/or microphone are positioned, and what they focus upon. They also reflect a selection: we tend to select clips that include some unusual or surprising event, that are relatively self-contained (i.e. have a beginning, middle and end) and last no longer than 5–7 minutes. Recordings are transcribed in detail, and the transcript often becomes the main object of participants' gaze. The transcript is a material representation that stabilises the ephemeral nature of interaction and affords close scrutiny of whatever the analyst has chosen to highlight. This naturally leads to greater attention to the most audible words spoken, and to the speakers, than to non-verbal communication, to intonation patterns, to quiet asides, and to non or less vocal participants. Though we often emphasise that the transcript is just a work-space, and that analysis must be performed on the recording itself, we typically return to the recording primarily when controversies arise around competing interpretations of specific sections of the transcript. (See also Lefstein & Snell [2011] on how the transcript lends itself to event-focused micro-analysis, and tends to limit possibilities for longitudinal analysis of processes and biographies).

Recognition of the differences between the material representations that each group is accustomed to working with is useful for making sense of the researcher-teacher encounters that took place in the data analysis workshops. By basing the discussions on video-recordings and detailed transcripts we required the teachers to work with materials to which they are relatively unfamiliar, and which are less well-suited to their pedagogical perspective. This imbalance was of course compounded by the fact that one of us was also the course lecturer, tasked with assessing the course participants.

Linguistic ethnography and pedagogy in conversation

In the preceding discussion we examined the main differences between the pedagogic and linguistic ethnographic perspectives on recordings of classroom practice, and explored their methodological, ideological and institutional roots. Before moving on to discussion of the actual and possible interactions between the two perspectives, it is worth noting that each perspective is better suited to some purposes than others. Indeed, it would seem that each perspective is relatively poorly suited for addressing the concerns central to the other. The pedagogic perspective's chief problem is its tendency to focus on what is missing rather than what is present in the recorded data. This tendency arises from participants basing their analyses on what they would have expected to find in a 'good' lesson, rather than what actually occurs. This is problematic on four counts: first, focusing on what is absent distracts us from making sense of what is actually going on. Second, it makes weighing opposing interpretations difficult, since they are only loosely related to the common object under discussion; in other words, the recorded lesson serves as a poor basis for assessing the relative merits of participants' different pedagogical preferences that they seek to project upon it. Third, discussion of good teaching that is based on idealised or imagined practice, rather than authentic representations of actual practice, can lead us to adopting or developing unrealistic pedagogical models. Finally, it is usually unfair to the recorded teachers and students: the practices that participants seek to find may have occurred prior to or after the very brief snapshot captured in the recorded episode. This final issue points to a further mismatch between the pedagogical perspective and the sort of materials we brought to the workshops: the 5–7 minute episode is not a good unit of analysis for studying pedagogic processes, which typically last for weeks or even months.

Conversely, linguistic ethnography is less well-suited for investigating learning. This limitation arises from a number of analytic prejudices: the tendency to privilege the 'here and now' of the recorded evidence over longer time scales, for which evidence is not as firm (see Lefstein & Snell, 2011a); the tendency to focus more on social interaction than on cognitive processes; and a preference for explanations based on visible social dynamics over inferences about what's going on inside actors' minds. Learning, which takes place over relatively long time-scales and to a certain extent within people's heads, is marginalised by these preferences. Nevertheless, since learning is not the only phenomenon – indeed, is often not the central phenomenon – to be found in classrooms, we argue that the sorts of issues that linguistic ethnography uncovers are crucial for a well-rounded and balanced understanding of pedagogy. Our challenge is to bring the two perspectives together.

How did the two perspectives interact in the workshops? Most of the time we talked past one another. Following acquaintance with the data (listening and/or watching the recording twice, raising and responding to questions about the context) we conducted an initial review of issues that participants were interested in pursuing. This review was typically dominated by comments originating in the pedagogic perspective: e.g., what participants would have expected to see, what the teacher *should* be doing, how good the teaching is, or how the events observed resonate with their own experience. Some of these comments were contested, and discussion of the pedagogic merits of the case typically ensued. The course leader interjected here and there a request for evidence from the text, or a reminder that we should try to understand the event before judging it, but for the most part this pedagogic discussion continued for about half the workshop session. Eventually, the course leader shut down the pedagogic conversation, and focused the participants' attention on a specific moment or issue that he claimed was worthy of deeper (i.e. linguistic ethnographic) examination. In the subsequent micro-analytic brainstorm the course leader typically deflected attempts to re-inject pedagogic issues by requesting that participants attend to what is happening in the episode (usually, in the specific 2–3 turns that were the object of analysis) and by demanding specific evidence for interpretations offered. In such a way, the workshops were divided into two more or less independent segments – the first pedagogic, the second, linguistic ethnographic – which rarely interacted with one another in any meaningful way. The main exceptions to this generalisation were events in which the linguistic ethnographic analysis directly challenged pedagogic assumptions and interpretations, or occasions in which the class engaged in meta-methodological reflection, e.g., about our tendency to rush to judgment about teaching quality even before fully understanding what is going on.

While these interventions are useful for teaching linguistic ethnography and its merits, we wonder if it might be possible to accomplish richer and more productive conversations between the perspectives. In moving forward, we want to experiment with making space for quality pedagogical reflection. One of the problems in the way we structured the workshops was that we rarely had time, conditions or tools to explore seriously participants' pedagogic reflections. Paradoxically, though we argued that the pedagogic discussion should follow the linguistic ethnographic one, in actuality the order was reversed, and we never managed to come back to the pedagogic issues that were raised at the outset. Perhaps if participants knew that we would devote the latter 40–60 minutes of each workshop to pedagogic discussion they would more readily delay their pedagogic reflections until then.

No less importantly, quality pedagogic exploration demands appropriate materials and tools, including:

(a) *Data about learning processes*, including e.g., examples of student work, sampling of discussions over time, etc. Comparative data may also be productive, e.g., data comparing two strategies for teaching the same materials or students.

(b) Some agreement about pedagogical goals and principles, i.e. about what is good teaching and what it should strive to achieve – at the very least provisional agreement for the sake of the workshop.

(c) Tools for analysing learning processes. Here we can build on micro-analytic and transcontextual methods that have been developed outside of the linguistic ethnographic community, for example Parnafes and diSessa's (2013) method for 'microgenetic learning analysis', or the way in which Wortham (2006) investigates the evolution of cognitive models articulated in classroom discourse over the course of multiple events of cognition. One limitation of these and related methods is that they require reduction and organisation of relatively large data sets prior to micro-analysis: one cannot simply apply them to whatever 5-minute strip of interaction students have brought to a workshop.

(d) Methods for relating analyses of learning processes and classroom interactional dynamics to conclusions about teaching. Just as we cannot derive *ought* from *is*, we cannot straightforwardly derive teaching strategies from theories or evidence of learning. We believe that a promising way forward is to focus on dilemmas, and to attempt to sharpen teachers' professional judgment by examining (a) What is happening (including, what are students learning)? (b) Why is it happening? (c) What are the possible strategies or moves the teacher can employ? And (d) What are the advantages and disadvantages of each? (See Lefstein & Snell, 2014, for an elaboration of the rationale behind developing teacher professional judgment through discussion of dilemmas, and for examples of analyses of classroom episodes.)

We view such tools and the pedagogic exploration they're intended to support as complementary to and potentially building upon linguistic ethnographic analysis. Our challenge is how to combine both perspectives in the limited time frameworks in which we work. We are convinced that linguistic ethnographic analyses have pedagogic value; indeed, it stands to reason that their relevance will become clearer when combined with quality pedagogic discussion (instead of competing with it).

In closing, we would like to reflect on the broader educational context of the issues discussed here. What's at stake is much larger than the success of a seminar course or its participants' satisfaction. It is now commonly accepted that what happens in the classroom is the key determinant of the quality of school education, and that teacher participation in critical, collaborative conversations about their practice is a crucial component of any attempt to improve teaching. However, not all professional conversations advance their participants' insights and judgment to the same extent. The analytic dispositions, forms of reasoning and breadth of considerations that linguistic ethnography offers can contribute significantly to teacher professional discourse and learning. Our challenge is to adapt, complement and mediate linguistic ethnography in ways that are constructive, have integrity, and are recognised as helpful by practitioners.

Note

This research was supported by THE ISRAEL SCIENCE FOUNDATION (grant No. 208/12).

References

Agar, M. (1986). *Independents Declared: The Dilemmas of Independent Trucking.* Washington, D.C.: Smithsonian Institution Press.

Bloome, D., Puro, P., & Theodorou, E. (1989). Procedural display and classroom lessons. *Curriculum Inquiry, 19*(3), 265–291.

Ecclestone, K., & Hayes, D. (2009). *The Dangerous Rise of Therapeutic Education.* London: Routledge.

Flum, H., & Kaplan, A. (2006) Exploratory orientation as an educational goal. *Educational Psychologist, 41*(2), 99–110.

Goodwin, C. (1994). Professional vision. *American Anthropologist, 96*(3), 606–633.

Jackson, P. W. (1990). *Life in Classrooms* (2nd edn). New York: Teachers College Press.

Lefstein, A., & Snell, J. (2011a). Professional vision and the politics of teacher learning. *Teaching and Teacher Education, 27*(3), 505–514.

Lefstein, A., & Snell, J. (2011b). Promises and problems of teaching with popular culture: a linguistic ethnographic analysis of discourse genre mixing. *Reading Research Quarterly, 46*(1), 40–69.

Lefstein, A., & Snell, J. (2014) *Better than Best Practice: Developing Dialogic Pedagogy.* London: Routledge.

Parnafes, O., & diSessa, A. A. (2013). Microgenetic learning analysis: a methodology for studying knowledge in transition. *Human Development, 56*(1), 5–37.

Rampton, B. (2006). *Language in Late Modernity: Interaction in an Urban School.* Cambridge: Cambridge University Press.

Roberts, C. (2001) *Language Learners as Ethnographers.* Clevedon, England: Multilingual Matters.

Snell, J., & Lefstein, A. (2012) Dialogic Teaching of 'Low Ability' Pupils: A Tale of Three Classrooms. School of Education and Social Work, University of Sussex, 5/3/2012.

Snell, J., & Lefstein, A. (2015) 'Moving from "interesting data" to publishable research article – some interpretive and representational dilemmas in a linguistic ethnographic analysis'. In Smeyers, Paul, Bridges, David, Burbules, Nicholas and Griffiths, Morwenna, (eds) *International Handbook of Interpretation in Educational Research Methods*, Springer.

Varenne, H., & McDermott, R. (1998). *Successful Failure: The School America Builds.* Boulder, CO: Westview Press.

Wortham, S., & Fisher, E. (2006). *Learning Identity: The Joint, Local Emergence of Social Identification and Academic Learning.* New York, NY: Cambridge University Press.

11
Partnerships in Research: Doing Linguistic Ethnography with and for Practitioners

Jeff Bezemer

Introduction

In this chapter I reflect on linguistic-ethnographic research that I conducted in partnership with surgeons. My focus is twofold: I explore how the partnership shaped my research; and I illustrate how linguistic ethnography can contribute to public and professional debates about health care.

Three joint research projects on learning and communication in the operating theatre form the backdrop to the chapter. In each of these projects I worked closely with Roger Kneebone, a professor in surgical education at Imperial College London. In the first project, 'Mapping Educational Activity in the Operating Theatre', we looked at on-the-job surgical training (funded by the London Deanery, the organisation responsible for postgraduate medical education; and the Royal College of Surgeons of England). In the second project, 'Digital Technologies in the Operating Theatre', we explored the role of video technology in surgery (funded by the Economic and Social Research Council (ESRC)). In the third project, 'Transient Teams in the Operating Theatre', we investigated communication between surgeons and nurses during operations (funded by the ESRC).

Keen to develop links with 'non-clinical' educationalists Roger took me on as a research fellow in 2009 when he obtained a grant for the first project. During that first project I was employed directly by the Department of Surgery at Imperial College London. I was licensed to observe in operating theatres of the hospitals attached to the College and shared an office inside one of the hospitals. I was an ethnographer 'in residence' and therefore in a position to interact with surgeons and other health care professionals, not only before, during, and immediately after operations, but also in departmental research seminars, lectures, official email circulations, and informal gatherings, such as Christmas parties. I also worked closely with another surgical partner, Alexandra Cope, a specialist surgical registrar (an experienced trainee) who was a clinical research fellow on the first project and worked on a PhD in surgical education. As we embarked on the second project, in 2011, I took up a post at the Institute of Education. I kept my licence to observe, and did more fieldwork in operating theatres, again with Alex. Two other researchers, Terhi Korkiakangas and Sharon-Marie Weldon, did the fieldwork for the third project, which started in 2012.

The chapter is based on my fieldnotes, email exchanges with my research partners, and memos I wrote after fieldwork. For the purposes of this chapter I define 'partnership' as collaboration with members of the community under study (in my case surgeons), based on a shared interest (e.g. surgical education) and a (formalised) commitment to a joint research project (in my case the commitment was formalised in e.g. funding applications). The chapter follows different stages in the partnership. First, I discuss the fieldwork I did with Alex. Second, I outline the theoretical and methodological perspectives that guided my initial engagement with the data. Third, I present two case studies that illustrate how I built on these perspectives to address the concerns of surgeons, health care professionals and the public more widely, which focus on the timely question of how to improve the safety and quality of health care.

Fieldwork in the operating theatre

As a 'non-clinical' research fellow at Imperial College London I had access to the operating theatres of the hospitals attached to the College. Roger introduced me to a couple of consultant surgeons and senior nurses there, who introduced me to their colleagues in theatres. Inside theatres I talked to and observed a range of staff and trainees: nurses, operation department practitioners, medical students, house officers, anaesthetic registrars, consultant anaesthetists, surgical registrars, and consultant surgeons. Nurses inducted me into the space, explaining where not to stand and what not to touch. I made sure I arrived before 8am, as they were getting ready for their case list, so that I would have an opportunity to ask if they would be happy for me to observe in their theatre on that day. I focused on the case lists of surgeons who had been notified of my work by Roger. As soon as they or their trainees arrived I introduced myself and asked whether they were happy for me to be observing. Nobody ever raised objections, and they hardly took any notice of me. There were small jobs I was asked to help with, such as helping somebody to gown up or helping to move a patient from bed to table, but otherwise I was left 'observing'.

When Alex joined the project a couple of months after I had started observing in theatres the fieldwork changed. Through her I got to interact with many more surgeons, and often found myself participating – peripherally – in informal conversations in between cases. While Alex was there with her 'researcher' hat on she was also at the same time a surgeon, a member of the department, and a trainee, and addressed in all of those roles during fieldwork. She participated in some of the normal routines in theatres, except that she would not operate. For instance, she joined surgeons as they went into the scrub room to scrub up (a place where I felt somewhat out of place). Here she often picked up essential 'contextual' information, for instance, about what had happened on the ward and how that had affected the mood of the consultant. She helped where that seemed appropriate. For instance, she relayed information required by a nurse, put up the x-ray on the theatre computer required by the surgeon, and articulated, on the surgeon's request, her view about the unfolding anatomy (see Transcript 2 in this chapter). That has shaped our data directly, and also indirectly in that through reciprocating willingness of staff to take part in our research she laid the foundation for the next step in our project: to video-record operations.

The operations we observed ranged from minor operations, described by surgeons as 'simple' and 'straightforward', such as removal of fatty lumps, lasting about 20 minutes, to major operations involving the removal and reconstruction of (parts of) the colon, stomach, and oesophagus, lasting up to six hours. The actual time we spent observing in theatres exceeded the operating time, covering also the preparations and cleaning up in the operating theatre and its adjacent rooms (the prep room, where nurses sort the instruments, and the anaesthetic room, where the anaesthetist puts the patient to sleep). We spent many hours waiting for the next case to start, during which time opportunities often arose to talk to staff and students. We took pictures of the spatial arrangement of staff during operations and made photocopies of documents circulating in theatres, such as operating lists, log books, and operative reports. We each made fieldnotes of every case we observed. By the beginning of 2010 we had documented about 30 operations in that way.

By then we had obtained ethical approval from the National Health Service's Research Ethics Committee to make audio- and video-recordings in operating theatres. Following approval Alex began informing staff and patients about the filming and gained their consent. Some nurses had reservations about being filmed and audio-recorded, but most of them and all surgeons almost always agreed to it. As a clinician Alex was in a better position to take consent than I was. I lacked the practical knowledge about when and how to approach staff. The same applied to consenting patients; my lack of know-how about how to find out who they were, where they were, and when and where they could be approached, while at the same time having to track down the surgeons and other staff and set up the recording equipment, would have been challenging to do on my own.

By the summer of 2010 we had audio- and video-recorded ten operations for the first project (on surgical education). In late 2011 we recorded another 12 for the second project (on video technologies) and for Alex' PhD research, generating a total of 33 hours of audio-visual material. We used a wireless microphone worn by one of the surgeons, and video cameras built into a light handle, which allowed us to capture that to which surgeons typically orient themselves, that is, their hands, their instruments, and the parts of the patient's body that they operate on. We also recorded the view of the laparoscope, that is the camera that is used in key-hole surgery to get a view inside of body cavities. These recordings were aimed at capturing activity around the operating table – they were focused on the actions of surgeons, not on those of nurses, anaesthetists and other professionals in the operating theatre.

Throughout fieldwork Alex and I discussed our observations and exchanged fieldnotes. We also watched many video clips together. Our post-observational conversations amount to at least 35 hours (1 hour after each jointly observed operation). Of course, our conversations were not framed as 'interviews'; Alex was not a 'research participant', and I did not record, transcribe and analyse these conversations. Yet the conversations have contributed to my research in at least two ways. First, Alex taught me about surgery and operations, which I used to make sense of the video clips that had drawn my attention. For instance, she commented on the embodied actions of the surgeons featuring in those clips: how particular instruments are designed, how they feel, how they were used in the clips we focused on. Second, by articulating *her* perspective she unwittingly provided directions along which to look. For instance, I focused on surgical training of registrars at her level of training, while largely ignoring medical students.

Looking back, I note that the partnership has allowed me to *extend* traditional fieldwork. As I was 'in residence' I was exposed to everyday

life in operating theatres and other work spaces of surgeons, while Alex
acted as a *mentor*, and *mediator* between myself and surgeons and other
health care professionals. Then, each time we had completed a significant part of fieldwork (after the first 30 operations were documented,
after the first ten operations were video-recorded and again after the
next 12 were recorded) we went our own ways to engage with the data.
I describe that engagement in the following section.

Linguistic-ethnographic perspectives on the operating theatre

The starting point for analysing the materials we had collected was that
people use linguistic and a range of other communicative resources,
such as gesture, gaze and body posture, to construct social realities.
In order to gain insight into these social realities I needed to analyse
in detail how people talk and use their body in situated interaction.
That's why I audio- and video-recorded interactions around the operating table, rather than making fieldnotes alone: one cannot record the
details of interaction as it unfolds in on-the-spot-note-taking. A number
of 'sensitising concepts' or theoretical pointers guided my initial explorations of these data.

The first pointer drew my attention to the range of *activity types*
inside the operating theatre. I noticed that while staff in operating
theatres frequently engaged in conversations their main focus is on
what Goffman (1981) calls 'coordinated task activity'. In this activity
speech only becomes 'critical when something doesn't go as expected'
(Goffman 1983: 4): surgeons and nurses often quietly coordinate their
collaborative work through embodied action, without using speech all
the time. It also struck me that bodily arrangements in surgical activity often run contra to conventional social expectations in relation to
interpersonal distance, bodily comportment and gaze in conversations
(Bezemer 2014).

The second pointer drew my attention to the *sequential ordering* of
actions and spoken utterances during operations. *Embodied actions*,
including gestures made with hands and with instruments, can prompt
or be prompted by other actions, or they can prompt or be prompted
by a spoken utterance. For instance, a surgeon ceasing to tie knots and
holding the end of the stitch in fixed position prompted an assistant to
cut the stitch (Bezemer et al. 2011a); and so did a surgeon saying, 'yeah
you can cut that'. Mondada (2011) calls such sequences 'paired actions';
indeed they are organised in the same way that, say, an 'adjacency

pair' of a question and an answer is. I also considered the *affordances* of speech and different kinds of actions. For instance, surgeons frequently make references to highly specific points in space; for example when one surgeon suggests to another where he thinks the other should cut. These references can only be achieved in gesture: speech does not allow them to be as spatially precise as one can be with the tip of an instrument (Bezemer et al., 2014).

The third pointer drew my attention to the 'gains and losses' involved in representing the social world inside the operating theatre in writing for specific audiences. For instance, I looked at the 'preference cards' of surgeons, that is, notes detailing for each consultant and for each of the procedures they perform the instruments that they want to have at their disposal. These cards distribute the work of surgeons and nurses in particular ways, and they help understand some of the observed interactions between them (Bezemer et al. 2011b).

While these perspectives draw on a significant body of literature they are underrepresented in *medical* journals. When we started the research only a handful of studies on learning and communication in the operating theatre had adopted linguistic and/or ethnographic perspectives, and all of them except one (Moore et al. 2010) were published in social science journals (see Weldon et al., 2013 for a literature review). The same applies to my methodological orientation, which is recognised in a range of social science journals yet rarely adopted in medical journals. I engaged with small excerpts from a purposive data sample, rather than coding much larger, representative data samples as other publications on learning and communication published in medical journals typically do (see Blom et al. 2007). My aim was to seek generalisable and falsifiable explanations. In the words of Burawoy, I sought to 'extract the general from the unique' (Burawoy 2009: 21).

Alex did her own analysis of the video-recordings. The audience for her work was the world of surgery. She knew that to be recognised by this world she was also going to have to publish in medical journals. Hence, she drew on a framework of theories cited in medical journals, such as Ericsson (2004); and coded larger data samples including the video-recordings of teaching and learning at the operating table and the audio-recordings of interviews surgical trainers and trainees (see Cope 2013). Notwithstanding our theoretical and methodological differences our partnership continued to be of mutual benefit. In the periods that we each worked on the data we met up on a weekly basis, giving detailed feedback on each other's emerging analyses and ideas. These interactions shaped my analysis in important ways. Rather than going back to the surgeons I studied, who were practically unavailable for post-observational conversations, Alex taught me about inter-professional dynamics in the operating theatre, and specific biographical details of staff. In return, I helped her where I could. For instance, we had lengthy discussions about the categories she defined as part of her coding schemes, and I was one of a number of 'raters' who coded a subsample of the data to test the 'inter-rater reliability' of her coding scheme.

I was well aware of the lack of familiarity among surgeons with linguistic ethnographic perspectives. However, I did aim to share my insights with them and other 'non-clinical' academic communities. The first papers I wrote drew directly on the observations I have outlined above and appeared in journals such as *Symbolic Interaction* and *Applied Linguistics Review*. These papers fed into guest lectures I gave for Imperial's Master's programme in Surgical Education and workshops I ran in national and international conferences attended by surgeons, such as the *Ottawa Conference*, a major conference on education and assessment in medicine. Attendees at these sessions expressed great interest in what I had to say about learning and communication in the operating theatre. Yet their comments on evaluation forms suggest that while some found my analyses useful, others were less convinced. They recognised what I rendered visible in detailed transcripts and ethnographic accounts, but they were not always clear as to how these analyses could be used to help improve surgical care. 'So what?', they asked, for instance, when I pointed out that teaching medical students in the operating theatre is often organised in sequences of Initiation, Response and Feedback.

Meanwhile, I moved on from the ethnographic ambition to 'understand', in my case, learning and communication in the operating theatre, to now also contribute, to 'make a difference', however small. Through my residency I had become familiar with the discourse of 'improvement' in health care (all my colleagues in the department were talking about it) and noted the frequent use of terms such as 'patient safety', 'human factors', 'situation awareness', 'non-technical skills', and 'decision making'. I realised that to make 'impact' I had to develop ways to connect my insights in, say, the sequential organisation of talk, with some of those categories. The two case studies I present in the following section illustrate how I did that.

Addressing questions from health care with linguistic ethnography

Case study I: Surgical training

Since we had done fieldwork in a teaching hospital we had hours of video-recordings of operations performed by surgical registrars under supervision of consultant surgeons. Alex, being a registrar herself, was particularly interested in this. Detailed transcription and interactional analysis seemed to be a good way to go about gaining new insight into the role of language and communication in providing surgical care and teaching safely.

Take Transcript 1. This is an excerpt from an interaction featuring a registrar (who had been in specialist training for about ten years) working under the supervision of a consultant surgeon. They had worked together for six months. Looking back on the episode, the consultant told us that he knew this trainee well and that he therefore felt comfortable handing the scalpel to him. In the episode they perform a keyhole operation, which means that they access the patient's abdomen through a number of keyhole incisions. They then insert a camera (a 'laparoscope') into the cavity, gaining a view which is magnified and projected on screens around them. Other instruments are then inserted to operate inside the patient's abdomen. In the focal episode, the trainee is dissecting an attachment to the abdominal wall. To achieve that, they need to identify 'planes' where they can separate tissue without damaging surrounding – and often vital – structures. For instance, the gonadal vessels and the ureters are delicate structures that run close to the colon and remain difficult to spot when dissecting the colon out. Surgeons therefore treat these structures as 'danger points' (Goffman 1961) which, if exposed to 'unskilled action', result in significant 'costs'. I selected the episode for close analysis as it is here that the trainer *orients to* a danger point (the trainer *warns* the trainee in the first line of Transcript 1), providing an opportunity to investigate how consultants see and deal with risks when they let their trainees operate.

In the focal episode the consultant holds the *camera*. He sets the frame, zooming in and out and changing the camera angle as and when he feels appropriate. The trainee is in control of the Harmonic, a laparoscopic scalpel that surgeons use to cut and coagulate tissue by burning it. Both direct their gaze at one of the screens that display what the camera captures. To make a cut the trainee grasps tissue, closes the instrument, and then presses a pedal to activate the electric circuit that runs through the grasper, so-called 'diathermy'. In Transcript 1 these actions

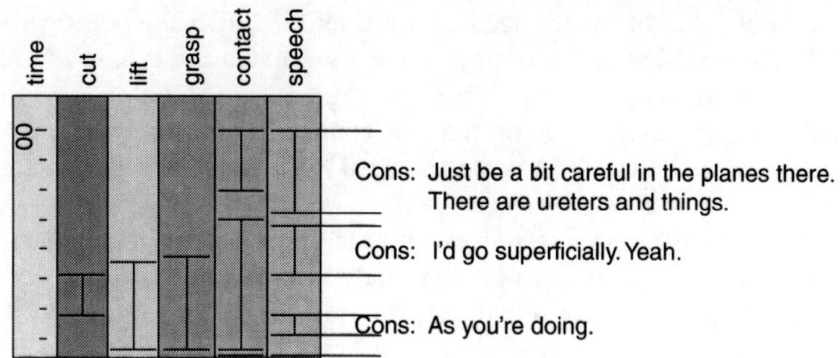

Figure 11.1 Transcript of interaction between supervising consultant and operating registrar

are marked on (vertical) time lines alongside the spoken utterances produced by the trainer. Every second is marked with a short hairline. The first vertical line marks the moments that the trainee keeps the scalpel in contact with tissue; the second line the moments that he lifts tissue up; the third line the moments that he grasps tissue; and the fourth line the moments that he actually cuts tissue (Figure 11.1).

The transcript helps us deconstruct – 'dissect' – what happens in this strip of interaction. As the trainee makes the first contact in this episode, the trainer tells the trainee to 'just be a bit careful with the planes there'. The trainee then withdraws the instrument from the tissue he was touching and the trainer explains why he wants the trainee to be 'careful' in the area he was in: 'there are the ureter and things'. The prompt change in the trainee's course of action suggests that the trainee is responding to what the trainer says, perhaps taking his comment as an indication that he had better find a different, 'safer' plane. Note that the trainer's 'there' in the first two utterances refers to a broad area, including but not specifically pointing to where the trainee had placed the scalpel.

In the next four seconds or so the trainee makes the first cut. As the trainee is approaching a different plane the trainer tells him to 'go superficially'. Staying superficial is a way to avoid getting in contact with structures such as the ureter, which are hidden further into the body. The latter part of the utterance overlaps with a grasping and a lifting action by the trainee. Then, just after the trainer has said (a very short) 'yeah', the trainee starts cauterising. As the trainer's 'yeah' is preceded by a lifting and grasping action and followed by a cauterising action we suggest that the trainer has interpreted the lift and the grasp as an indication of the trainee's commitment to cut at the point where he is grasping; and that the trainee has interpreted the trainer's 'yeah' as a ratification to cauterise. After the cauterising the trainer says, 'as you're doing', acknowledging that the trainee has indeed gone 'superficially', as he had suggested. As the tissue that is cauterised separates, the trainee withdraws the instrument.

We used this form of analysis of teaching episodes to make two points. First, we proposed that the analysis shows how patient safety is actually achieved. We noted that the trainee's actions signify to the trainer a trajectory of actions. This is an important resource for achieving surgical care in a learning environment where the trainee holds the scalpel: trainers can read and anticipate, and trainees can signal what they are up to. We also explored the potentials and limitations of using speech to give instructions. We saw what the effects were of the trainer's spoken utterances: they prompted the trainee to withdraw his instrument, start a new contact, or proceed to cut. In other words, speech is an important resource for achieving surgical care in learning environments, allowing the trainer to prompt the trainee to *act* or to *cease to act*. We also rendered visible some of the challenges in using speech. Surgeons do not have names for everything they see inside a body, so you'll often hear them saying something like, 'that stuff there', for instance, when directing a trainee *where* to act. At these moments *pointing* is an essential semiotic resource, yet supervising surgeons often do not have a spare hand to point with at these moments as they hold the camera in one hand and provide traction with the other (Bezemer et al., 2014). This challenge could be addressed, for instance, by introducing head mounted laser pointers.

Another point we were able to make with this analysis was to do with the limitations of more common qualitative and quantitative medical research. For instance, we pointed out that the kinds of teaching strategies made *visible* by the transcript are not articulated in interviews and they would be difficult to note on-the-spot in structured observation sheets, yet they play a key role in safely training up the next generation of surgeons – and in training them how to support the training of others. We also drew attention to the way in which operations are reported. In research and assessment, surgeons often distinguish between 'doing' an operation, either independently or under supervision, and 'assisting in' an operation. Classifying participation in that way enables surgeons to calculate 'how many' cases of a procedure they 'have done' ('I've assisted in 100 and did 50'). Using examples such as the one above we highlighted that operating is always a *joint achievement*. Trainees do not simply 'do' the operation, nor are they merely passive 'recipients' of instruction: control over operations is distributed, and this distribution (the degree of guidance) varies significantly from moment to moment: some actions are performed by trainees without any visible or audible guidance, whereas others are strongly mediated by instructions. In a paper for the *World Journal of Surgery* (2012), we therefore concluded that the common classification of participation in operations is 'an oversimplification of a complex picture'.

That paper didn't get accepted in its original form. In the first version we didn't include any numbers; it focused entirely on a transcript. As noted in the previous section such a focus on a small excerpt was highly unusual for a surgical journal. The response from our reviewers was that we had an important message, but not the numbers to back it up. In the mean time, Alex had done additional fieldwork for her PhD, observing 122 operations (Cope 2013); and together we had audio- and video-recorded another 12 operations. Using these materials we were able to *sandwich the transcript between tables*. One table showed how many of the 122 operations Alex had classified as 'done' by trainees in her fieldnotes, and another table showed our classification of who 'did' which *phase* in the 12 video-recorded operations. Thus we looked at 'participation' at three levels: at the level of an operation, at the level of a stage within the operation, and at the level of situated interaction. That 'mixed method' approach ('coding' 122 operations, plus transcribing a small excerpt from one operation) proved successful: the next version of the paper was accepted.

Case study II: decision making

Another area of the research focused on decision making. Decision making has received ample attention in social studies of medicine. Much of that work explores how doctors discuss treatment options and reach decisions with the patient and other specialists. Other research in this area is on how doctors make decisions as they 'do' clinical work, such as performing a surgical procedure. While some research on decision making involves micro-analysis of interactions (see for instance Sarangi and Roberts 1999) the work on *intra-operative* decision making is dominated by psychological research. These studies describe decision making as an important cognitive skill that enables surgeons to consider and choose between multiple courses of action in situations of uncertainty and high time pressure. They draw on observations, think aloud sessions and retrospective interviews (Fioratu et al. 2011). Each of these sources has limitations. Think aloud sessions and interviews only capture decisions that the surgeon is aware of and able to articulate verbally. The observational studies (which usually do not involve video-recordings) only capture decisions that the observing researcher notices on the spot.

That provides a strong rationale for a linguistic ethnographic contribution to research on decision making during operations. First, decision making is recognised by the medical world, including surgeons, and connects with current debates about transparency and 'speaking up' in clinical teams when important decisions are being made (see for example Reid & Bromiley 2012). Second, we had relevant data: *video-recordings* of laparoscopic operations, which we can play back alongside the audio to produce a detailed picture of how the operation unfolded. Third, we render decision making *visible* and *audible* in interactions between surgeons, moving beyond the notion that decision making is lodged inside a single surgeon's mind.

Consider the next example, taken from another keyhole operation: a gall bladder removal operation. A registrar (Registrar 1) is operating, assisted by another registrar (Registrar 2). Alex (Registrar 3) and I are observing. Transcript 1 details a small strip of interaction from about 5 minutes into the operation (Figure 11.2).

Using a special type of grasper the operating registrar separates tissue, rendering anatomical structures visible. He then says, 'there you go'. The assistant responds to this by saying, 'nice'. The operating surgeon then sweeps his closed instrument up and down the structure he has

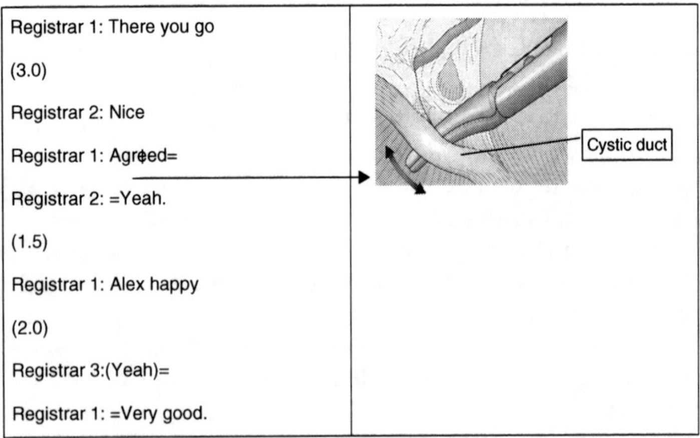

Figure 11.2 Transcript of interaction between operating (1), assisting (2) and observing (3) registrars

just freed up, while asking, 'Agreed?' The assistant responds affirmatively. He then asks Alex if she's happy, Alex responds that she is, and he then closes the exchange by saying, 'very good'.

So what is being decided here, and how? We might say that the operating registrar's 'agreed' and 'happy' serve as *proposals*, which are accepted by the assistant and by Alex. However, it is not clear from the spoken interaction *what* they agree on. For that we need to look more closely at the unfolding anatomy and the actions they perform. What they are looking at here is the cystic duct, which they need to clip and cut before they can remove the gall bladder. When the operating registrar says, 'agreed' he makes a sweeping movement alongside this duct. To them, this gesture and question marks a decision point in the operation that surgical textbooks also highlight: the decision whether or not to proceed with the clipping and cutting of the duct. The textbooks insist that surgeons need to obtain a 'critical view' of the anatomy. They need to have freed up the cystic duct from surrounding tissue, such as fat, in order to ascertain that it is indeed the cystic duct, and not the main, 'common bile' duct from which it branches off. Accidentally taking down the common bile duct would lead to serious complications, which would only become manifest when the patient is already out of the operating room. In light of that, the operating registrar's question – 'agreed' – signifies that he is proposing to proceed to clip and cut the structure that he is drawing attention to with the sweeping gesture. Indeed, immediately after this exchange he cuts this structure.

This analysis can feed directly into questions about surgical care. We rendered something visible which some audiences may see as illustrations of 'good practice', suggesting, for instance, that surgeons should always seek agreement from other surgeons co-present prior to making important decisions such as this one. We were keen to look at a *collection* of examples of the same decision point from a number of different operations. Looking across 12 gall bladder removal operations we were able to notice, for instance, that only on some occasions did the operating surgeon make a *verbal* proposal to cut prior to cutting the cystic duct. Yet on all occasions they made a *gesture* with their instrument to exhibit that the structures are 'clean' and sufficiently freed up prior to cutting. We also noticed that only registrars got involved in this decision making: house officers never reply to a question such as, 'Agreed?'.

The case studies illustrate one version of linguistic ethnography. Using video-recordings I explored, not only the role of language, but also the role of gesture, gaze and body posture in operating theatres. Through *micro-analysis* of social action in all these modes I was able to address a range of different 'issues' in surgery, including surgical training and decision making. Approached in that way linguistic ethnography can be used to shed light on what happens in any site, even on activity which is not always organised around spoken interaction, such as operations. Exploring language and communication *ethnographically* meant that I also looked beyond my video-recordings. For instance, the first case study was informed by explorations of how operations are recorded by the surgical community themselves, for example in the portfolios of surgical trainees. The analysis in the second case study is informed by explorations of how the surgical procedure in focus is presented in surgical textbooks. These documents provided useful insights into wider institutional and professional discourses, respectively, which I linked to the micro-analysis of small excerpts of video-recorded interaction. This form of *trans-contextual* analysis is one the distinctive features of an ethnographic approach to language and communication.

The case studies also illustrate how I produced linguistic ethnographic accounts that resonate with the concerns of surgeons. My strategies for achieving that can be summarised as follows: (1) translating linguistic-ethnographic perspectives into pertinent questions (for example, 'How do surgeons mark the decision to proceed to perform a highly conse-quential action in their interaction?'); (2) problematising and comple-menting categories circulating in the surgical community by showing how interaction unfolds in situ (for example showing that 'doing' an operation can refer to many different degrees of control by operating and assisting surgeons); (3) combining detailed analysis of data excerpts with coding of larger samples; (4) building up categorical collections of interactional data (for example looking at a decision point across mul-tiple cases of the same procedure). These strategies were helpful ways to bridge my theoretical and methodological stance with that of the majority of the surgical community.

As I was making an effort to reach out to the wider surgical com-munity I again benefited greatly from the partnership. As co-authors of most papers my partners helped mediate the linguistic ethnographic perspective through detailed track changes and comments such as, 'sur-geons won't understand this'. Having published extensively in medical journals they were much more familiar with the standard formats of these journals, such as its background-aims-methods-results-conclusion structure, and the expected writing style (for instance, concise and with no active constructions). To make a 'real' impact the analysis needs to be pushed further still, leading to actual proposals for change. At the time of writing we have not reached that point, but we are getting close.

Closing remarks: Learning through participation and partnerships

Ethnographers are committed to understanding the life worlds, concerns, rationalities, and perspectives of the people they study. They get at these understandings through participation, however peripherally, in their everyday practices. Some ethnographers are already familiar with the environments they enter as a researcher (for instance, a former teacher may turn to ethnography, in studying classroom activities). Yet other ethnographers focus on communities or practices that they have never been exposed to before. That applies to the work discussed in this chapter. I had never seen an operating theatre before, so I had a lot to learn: How, where and when to stand, for instance, or how to wear a surgical hat; when to speak and when to remain quiet; what the tallies on the whiteboard mean; who is who; what a liver looks like, how organs are taken out, and so on. Much of that *learning* was through observation and some 'explicit teaching' by my research partners, much like medical students who enter the operating theatre for the first time.

Some ethnographers go one step further: they also learn by 'doing' the work that they're studying, much like the apprentices described by Lave and Wenger (1991). For instance, Charles Briggs (2010) learnt some of the crafts of the people he studied by doing it himself, under the watchful eye of the expert. Yet for each practice one studies there is a boundary, a cap on how far the participation can go. These boundaries may be shaped by practical considerations – Charles must have run out of time to practise before becoming an 'expert' himself – as well as ethical considerations. In my case, the limits of participation were based on patient safety. Through my partnerships I had peripheral access to surgery, yet I could not increase my participation beyond that point and experience what it is like to operate on a patient, or to hand instruments to a surgeon, or even to hold a retractor. This is a common limitation for ethnographers of work. Perhaps more so now than in the past as contemporary ethical codes of conduct and legal frameworks for doing research demand careful consideration of possible harm to anyone involved, both researcher and research participants. Indeed, in the current climate, the participatory observation of Bosk (1979), who occasionally scrubbed in and held retractors, would be difficult to replicate.

That makes partnerships a *timely* arrangement. By attaching oneself to a committed member of the community one studies who is also co-researcher (and therefore benefits from the institutional rewards for that role) one can get closer to the 'life world' or 'lived experiences' of that community than solely on the basis of 'visiting' a research site, interviewing 'research participants' and studying fieldnotes and video-recordings in isolation. In a way, the partners can compensate for the limits on fuller participation, which is depriving the ethnographer of an embodied experience of what it is like to do what is central to the community one is interested in.

There are limitations to the partnership. We must not idealise research partners as 'native speakers' of a universal language of practice, whom we can consult to check what an action means and whether it is 'grammatical' or not. Surgical ways of doing come in many 'accents' and change rapidly as a result of technological change. Surgeons working in London have trained around the world, and bring in a range of different culturally and socially shaped 'accents'. There is another risk attached to partnerships: it may take away an incentive to talk to other members of the community. Yet in research partnerships 'infidelity' ought to be encouraged; it is only beneficial to a linguistic ethnographic analysis to collect as many perspectives on one's data as possible.

The case studies that I have discussed show how linguistic ethnography can make a distinct contribution to pertinent questions that are at the heart of public debate (see also Iedema 2009; Vincent 2009). My efforts to make such a contribution were strongly influenced by and dependent on a partnership with two surgeons throughout all stages of the research, from data collection to writing up linguistic ethnographic accounts for medical journals. My experience suggests that partnerships enable linguistic ethnographers to gain peripheral access to, and produce accounts of, a practice that they were entirely unfamiliar with prior to studying it. These accounts can resonate with the community under study and potentially have impact. It is well worth replicating this model of collaboration to access the world of health care professionals and other practitioners and to join more public and professional debates from which linguistic ethnographers are currently absent.

Acknowledgements

The writing of this chapter was supported by the Economic and Social Research Council through MODE, a node of the National Centre for Research Methods (2011–2014, RES-576-25-0027). The research it draws on is funded by the Economic and Social Research Council (RES-576-25-0027 and RES-062-23-3219), the London Deanery (Simulation and Technology-Enhanced Learning Initiative), and the Royal College of Surgeons of England (Alex's fellowship). Needless to say that I am deeply grateful to Alex Cope and Roger Kneebone for our fruitful partnerships. I would also like to thank the editors of this volume for their helpful comments on earlier versions of the chapter

References

Bezemer, Jeff (2014). Gesture in operations. In C. Jewitt (ed.) *Handbook of Multimodal Analysis* (second edition). London: Routledge (pp. 352–362).

Bezemer, Jeff, Alexandra Cope, Omar Faiz and Roger Kneebone (2012). Participation of surgical residents in operations: challenging a common classification. *World Journal of Surgery* 36, 9, 2011–2014.

Bezemer, Jeff, Ged Murtagh, Alexandra Cope, Gunther Kress and Roger Kneebone (2011a). 'Scissors, Please' The Practical Accomplishment of Surgical Work in the Operating Theatre. *Symbolic Interaction* 34, 3, 398–414.

Bezemer, Jeff, Alexandra Cope, Gunther Kress and Roger Kneebone (2011b). 'Do You Have Another Johan?' Negotiating Meaning in the Operating Theatre. *Applied Linguistics Review* 2, 313–334.

Bezemer, Jeff, Alexandra Cope, Gunther Kress and Roger Kneebone (2014). Holding the Scalpel: Achieving Surgical Care in a Learning Environment. *Journal of Contemporary Ethnography* 43, 1, 38–63.

Bosk, Charles (1979). *Forgive and Remember: Managing Medical Failure*. Chicago: The University of Chicago Press.

Briggs, Charles (2010). The Research Interview and the communicability of daily life. Keynote at the *Explorations in Ethnography, Language and Communication* conference, Aston University, 24 September 2010.

Burawoy, Michael (2009). *The Extended Case Method: Four Countries, Four Decades, Four Great Transformations, and One Theoretical Tradition*. University of California Press.

Cope, Alexandra (2013). *The Pedagogy of the Operating Theatre*. Unpublished PhD thesis, Imperial College London.

Ericsson, K. Anders (2004). Deliberate practice and the acquisition and maintenance of expert performance in medicine and related domains. *Academic Medicine* 79, 10: s70–s81.

Goffman, Erving (1961). *Asylums: Essays on the Social Situation of Mental Patients and Other Inmates*. New York: Anchor Books.

Goffman, Erving (1981). *Forms of Talk*. Philadelphia: University of Pennsylvania Press.

Goffman, Erving (1983). The Interaction Order. *American Sociological Review* 48, 1, 1–17.

Iedema, Rick (2009). New approaches to researching patient safety. *Social Science & Medicine* 69, 1701–1704.

Mondada, Lorenza (2011). The Organisation of Concurrent Courses of Action Surgical Demonstrations. In Jürgen Streeck, Charles Goodwin and Curtis LeBaron (eds) *Embodied Interaction: Language and Body in the Material World*. Cambridge: Cambridge University Press.

Moore, Alison, David Butt, Jodie Ellis-Clarke, and John Cartmill (2010). Linguistic Analysis of Verbal and Non-verbal Communication in the Operating Room. *ANZ Journal of Surgery* 80, 12, 925–929.

Lave, Jean, and Etienne Wenger (1991). *Situated Learning: Legitimate Peripheral Participation*. Cambridge: Cambridge University Press.

Reid, J. and M. Bromiley (2012). Clinical Human Factors: The Need to Speak up to Improve Patient Safety. *Nursing Standard* 26, 35, 35–40.

Sarangi, Srikant and Celia Roberts (1999). *Talk, Work and Institutional Order Discourse in Medical, Mediation and Management Settings*. Berlin: Mouton de Gruyter.

Vincent, Charles (2009). Social Scientists and Patient Safety: Critics or Contributors? *Social Science & Medicine* 69, 1777–1779.

Weldon, Sharon-Marie, Terhi Korkiakangas, Jeff Bezemer and Roger Kneebone (2013). Communication in the Operating Theatre: A Systematic Review of Observational Research. *British Journal of Surgery* 100, 1677–1688.

12

Linguistic Ethnographic Perspectives on Working-class Children's Speech: Challenging Discourses of Deficit

Julia Snell

Introduction

In February 2013 it was widely reported in national newspapers that the head teacher of a primary school in Teesside, north-east England, had banned the use of spoken Teesside dialect forms in the classroom and written to her pupils' parents to ask that they do the same at home (e.g. Furness 2013; Williams 2013). The stated reason for this move was the need to give the working-class pupils involved the best possible chance of educational (and later career) success, which for this head teacher meant eradicating eleven 'incorrect' words, phrases and pronunciations from the children's speech (represented in Figure 12.1). This story was of particular interest to me because I happen to be a native of Teesside – one who uses all eleven of these 'problem' features – and I have also conducted research on children's language in this area. As such, I was especially infuriated by the inaccuracies and flawed assumptions evident in this head teacher's letter to parents (and the media reporting of it) and troubled by the potential damage these might cause to young working-class children. I responded publicly in an article published in *The Independent* (Snell 2013a), but it was of course impossible to do justice to the issue in the less than 600 words afforded to me. In this chapter I pick up on some of the points addressed in this article, as well as the issues and questions that were raised in the debate surrounding it.

The Teesside story is by no means unique. Similar reports have emerged based on the actions of schools elsewhere in the UK, including Essex, Sheffield, the Black Country, and London (where ethnicity and related prejudices enter the fray). Indeed, the issue of dialect prejudice in education has a long history, both in the UK and elsewhere. Sociolinguists have been fighting this kind of prejudice since the 1960s;

<table>
<tr><td colspan="2">If you hear your child saying the following phrases or words in the left hand column please correct to the phrase or word in the right hand column. I'm sure if we tackle this problem together we will make progress.</td></tr>
<tr><td>Incorrect</td><td>Correct</td></tr>
<tr><td>I done that</td><td>This should be, I have done that or I did that</td></tr>
<tr><td>I seen that</td><td>This should be, I have seen that or I saw that</td></tr>
<tr><td>Yous</td><td>The word you is NEVER plural e.g. we should say, "You lot come here!"</td></tr>
<tr><td>Dropping the 'th'</td><td>"School finishes at free fifteen," should be, "School finishes at three fifteen."</td></tr>
<tr><td>Gizit ere</td><td>Please give me it</td></tr>
<tr><td>I Dunno</td><td>This should be. I don't know</td></tr>
<tr><td>It's nowt</td><td>This should be, it's nothing</td></tr>
<tr><td>Letta, butta etc</td><td>Letter, butter, etc</td></tr>
<tr><td>Your</td><td>Your late should be, you're late (You're is the shortened version of you are)</td></tr>
<tr><td>Werk, shert etc</td><td>I will wear my shirt for work</td></tr>
<tr><td>He was sat there</td><td>He was sitting there</td></tr>
</table>

Figure 12.1   Letter sent to parents of pupils at Sacred Heart Primary School in Teesside. (The original letter can be seen in Williams 2013).

yet negative and uninformed views remain. In this chapter I consider what a linguistic ethnographic approach might be able to add to the long tradition of sociolinguistic work in this area. This approach aims (1) to understand the meanings children invest in their use of local dialect forms, and (2) to highlight the social and ideological embedding of teachers' responses to it.

Traditional sociolinguistic responses to dialect prejudice

Sociolinguists believe that negative attitudes towards non-standard speech reflect social rather than linguistic value judgements (Trudgill 1975: 28). Beginning in the 1960s, they sought to counter these 'subjective' value judgements with 'objective' linguistic facts. This was the approach taken by William Labov in his defence of Black English Vernacular in the US. In 'The Logic of Nonstandard English' (1969) he addressed misunderstandings about the relationship between concept formation on the one hand, and dialect differences on the other, in order to challenge those who argued that the language of Black children lacked the means necessary for logical thought. In the UK, Peter Trudgill (1975) responded to concerns about the use of regional dialects in the classroom by writing a book on dialect variation for teachers. The book aimed to bring linguistic concepts and research to bear on educational issues related to language, and in particular to help teachers understand the grammatical structure of regional varieties of British English.

Labov and Trudgill were seminal figures in the emergence of a sub-field of sociolinguistics that has come to be known as variationist socio-linguistics. Variationist sociolinguists focus on variation in dialects and examine how this variation is structured. They have shown that linguistic difference has regularity and can be explained. Scholars in this field have been central figures in the fight against dialect prejudice. Speaking from a position of 'scholarly and scientific detachment' (Labov 1982: 166), variationist sociolinguists have been able to show that the grammar of non-standard dialects is not wrong, lazy or inferior; it is simply *different* to 'Standard English' and should therefore be respected. Some of these researchers have worked directly with teachers and teacher trainers and have designed curriculum materials on language variation for use in the classroom (see Cheshire 2005 for a review).

The argument that the grammar of regional dialects is simply different from (but equal to) Standard English can be applied to the letter written by the head teacher of Sacred Heart Primary. For example, the letter warns against the use of 'yous' because 'you is NEVER plural'. This information is misleading. In Standard English 'you' is the pronominal form used for both second person singular *and* plural. In fact, historically 'you' was the plural form while 'thou' was singular. Many languages still differentiate between second person singular and plural address (e.g. 'tu' and 'vous' in French). Standard English no longer makes this distinction, but many other dialects of the UK (e.g. Glasgow, Liverpool, and Newcastle), as well as Irish English, use 'yous' to fill the gap (Hickey 2003). US English has also developed similar strategies, using forms such as 'y'all' (Crystal 2004: 449) and 'yinz' (Johnstone et al., 2006). It would appear, then, that 'yous' is part of a wider global tendency to innovate within the pronominal system. It allows speakers to disambiguate between singular and plural address in spoken interaction, and is therefore a useful addition to the grammar of the local dialect.

I made this point (amongst others) in the article I wrote for *The Independent*. While most readers were supportive, others raised objections. The following comment was posted to the online version of the article:

> This article is, to use the author's words, unhelpful and damaging, and is typical of an academic's view. So you are a native of Teesside and still use the 'problem' words and phrases? Well that's all well and good, but not everyone can be a lecturer at King's College. Teesside is amongst the most deprived areas in the UK and as such most of

the kids in school here today will find their lives defined by trying to get and hold onto jobs. You may find the words 'Gizit' and 'Yous' to be perfectly acceptable but few employers will agree with you. I can assure you that the historic use of 'you' as a plural of 'thou' will be utterly lost on the small business owner who just wants to find decent staff for the shop floor. I can only pray that the Carol Walkers [the head teacher of Sacred Heart Primary] of the world are given heed and that the Russell Group academics poke their heads into the real world from time to time.

(Tom Carney, comment posted to The Independent
website on 10th February 2013)

This comment highlights a valid point. Linguists may be able to prove objectively that stigmatised dialects of English, like Teesside English, are linguistically equal to other varieties (including 'Standard English'), but teachers, parents and pupils know very well that these varieties are not *socially* equal. As Bourdieu (1977: 652) pointed out some time ago, this means that '[a]rguments about the relative value of different languages [or language varieties] cannot be settled in linguistic terms'. While sociolinguists have long recognised this fact, we may have failed to account for it adequately within our responses to discourses of linguistic deficit. This has left us open to being accused of living in an 'ivory tower', unaffected by the 'real' world.

Tom Carney's comment also raises a second relevant point: if local dialect forms incur such heavy social sanctions, not just within schools but within the workplace too, why do speakers continue to use them? Addressing these related issues – (1) how we (as researchers) might more effectively challenge dialect prejudice, and (2) why non-standard varieties persist in the face of this prejudice – requires more than a descriptive linguistic analysis of standard versus non-standard grammar. In the rest of the chapter I aim to show how adopting a linguistic ethnographic perspective is helping me to address these issues, and further, how this has led to more general shifts in my research practices. In doing so, I draw upon an ethnographic study of language variation in two social class differentiated primary schools in Teesside. I begin in the next section with a brief account of this study.

Background to study

Between November 2005 and January 2007 I conducted ethnographic fieldwork in two Teesside primary schools. These schools were chosen deliberately to highlight a social contrast. Ironstone Primary was situated in a lower-working-class area of Teesside, and Murrayfield Primary in a lower-middle-class area (all names used in this chapter are pseudonyms). These class designations were based on 2001 Census statistics (taking into account factors such as housing and levels of employment) and government measures of deprivation. Since the pupils were living in the areas immediately surrounding their schools, the two groups of children were broadly classified as 'lower working class' and 'lower middle class'. Through ethnographic fieldwork I began to understand how these demographic differences translated into actual experience.

I made weekly visits to the Year 4 (aged 8 to 9 years) classroom in both schools and participated in school life as a classroom helper. I followed the same children into Year 5 (aged 9 to 10 years). Throughout, I spent time with the children in the playground, chatting and playing games. As a result, I was able to develop some knowledge of the children's personalities, interests and friendships, and engage with their activities both inside and outside of the classroom. As a native of Teesside, I spoke with a familiar dialect and shared knowledge of the local area. I was thus closer to the children and the community I was studying than a researcher originating from outside of the area might have been (at the time I was a 25 year-old PhD student staying with family in Teesside, and thus not quite as removed from the experiences of children in Teesside as Tom Carney's comment implies).

After seven months of making weekly visits to the two schools, I began recording the children using a radio-microphone. This method meant that the children could move around freely while being recorded, participating as normal in their daily school activities. I was not necessarily (in fact not usually) a participant in the recorded interactions. This method produced a rich repository of children's spontaneous speech. The quantitative and interactional analyses presented in this chapter are based on 50 hours of radio-microphone recordings (25 hours from each school), collected when ten pupils from each school wore the radio-microphone for half a day. These recordings were supported by the observations and fieldnotes I made throughout 15 months of ethnographic fieldwork.

In the early stages I viewed ethnography as a method of data collection, a way of obtaining naturally occurring speech, or what Labov (1972) termed the 'vernacular' (which is still considered to be the 'holy grail' of variationist sociolinguistic study). I gradually realised, however, that it had a much bigger role to play. The accumulated experiences gained from participating in school activities combined to form the 'ethnographically informed lens' (Maybin 2006: 13) through which I could begin to understand the children's linguistic practices, not from a position of 'scholarly and scientific detachment' (Labov 1982: 166), but from the position of participant observer closely involved in the focal communities. This shift forced me to reflect on my own role in the research process. While the primary aim of the study was to understand the linguistic practices of these two groups of children, a secondary aim was to use these understandings to challenge misconceptions about working-class children's speech. This aim arose from my own experiences of growing up in a working-class community in Teesside. I therefore had a personal investment in the research from the beginning, and this further intensified as I developed close relationships with the children involved. I was aware of the possibility that this could bias my analyses, and in particular that it might lead me to romanticise the speech of the working-class participants (cf. Bourdieu's [1991: 53] criticisms of Labov). I sought to mitigate these risks by subjecting the data to rigorous and accountable analytic procedures (as demonstrated below). At the same time, however, I was aware that my background and experiences helped me to tune in to the activities, concerns and values that were important to the children I was studying, and to sustain positive relationships with them over time. I did not, therefore, aim to 'exorcise my subjectivity' but to 'manage it – to preclude it from being unwittingly burdensome' (Peshkin 1988: 18).

Analysis: from variationist sociolinguistics to linguistic ethnography

When I began my analysis of the linguistic data I was situated quite firmly within the variationist sociolinguistic paradigm. In line with this approach, I identified linguistic variables and associated variants, and examined the social distribution of these variants across my data set. The linguistic variable is one of the most fundamental constructs in variationist sociolinguistics. Two or more forms are said to be variants of a linguistic variable if they have the same basic referential meaning and fulfil equivalent functions. One of the variables I investigated was the first person objective singular, which has two variants in Teesside: standard *me* and non-standard *us*. The non-standard variant is fifth in Sacred Heart's list of prohibited forms ('Gizit' is a condensed form of 'give us it'). The distribution of the two variants across the data set confirmed the familiar variationist finding (and lay perception) that working-class speakers use a greater frequency of non-standard variants than

Table 12.1   First person objective singular by school

	Ironstone		Murrayfield	
	N	**%**	**N**	**%**
Me	285	83.1%	300	96.2%
Us	58	16.9%	12	3.8%
	343		**312**	

their middle-class counterparts (Table 12.1). I was struck, however, by the fact that neither group of children used singular 'us' very frequently. Even in working-class Ironstone Primary it occurred in only 16.9% of all tokens of the objective singular. Upon further investigation I found a possible explanation for this low relative frequency: the non-standard variant, singular 'us', occurred only in imperative clauses, such as 'Give us my shoe back'. In order to proceed with the analysis, therefore, I had to revise my definition of the linguistic variable from 'first person objective singular' to 'imperative with first person singular pronoun object'.

Table 12.2 shows the frequency with which children in both schools used imperatives with 'me' versus imperatives with 'us'. The difference between the two schools appears more marked here, and the use of singular 'us' is shown to be a more significant feature of the children's speech, especially in Ironstone Primary. While more accurately defined, however, this new variable and accompanying analysis still does not give a complete picture. Imperatives (whether with 'me' or 'us') are just one form of directive (i.e. the speech act issued by speakers in order to attempt to get their addressee(s) to do something). Table 12.3 lists a selection of grammatical forms that are typically recognised as fulfilling a directive function (e.g. by Mitchell-Kernan and Kernan 1977; Gordon and Ervin-Tripp 1984). It shows the frequency with which children in both schools used these different types of directive, and thus allows us to situate their use of imperatives with singular 'us' relative to the broad range of other possibilities available to them. At this point we have to give up on the notion of the linguistic variable, however, because it is not possible to delimit the full range of potential options; and as we shall see, it is debatable to what extent the different options can be said to 'mean' the same thing.

The high incidence of imperatives across both schools is in line with other studies of children's directives (e.g. Mitchell-Kernan and Kernan 1977). Imperatives function as commands. They imply the speaker's

Table 12.2 Imperatives with first person pronoun objects: comparison across schools

	Ironstone		Murrayfield	
	N	%	N	%
Imperatives with 'me' e.g. 'Pass me it'	38	39.6%	26	76.5%
Imperatives with 'us' e.g. 'Give us my shoe back'	58	60.4%	8*	23.5%
	96		34	

Note: *This figure does not agree with Table 2, which shows 12 instances of singular 'us' in the Murrayfield Primary data. This is because 4 examples of singular 'us' occurred in direct repetitions within a single utterance (i.e. the same directive was repeated 4 times, with no variation, one after the other). Immediate repetitions like this were counted as just one token within my analysis of directives.

Table 12.3 Children's directives: a comparison across schools

	Ironstone		Murrayfield	
	N	%	N	%
Imperative with 1st person pronoun object – 'me' e.g. *Pass me it*	38	5.0%	26	3.3%
Imperative with 1st person pronoun object – 'us' e.g. *Give us my shoe back*	58	7.6%	8	1.0%
Other imperatives e.g. *Get off my shoe*	448	58.5%	447	57.2%
'Howay' *	41	5.4%	7	0.9%
1st person modal interrogatives e.g. *Can I have your pencil?*	55	7.2%	134	17.2%
2nd person modal interrogatives e.g. *Will you pass me my plan?*	30	3.9%	51	6.5%
3rd person modal interrogatives e.g. *Miss, can he have it?*	5	0.7%	3	0.4%
1st person expression of obligation e.g. *We have to go*	6	0.8%	4	0.5%
2nd person expression of obligation e.g. *You have to sit somewhere else*	28	3.7%	29	3.7%
1st person expression of need/want e.g. *Miss we need some felt tips*	42	5.5%	42	5.4%
2nd person expression of need/want e.g. *You need to write it in your book*	10	1.3%	18	2.3%
3rd person expression of need/want e.g. *Miss, Harry wants you*	5	0.7%	12	1.5%
TOTAL	766	100%	781	100%

Note: *Dialect feature specific to the north-east of England, which means something like 'come on'.

belief that their addressee will perform the action, and do not allow that the addressee has any choice in the matter (Leech 1983: 109). In routine and cooperative activities among peers (like the kind of activities children typically participate in at school), this type of speech act is frequent and unremarkable. In other situations it has been pointed out that the use of commands may be considered 'face-threating' for the addressee, and thus risky for the speaker (Brown and Levinson 1987: 191). Other strategies are less direct (and thus less risky). For example, modal interrogatives are less direct because they frame the directive as a question (e.g. 'Can you pass me that book?'). This kind of 'conventionalized indirectness' (Brown and Levinson 1987: 70) is considered polite in English. Children in both schools used this strategy, especially with adults, but it was more frequent at Murrayfield Primary (Table 12.3).

The quantitative analysis represented in Table 12.3 demonstrates that both groups of children have an extended *repertoire* of directive forms, some considered 'standard', and others (like imperatives with singular 'us') considered 'non-standard'. The term 'repertoire' has circulated within sociolinguistics for several decades, being used to refer to the set of communicative resources that a speaker commands, together with knowledge of how to use those resources (see e.g. Gumperz 1986: 20–21; Hymes 1996: 33). Resources within a speaker's repertoire are associated not just with referential meaning, but also with non-referential or 'indexical' meanings and social values:

> The resources that enter into a repertoire are indexical resources, language materials that enable us to produce more than just linguistic meaning but to produce images of ourself, pointing interlocutors towards the frames in which we want our meanings to be put.
>
> (Blommaert and Backus 2012: 26)

The concept of indexical meaning can be traced back to the work of the American philosopher Charles Sanders Peirce, where it was used to refer to signs whose meaning is context-dependent (e.g. deictics such as 'this', 'that', 'here' and 'now'); but more recently the term has been used in linguistic anthropology and sociolinguistics to describe the processes through which linguistic forms acquire social (rather than referential) meaning. If a linguistic form (unit of grammar or discourse, word, phrase, pronunciation) regularly co-occurs with a particular attitude, way of dressing, social identity or activity, it may take on the meanings associated with these social phenomena and come to 'index' (i.e. evoke) these meanings in other contexts. For example, the use of the glottal stop for 't' in the middle and end of words in English is associated with urban working-class speech. Because of this, some UK politicians have adopted the glottal stop when making speeches in order to index meanings like 'informality' and 'lack of pretention', and to try to appear to be just like 'ordinary working people' (a phrase they often use). As this illustration indicates, a linguistic form does not have just one precise or fixed indexical meaning, but rather a range of related meanings, an 'indexical field' in Eckert's (2008: 454) terms. The particular meaning that is activated in a particular context of use will depend, amongst other things, on the perspective of the hearer and the other semiotic resources at play (Eckert 2008: 466). For example, if when talking to a group of factory workers a politician uses the glottal stop together with other linguistic features more characteristic of upper-middle class speech, while wearing an expensive suit, he or she may end up constructing an overall style that indexes meanings like 'inauthenticity' and 'condescension'.

Building on this notion of indexicality, I wanted to understand the range of potential meanings singular 'us' had for the children in my study. This would help me to explain, first, why they chose to use this form on some occasions but not others, and second, why they chose to use it at all, given that it is stigmatised by wider society, and in some cases, explicitly prohibited by teachers. Other scholars have made tentative statements about the meaning of singular 'us', suggesting that it appears to be restricted to imperatives and may be used as a politeness device to soften the force of the request (e.g. Anderwald 2004: 178; Carter and McCarthy 2006: 382). While this explanation seems plausible – singular 'us' was restricted to imperatives in my data, occurring only as part of requests like 'Give us that book' – it is based on a rather static view of language in which the meaning of a linguistic form is seen to be fixed regardless of context of use. In line with Eckert (2008: 464), I proceeded instead on the assumption that '[p]articipation in discourse involves a continual interpretation of forms in context, an in-the-moment assigning of indexical values to linguistic forms' (Eckert 2008: 463). This meant extending my analysis beyond an exclusive focus on linguistic form and towards an analysis of language use in its full ethnographic context.

For each token of singular 'us' in the data set I went back to the original recording and transcribed in detail the interaction five minutes either side of the occurrence of singular 'us' (the remainder of the recordings had been transcribed very broadly i.e. without any detail on pauses, fillers, and hesitations or any paralinguistic information). I subjected each of these episodes to micro-ethnographic analysis. This involved listening repeatedly to the recording, moving through the interaction moment by moment, attending to how participants build up the interaction, and asking at each moment: What is happening here? How do we know? (Rampton 2006). I drew upon my fieldnotes to provide contextual information and visual detail about the event (e.g. the areas within the classroom/playground that the children inhabited during the interaction, the props and other artefacts involved). I also relied upon my fieldnotes for more general information about the changing status of the children's peer-relationships, their attitudes to school and to each other, their behaviour in and out of the classroom, and any other ethnographic detail that might prove consequential to my analyses. I used the transcripts as a workspace to record all of these observations and to work through competing interpretations of participants' utterances, focusing in particular on their use of local dialect forms. Methodologically, this involved a shift away from variationist sociolinguistics to linguistic ethnography. While scholars working within the variationist tradition have certainly used ethnographic methods to inform their analyses of sociolinguistic variation (e.g. Labov 1963; Cheshire 1982; Milroy 1987; Eckert 2000; Mendoza-Denton 2008; Moore 2010) – and in doing so have contributed to theory and method in linguistic ethnography (e.g. Eckert's work on style has been particularly influential) – they have usually stopped short of analysing the use of linguistic variants in their discursive context (Coupland's early work [e.g. Coupland 1988] was an important exception; see also Kiesling 2009; Moore and Podesva 2009).

Micro-ethnographic analyses of all 66 examples of singular 'us' in the data set indicated that this form did not have a fixed meaning, but rather an indexical field comprising a constellation of meanings related broadly to issues of inclusion versus exclusion (such as in-group versus out-group, shared participation versus peripherality). By way of illustration, I share below my analysis of one episode involving the use of singular 'us'. I have selected this particular episode because it includes repeated occurrences of imperatives with singular 'us', and because Clare (who is wearing the radio-microphone) was the most prolific user of this form (22 of the 66 occurrences in the data set can be clearly attributed to Clare).

The interaction in Extract 1 took place during the lunch break at Ironstone Primary on 3rd November 2006 (see also Snell 2013b). Clare approaches a group of girls who are playing a game that involves stealing each other's shoes. She wants to join in with the fun, but the girls then steal Clare's shoe.

Extract 1: Clare's missing shoe

```
1    Jane:        ((chanting)) we got a boot
2                 we got a boot
3                 we got a boot
4                 we got a boot
5    Clare:       she's got my shoe ((laughs while saying 'shoe'))
6    Anon:        Clare's shoe
7                 Clare's shoe
8    Inaudible:   ((Background noise - 3 seconds))
9    Danielle:    kinky boots
10               kinky boots
11   Anon:        pass us it
12   Anon:        Clare's shoe
13               get off Gemma (xxxxx)
14   Inaudible:   ((Background noise - 3 seconds))
15   Clare:       give us it
16   Anon:        Clare's shoe ((chanting))
17               Clare's shoe
18               [Clare's shoe
19   Anon:        [(pass us it)
20               (3)
21   Clare:       give us i::t ((hyperarticulated /t/ release))
22   Anon:        (I know I haven't got it)
23   Clare:       ROSIE
24               (2)
25               Rosie give us i:t
26               ((Background noise - 12 seconds))
27   Anon:        get Clare's [feet
28   Clare:                   [Give us back my shoe
29   Jane:        get Clare's feet
30               (2)
31   Anon:        get it get it
32   Joanne:      Danielle Danielle
33               get it ((laughing))
34   Anon:        we've got one
35   Anon:        alright you may as well give (us) the other one
36   Gemma:       can I get that one?
37   Jane:        yeah lay down on the floor
38   Gemma:       yeah lay down (Clare xxxxxx)
```

39	Julia:	(what's going on)
40	Tina:	because Clare's got one shoe on
41		*((Background noise and sound of children running – 17 seconds))*
42	Clare:	he::lp
43		*((Sound of Clare running and making strained noises, perhaps grabbing for the shoe – 12 seconds))*
44	Clare:	**give us my shoe back** *((said with resignation))*
45	Tina:	she hasn't got her shoe (**xxxxxxxxxxxx**)
46		(she's a) lucky woman
47	Clare:	Jane you- *((breathing heavily))*
48		(3)
49		**give us my shoe back**
50		(1)
51		**give us my ba::ck**
52		(1)
53		**give us my shoe ba:ck**
54	Danielle:	Clare I've got <u>my</u> shoes off
		I'm not com[plaining
55	Clare:	[I KNOW but <u>my</u> feet are freezing
56	Danielle:	[so are mine
57	Jane:	[so are hers (.) she's got tights on
58	Clare:	I HAVE
59	Danielle:	no you haven't
60		(1)
61		so my are thinner than yours
62		have you seen mine compared to yours Clare
63		mine are thinner

Clare appears to find herself in a difficult situation in this episode: it is a wet November day and she has an exposed foot because one of her shoes has been stolen by some of the other girls. Clare's situation is not unique, however. I was in the playground during the game and know that several other girls had also had their shoes taken. I documented in my fieldnotes that, generally speaking, spirits were high and the girls seemed to be having fun. It is evident from the recording that Clare's initial response is also positive, even jovial: she laughs through her utterance on line 5. Ten seconds later, however, when Clare makes an attempt to get her shoe back (line 15) there's a change in footing

(Goffman 1981) to a more serious stance: this time there is no laughter and Clare's intonation is flat. It is not easy to decipher from the recording exactly what happened during this ten second period, but it seems that Clare's shoe was being passed around (see e.g. lines 11–13) amidst chanting (lines 6–7, 9–10), and that Clare was being positioned by her peers as a non-participant (in addition to the teasing implicit in the chanting, notice the use of the third person in lines 6, 7, 12, and then later in lines 16–18, 27, 29). We might reasonably assume that all of this was frustrating for Clare, and perhaps also that her foot had started to get cold (see her later comment on line 55). It appears, then, that by line 15 Clare is no longer a willing participant sharing in the fun. When she makes a second request to retrieve the shoe on line 21, the stress on 'give', the lengthened vowel in 'it' and the final hyperarticulated /t/ index her sense of building frustration (stop release has commonly been found to index exasperation and sometimes anger [Eckert 2008: 469]).

Clare wants to get her shoe back and has available to her several options for formulating a directive, ranging from the standard direct command 'Give me my shoe back' to the indirect modal interrogative 'Can I have my shoe back?'. Clare uses both of these forms (and other alternatives) elsewhere in the data (see Snell 2013b for further analysis). On this occasion she chooses an imperative with singular 'us'. As noted earlier, one explanation for her choice is that singular 'us' softens the command. This explanation seems less plausible, however, when ethnographic data is taken into account. In an interview, the class teacher told me, somewhat euphemistically, that Clare 'falls in and out of friends with people a lot' (Interview, 29th January 2007), and this was certainly my impression of her too. My fieldnotes are littered with references to Clare's arguments. Here are two examples:

Extract 2 (Fieldnotes, 20th October 2006):

When I got back into the class, Helen, Clare and Caroline came in with the lunch boxes ... Helen was saying that Mrs Monk was going to sack Joanne and Danielle from their role as librarians and Clare was defending them. Clare and Helen seem to enjoy arguing! They're very confrontational with each other.

Extract 3 (Fieldnotes, 12th January 2007):

The children had Mass first thing but I didn't go. I hung back in the classroom and had a chat with Mrs Trotter [the class Teaching

Assistant] – she always knows the school gossip! ... I discussed some of the children with Mrs Trotter ... She commented on the table of girls (Clare, Helen, Caroline and Rosie) and said that they're always arguing and bickering. Apparently, they play together outside of school and are always falling out. I noted that I've seen Clare and Helen arguing a lot, and she said that Clare would find an argument in an empty room!

My overall impression of Clare, then, was of a confident, outgoing girl who regularly courted confrontation and was not overly concerned with protecting the feelings (or in pragmatic terms, the 'face wants' [Brown and Levinson 1987]) of her interlocutors. In the episode presented in Extract 1, she appears frustrated and thus perhaps even less likely to be concerned with politeness. What does seem important in this episode is that the other girls position Clare as outside of their group, a target rather than a participant in the fun. Clare's use of singular 'us' may, then, be an attempt to appeal to some sense of group support or solidarity in response to her exclusion. These indexical meanings may derive in part from the fact that this form is a salient feature of the local dialect (salient enough to have become part of Sacred Heart's list). In addition, the important role of plural pronouns more generally in negotiating relationships of solidarity and power has been well documented (e.g. Brown and Gilman 1960; Head 1978).

On this occasion, Clare's strategy does not work, because the other girls reject her appeal to group solidarity. On line 45, Tina points to another girl who has a missing shoe, and later Danielle emphasises 'I've got <u>my</u> shoes off. I'm not complaining' (line 54), with the stress on 'my' indicating contrast (i.e. Danielle also has bare feet, but unlike Clare, she isn't complaining). These girls seem to be pointing out that there are other children in the same position as Clare who are making less fuss, and thus Clare's appeal to group support is futile. The interaction in this episode tells a different story. Danielle might have a missing shoe, but she is clearly still part of the in-group, which makes her position different from Clare's. Friends like Joanne are keen to include Danielle in the fun (line 32), and allies like Jane give her support when necessary (line 57). Clare, on the other hand, remains firmly on the periphery of this group throughout the interaction.

In summary, the participants in my study used singular 'us' exclusively in imperative clauses in order to form commands or requests like 'Rosie, give us it' and 'Let us talk through that'. Detailed analyses (of the kind demonstrated above) indicated that singular 'us' was used when these commands/requests occurred amidst negotiations related to issues of inclusion versus exclusion (i.e. who's in and who's out?), though the precise meanings attached to singular 'us' depended on the specific context of use. In these situations the imperatives were not necessarily 'face-threatening' (in Brown and Levinson's terms), but they were different to the many other 'standard' imperatives that cropped up elsewhere in the data as part of routine tasks and shared activities. In other words, imperatives with singular 'us' were able to do social work that the 'standard' options did not allow (see also Snell 2010 for discussion of possessive 'me').

Discussion: use-value and exchange value

On page 228, I asked why children in Teesside persist in using non-standard forms like singular 'us' despite their teachers' protestations and wider social prejudice. One answer, based on the analysis presented in this chapter, is that they do so (at least in part) because these forms are interactionally very useful, indexing social meanings that are important to speakers. These forms have *use-value*, a particular worth to the speaker and to others in the community (Skeggs 2004). It is therefore unlikely that children will stop using such forms just because their teachers tell them to. This is why attempts to eradicate local dialect forms will not work, and rather than having the desired effect – to empower working-class children – they may have unintended negative consequences, damaging children's sense of self and discouraging their active participation in class discussion. We cannot simply dismiss such attempts as ill-informed, however, because use-value is only part of the picture. We must also account for *exchange value*, the more abstract value linguistic forms carry beyond local contexts of use.

The notion of exchange has long been fundamental to ways of understanding social and economic relations (Skeggs 2004: 10). For Bourdieu (1977, 1991), exchange involved different forms of capital, and this has been a useful way of thinking about the relationship between language and power. Standard English and prestige accents (such as Received Pronunciation) are dominant or 'legitimate' ways of speaking in UK society. In Bourdieu's terms they have 'symbolic capital' because of their association with the economic and cultural power of those who use them. Symbolic capital can be transformed into real life advantages. Speakers can 'cash in' (i.e. exchange) their prestigious language for formal educational qualifications and prestigious occupations, and thus for economic capital (Coupland 2007: 85). Teachers are aware of this fact. They recognise that non-standard forms such as 'Gizit' and 'yous' lack positive exchange value on the legitimate linguistic markets (education, public administration, national media, and so on), and thus they encourage children to replace these forms with more prestigious alternatives. Set against this background, negative responses to non-standard dialect at school appear reasonable, or at the very least, understandable. This is why there is some public support for the kind of action taken by schools like Sacred Heart (this support is clear in the online comment from Tom Carney cited above). But attempts to ban local dialect forms reduce everything to exchange value. They ignore the fact that 'Gizit' and 'yous' have value beyond the exchange relations of the legitimate linguistic markets. One way to challenge dialect prejudice, then, might be to share with educational practitioners evidence of the local use-value of non-standard dialect forms. Linguistic ethnographers have developed a number of models for working with non-academic professionals (see Rampton, Maybin and Roberts, this volume, pp. 37–44; there are also several specific case studies in this volume – see for example chapters by Bezemer and Lefstein & Israeli). One of these is the joint data session, where researchers and practitioners work together to analyse research data. In an educational context, this might involve sharing with teachers recordings of children's interactions (like that presented in Extract 1), thus giving them the opportunity to see working-class pupils' speech in new ways. Research data can be used to highlight the meanings and values attached to local dialect forms and to demonstrate that children are able to style-shift; that is, they can use 'standard' forms on some occasions and 'non-standard' forms on others.

Speech is always situated within specific contexts and interactions. What counts as 'standard' or 'acceptable' speech will change from one situation to the next, and over time, leaving considerable scope for variation (and disagreement) in any definition of 'spoken Standard English'. This is why I have argued elsewhere that rather than attempt to erase local dialect it is more appropriate to work on extending children's linguistic repertoires (Snell 2013b). This involves understanding and valuing children's use of local dialect forms (as described above), but at the same time, explaining that in some arenas (e.g. formal educational contexts and job interviews) these forms will be judged against 'standard' ways of speaking (valued as such solely through their association historically with powerful people in society) and may be stigmatised.

Conclusion

There is still a pressing need to respond to deficit accounts of working-class children's speech within educational contexts. In this chapter, I have considered what linguistic ethnography might be able to add to the strong tradition of sociolinguistic efforts to challenge dialect prejudice. In doing so, I have tracked my own trajectory away from a traditional approach to analysing language variation and towards a linguistic ethnographic approach. I should make clear, however, that in adopting a linguistic ethnographic perspective I am not arguing for a rejection of variationist sociolinguistics. As Rampton, Maybin and Roberts point out in Chapter 2 of this volume, 'paradigms don't have to be swallowed whole ... if one is careful and willing to separate findings and methods from the explanations and interpretations with which they are conventionally packaged'. For me this meant using quantitative analyses of language variation to uncover patterns in the data, without accepting the basic tenet of variationist sociolinguistics that 'standard' and 'non-standard' variants of a linguistic variable necessarily *mean* the same thing.

In my work on children's language in Teesside I have found the combination of quantitative variationist analyses and linguistic ethnographic micro-analyses very productive. In this chapter, quantitative analyses of the frequency with which the children used different directive forms made it possible to locate their use of singular 'us' relative to the range of other options available to them, and highlighted the breadth of their linguistic repertoires. Linguistic ethnographic micro-analyses of the children's situated practice highlighted the local use-value of singular 'us', and thus shed light on the motivations behind children's continued use of this form despite pressure from their teachers to conform instead to prestige standards. Adopting a linguistic ethnographic perspective also prompted me to expand my notion of context, embedding my analyses of the children's interactions within broader social, cultural and economic processes, thus acknowledging exchange value as well as local use-value.

Linguistic ethnography therefore contributes a new analysis to longstanding sociolinguistic efforts to challenge prejudice against non-standard dialects, one which may help teachers to better understand why non-standard forms persist and why attempts to ban them are unlikely to work; but the extent to which this analysis can have real impact in the high profile debate outlined in the introduction to this chapter is as yet unclear. Further research is required to consider how best to disseminate sociolinguistic knowledge outside of academia. We need to research the textual trajectories involved in these debates, especially in an era where online forums and social media give academics even less control over the meanings given to their words in the public domain (cf. Graddol and Swann 1988). Whose voice(s) succeed in carrying forward in debates on non-standard language? How, and in what form? These questions are part of the bigger picture of challenging dialect prejudice.

Appendix

Transcription notations include:

(text)	- Transcription uncertainty
(xxxxxxx)	- Indistinguishable speech
(.)	- Brief pause (less than one second)
(1)	- Longer pause (number indicates length to nearest whole second)
(( ))	- Description of prosody or non-verbal activity
[[	- Overlapping talk or action
<u>text</u>	- Emphasised relative to surrounding talk (underlined words)
te::xt	- Stretched sounds
sh-	- Word cut off
>text<	- Speech delivered more rapidly than surrounding speech.
(hhh)	- Audible out-breath

References

Anderwald, Lieselotte. 2004. The varieties of English spoken in the Southeast of England: morphology and syntax. In Bernd Kortmann, Kate Burridge, Rajend Mesthrie, Edgar W. Schneider and Clive Upton (eds) *A Handbook of Varieties of English Volume 2: Morphology and Syntax*. Berlin: Mouton de Gruyter, 175–195.

Blommaert, Jan and Ad Backus. 2012. Superdiverse repertoires and the individual. *Tilburg Papers in Cultural Studies*. 24.

Bourdieu, Pierre. 1977. The economics of linguistic exchanges. *Social Science Information* 16(6): 645–668.

Bourdieu, Pierre. 1991. *Language and Symbolic Power*. Cambridge: Polity Press.

Brown, Penelope and Stephen C. Levinson. 1987. *Politeness: Some Universals in Language Usage*. Cambridge: Cambridge University Press.

Brown, Roger and Albert Gilman. 1960. The pronouns of power and solidarity. In Thomas A. Sebeok (ed.) *Style in Language*. Cambridge, MA: MIT Press, 253–276.

Carter, Ronald and Michael McCarthy. 2006. *Cambridge Grammar of English*. Cambridge: Cambridge University Press.

Cheshire, Jenny. 1982. *Variation in an English Dialect*. Cambridge: Cambridge University Press.

Cheshire, Jenny. 2005. Sociolinguistics and mother-tongue education. In Ulrich Ammon, Norbert Dittmar, Klaus J. Mattheier and Peter Trudgill (eds) *Sociolinguistics: An Introductory Handbook of the Science of Language and Society*. Berlin: Mouton de Gruyter, 2341–2350.

Coupland, Nikolas. 1988. *Dialect in Use*. Cardiff: University of Wales Press.

Coupland, N. 2007. *Style: Language Variation and Identity*. Cambridge: Cambridge University Press.

Crystal, David. 2004. *The Stories of English*. London: Allen Lane.

Eckert, Penelope. 2000. *Linguistic Variation as Social Practice*. Cambridge: Cambridge University Press.

Eckert, Penelope. 2008. Variation and the indexical field. *Journal of Sociolinguistics* 12(4): 453–476.

Goffman, Erving. 1981. *Forms of Talk*. Philadelphia: University of Pennsylvania Press.

Gordon, David and Susan Ervin-Tripp. 1984. The structure of children's requests. In Richard L. Shiefelbusch and Joanne Pickar (eds) *The Acquisition of Communicative Competence*. Baltimore: University Park Press, 295–321.

Graddol, David and Joan Swann. 1988. Trapping linguists: an analysis of linguists' responses to John Honey's pamphlet 'The Language Trap'. *Language and Education* 2: 95–111.

Gumperz, John. 1986 [1972]. Introduction. In John Gumpertz and Dell Hymes (eds) *Directions in Sociolinguistics: The Ethnography of Communication*. London: Blackwell, 1–25.

Furness, Hannah. 2013. Middlesbrough primary school issues list of 'incorrect' words. *The Telegraph*, 5th February 2013. Available online at <www.telegraph. co.uk/education/primaryeducation/9851236/Middlesbrough-primary-school-issues-list-of-incorrect-words.html> [Accessed 21st November 2014]

Head, Brian F. 1978. Respect degrees in pronominal reference. In Joseph H. Greenberg (ed.) *Universals of Human Language*. Stanford: Stanford University Press, 151–211.

Hickey, R. 2003. Rectifying a standard deficiency: second person pronominal distinctions in varieties of English. In I. Taavitsainen and A. H. Jucker (eds) *Diachronic Perspectives on Address Term Systems*. Amsterdam: John Benjamins, 345–74.

Hymes, Dell. 1996. *Ethnography, linguistics, narrative inequality*. London: Taylor and Francis Ltd.

Johnstone, Barbara, Jennifer Andrus and Andrew E. Danielson. 2006. Mobility, indexicality, and the enregisterment of 'Pittsburghese'. *Journal of English Linguistics* 34: 77–102.

Kiesling, Scott. 2009. Style as stance: stance as the explanation for patterns of sociolinguistic variation. In Alexandra Jaffe (ed.) *Sociolinguistic Perspectives on Stance*. Oxford: Oxford University Press, 171–194.

Labov, William. 1963. The social motivation of a sound change. *Word* 19: 273–309.

Labov, William. 1969. The logic of non-standard English. *Georgetown Monograph on Languages and Linguistics* 22: 1–44.

Labov, William. 1972. Some principles of linguistic methodology. *Language in Society* 1: 97–120.

Labov, William. 1982. Objectivity and commitment in linguistic science: the case of the Black English trial in Ann Arbor. *Language in Society* 11: 165–201.

Leech, Geoffrey N. 1983. *Principles of Pragmatics*. London: Longman.

Maybin, Janet. 2006. *Children's Voices: Talk, Knowledge and Identity*. Basingstoke: Palgrave Macmillan.

Mendoza-Denton, Norma. 2008. *Homegirls: Language and Cultural Practice among Latina Youth Gangs*. Oxford: Blackwell.

Milroy, Lesley. 1987. (2nd edition). *Language and Social Networks*. Oxford: Basil Blackwell.

Mitchell-Kernan, Claudia and Keith T. Kernan. 1977. Pragmatics of directive choice among children. In Claudia Mitchell-Kernan and Susan Ervin-Tripp (eds) *Child Discourse*. New York: Academic Press, 189–208.

Moore, Emma. 2010. The interaction between social category and social practice: explaining *was/were* variation. *Language Variation and Change* 22: 347–371.

Moore, Emma and Robert J. Podesva. 2009. Style, indexicality, and the social meaning of tag questions. *Language in Society* 38(4): 447–485.

Ochs, E. 1992. Indexing gender. In A. Duranti and C. Goodwin (eds). *Rethinking Context: Language as an Interactive Phenomenon*. Cambridge: Cambridge University Press, 335–358.

Peshkin, Alan. 1988. In search of subjectivity – one's own. *Educational Researcher* 17: 17–21.

Rampton, Ben. 2006. *Language in Late Modernity: Interaction in an Urban School*. Cambridge: Cambridge University Press.

Silverstein, Michael. 2003. Indexical order and the dialectics of sociolinguistic life. *Language and Communication* 23: 193–229.

Skeggs, Beverley. 2004. *Class, Self, Culture*. London: Routledge.

Snell, Julia. 2010. From sociolinguistic variation to socially strategic stylisation. *Journal of Sociolinguistics* 14(5): 618–644.

Snell, Julia. 2013a. Saying no to 'gizit' is plain prejudice: a war on dialect will quash curiosity and ideas. *The Independent*, 10th February 2013. Available online at <www.independent.co.uk/voices/comment/saying-no-to-gizit-is-plain-prejudice-8488358.html> [Accessed 7th December 2013]

Snell, Julia. 2013b. Dialect, interaction and class positioning at school: from deficit to different to repertoire. *Language and Education* 27(2): 110–128.

Trudgill, Peter. 1975. *Accent, Dialect and the School*. London: Edward Arnold.

Williams, Olivia. 2013. Primary school tells parents to stop children using slang phrases as it is preventing them from learning 'standard' English. *The Daily Mail*, 5th February 2013. Available online at <www.dailymail.co.uk/news/article-2273821/Middlesbrough-parents-clamp-local-expressions-home-children-learn-standard-English.html#axzz2KWn3AVOG> [Accessed 21st November 2014]

13
Hip Hop, Education and Polycentricity

Lian Malai Madsen and Martha Sif Karrebæk

Introduction

Hip hop has been one of the most influential global forms of popular culture among youth during the past two decades (Bucholtz 2011), and it has received increasing attention in sociolinguistics, linguistic anthropology and educational studies. The studies of critical hip hop (language) pedagogies, in particular, has focused on hip hop as a means of drawing out-of-school experiences of language closer to classroom pedagogy and curriculum (Hill 2009; Alim, Ibrahim and Pennycook 2009; Alim 2011). These frameworks often emphasise creative, limitless and counter-hegemonic linguistic practices as a significant part of the pedagogical and political potentials of hip hop culture. In this chapter we focus on the way hip hop practices are appropriated by a group of adolescents in positioning themselves as educationally ambitious. We investigate what local meanings these practices achieve and their relations to wider semiotic models and norms to discuss the interplay between education, activities, and popular cultural resources. Against the background of previous hip hop research, the case study we report from involved some surprising discoveries. The boys we studied formed a rap-group and engaged in various local hip hop events and initiatives led by different mentors. They were certainly creative in enacting street-wise and school-positive personae, but their hip hop literacy and linguistic practices fell short of challenging hegemonic educational norms.

In order to make, and make sense of, such surprising discoveries one needs a research approach which is sensitive to both situated activities and the broader context in which they occur, and we have found Linguistic Ethnography (LE) a particularly fruitful methodological framework for grasping the links between communicative actions, linguistic forms, activities and background understandings. Our self-identification as linguistic ethnographers has been the result of a gradual drift from our academic starting points in Language Socialisation (Kulick and Schieffelin 2004; Schieffelin and Ochs 1986) and Interactional Sociolinguistics (Gumperz 1982; Rampton 1995) rather than of a drastic shift of methodology and epistemology. This drift for us has meant that ethnography has come to play an increasingly significant part in our research, which began from a linguistic and micro-analytic starting point. LE is important because it offers a theoretically informed platform to pursue interests that go beyond traditional methods and foci of sociolinguistic analysis. At the same time, sociolinguistic analysis, attention to linguistic form and more indirect meanings of communication also contribute to the field of LE, as we hope to show in this chapter.

Our study of adolescents' engagement with hip hop cultural practices in and outside a school setting will illustrate the following three points. First, we will show that dominating educational norms are not only implemented by official educational institutions, but that they can also play a vital role in street and community initiatives and peer-cultural activities. Second, we will demonstrate that the adolescents orient to different centres of cultural norms, at times even within one and the same communicative unit. Their engagement with hip hop is polycentric, but traditional educational norms appear to dominate. Third, it will be clear that a combination of linguistic micro-analysis, meta-pragmatic analysis and ethnographic accounts is necessary to reach these conclusions.

Education, minority boys and popular culture

Recent surveys and reports document how boys with cultural and linguistic minority background in Denmark tend to be educational underachievers and have weak affiliations to the labour market (Egelund, Nielsen and Rangvid 2011; OECD 2006). It is often argued that minority children's problems are motivated (or even caused) by cultural differences, linguistic deficiencies, lack of educational aspirations, and reluctance to accept mainstream society's value-ascriptions (Andersen 2010). However, as McCarthy, Giardina, Harewood and Park (2003) point out, globalisation complicates these assumptions and should force educational institutions to reorient:

> The great task confronting educators as we move into the 21st century is to address the radical reconfiguration and cultural rearticulation now taking place in educational and social life. These developments are foregrounded and driven by the logics of globalization, the intensification of migration, the heightened effects of electronic media, the proliferation of images, and the everyday work of imagination. All these developments have shifted the commonly taken for granted stabilities of social constructs such as 'culture', 'identity', 'nation', 'state,' and so forth.
>
> (McCarthy et al. 2003: 462)

Educational institutions have been described as key sites for the reproduction of existing sociolinguistic economies and communicative inequalities (e.g. Bourdieu and Passeron 1977). At the same time students negotiate and challenge (sociolinguistic) order and hegemony (Blackledge and Creese 2010; Jaspers 2005; Rampton 2006). Formal education is frequently framed, and possibly experienced, in terms that contrast with popular culture. For instance, in general the National is accorded primacy in formal education, and the reproduction of traditional cultural values is a declared aim; studies of popular culture focus on present and future, rather than on tradition and custom; and *culture* becomes related to what people desire and aspire to, rather than what they are and do (Appadurai 2004; Vigh 2008: 20). Accordingly people's shared experiences, social solidarity (Fedorak 2009: 3) and translocal alignments (Hall 1985; Hebdige 2006; Pennycook 2005: 593) are key elements in such studies. Yet, popular culture practices and phenomena do pervade educational settings, thereby creating an interesting normative tension. Spaces of learning and socialisation develop within learners' networking practices, and formal education is just one among a range of institutional and non-institutional settings: clubs, afterschool centres and virtual gatherings. It is worth studying how language and other semiotic resources circulate, are learnt and appropriated in school-related popular culture activities as they often involve complex forms of cultural, linguistic and semiotic diversity, and for this purpose we focus on appropriations of hip hop.

Research site and data

Our case study comes from an extensive empirical collaboration which took place in a culturally and linguistically diverse urban school in a former traditional working class area in Copenhagen, the capital of Denmark.

We have carried out fieldwork alone, in pairs, and in teams from 2009 until today (2015; and continuing) among students in their final years of school (grade 7–9) as well as middle-school students (grade 4–6) and school-starters (grade 0–2). Our analytical starting-point is the students' local realities and everyday encounters, and although the project is school-based, our approach exceeds the school context and involves peers as well as institutional and non-institutional adults, leisure activities as well as school. Over the years we have collected a range of data types: field diaries, self-, group- and home-recordings, video-data, ethnographic interviews, written texts, CMC (Madsen, Karrebæk and Møller 2013). In this chapter we focus on three boys during grade 7 and 8 (year 2009) and attend to field diaries, interviews, self-recordings, classroom recordings, text from the webpage of a local grassroots organisation, and video-clips of the boys' hip hop productions from YouTube. The data is anonymised and the participants have given permission for us to quote their lyrics.

Hip hop in and outside school

When we began our observations among the adolescents it soon became clear that three boys, Mahmoud, Isaam and Bashaar, were heavily engaged in a rap-band. They signalled affiliation with hip hop culture through the way they dressed and the music they listened to. They composed their own music and lyrics, and it was a topic they often discussed in school breaks and in the youth club. During our fieldwork they also participated in various local and national hip hop and rap events (see also Stæhr 2010; Madsen 2011; Stæhr and Madsen 2015).

As a cultural form hip hop is a musical and lyrical means of expression. The production and performance involve literacy, musical, rhythmical, and kinaesthetic skills, and the expression of values and positioning in the social world are also central elements (Hill 2009). Hip hop has become a rather well-described vehicle for educational projects (e.g. Pennycook 2007; Hill 2009; Alim 2011), but still it is not conventionally included in curricular activities. Within the critical hip hop (language) pedagogies attempts are made to transfer semiotic competencies from particular popular culture niches into more formal, official contexts of school and training (cf. Ibrahim 1999; Bruce and Davis 2000; Dimitriadis 2001; Hill 2009; Ibrahim, Alim and Pennycook 2009; Alim 2011). The local hip hop environment in the context of our study emphasised such educational dimensions, and the boys' hip hop mentors were heavily involved in several initiatives. One of these was

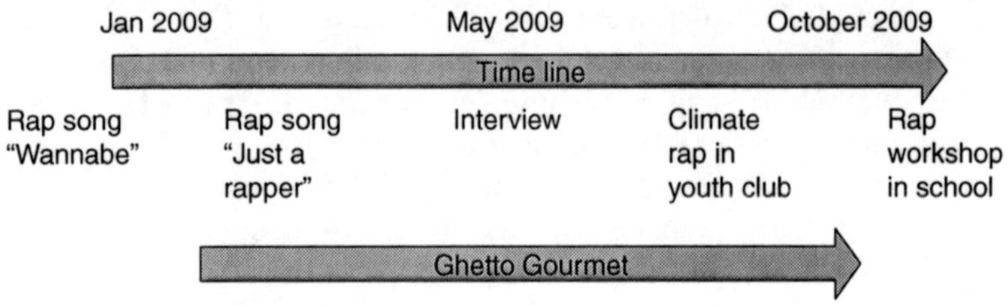

Figure 13.1   Timeline of data excerpts

the organisation *Ghetto Gourmet,* which had a so-called rap academy (workshops led by the rap mentors for youth interested in practicing rap music) as one of its activities. This organisation offered workshops to Copenhagen schools, and we will attend to several data types that illuminate different aspects of the adolescents' involvement with hip hop and Ghetto Gourmet as well as their school's participation in a hip hop course organised by this initiative. The data we discuss covers a period of ten months where the adolescents became increasingly involved in the Ghetto Gourmet activities and the links between hip hop and school activities became stronger. The different data types are presented in chronological order in our analysis and a timeline with an overview of the excerpts we discuss is pictured in Figure 13.1.

Linguistic practices in rap songs

Sociolinguistic studies of hip hop often attend to the linguistic practices used in the musical and lyrical productions, and to open our data discussion we carry out a similar analysis. The three boys regularly met their rap mentors in a studio and recorded their own rap songs, some of which they posted on YouTube. When we looked at the linguistic practices used in the hip hop productions of *the boys' rap group* we noticed a striking development in the direction of more standard language use. We will initially illustrate this with two short excerpts from their lyrics. The first is from an early rap the boys made when they self-identified as 'gangster rappers':

Excerpt 1: 'Wannabe'

Eow *yeah wannabes*   **Eow** *yeah wannabes*

De kan ikke blive som Mini G's   They can't be like the Mini G's

(Exkaran) han er alt for <u>klam</u>	(Exkaran) he is way too <u>gross</u>
Eow I ' nogle tabere I efteraber	**Eow** you're looser you copy
I kalder jer selv for en *G do you wannabe?*	You call yourself a *G do you wannabe?*
I har intet værdi *do* jeg er ikke	You have no value *do* I'm not
Dansk Folkeparti	'Danish Folk Party'
Så prøv at hør' det ' os der før'	So try to listen – we are in front
For det' her på Ama'r vi taler vores sprog	'cause it's here in Amar' we speak our language
acra para vur abow?	**acra para vur abow?**

The content of the song is about dissing wannabes, claiming authority, and local street credibility, and linguistically it clearly highlights the diversity associated with a vernacular speech style that the participants refer to as street language (Madsen 2013). The lyrics contain slang expressions (e.g. *klam*), non-standard expressions historically associated with English (e.g. *Do you wannabe*), and features historically associated with Kurdish and Arabic (*acra* 'police', *para* 'money', *vur* 'fist fight', *abow* 'an exclamation'). The boys list these expressions as belonging to their local language on Amager (or *'Ama'r'*). In this way the lyrics contain explicit commentary on language use and associated values as they address local speech practices and demonstrate what the boys refer to as 'our language'. In contrast, Excerpt 2 demonstrates a different attitude and style. The boys describe this rap as representing their development towards 'serious rappers'. Furthermore, this rap is produced during their involvement with the rap academy of Ghetto Gourmet:

Excerpt 2: 'Just a rapper'

Vi er her vi er mini ghetto gourmeter	We are here we are mini ghetto gourmets
Lad mig lige prøve at **argumentere**	Just **let me** try to **argue**
Jeg er bare en rapper du må **acceptere**	I'm just a rapper you have to **accept**
De ting jeg **leverer** plus mine rim de eksploderer	The things I **deliver** plus my rhymes they explode
Jeg er bare en rapper der rapper om mit liv	I'm just a rapper who raps about my life
Gider ikke spille smart og være **aggressiv**	Don't want to play smart and be **aggressive**
Jeg er bare mig selv og ikke andet	I'm just me and nothing else

Mine rim de er ikke for **fin** den er ikke for vandet	My rhymes they're not too**posh** it's not too vague
Den er **ren** den er **flot** den er **venlig**	It's **clean** it's **nice** it's **friendly**
Mine raptekster er helt **uimodståelige**	My rap lyrics are **irresistible**
Chorus:	Chorus:
I ved jo godt hvem vi er	Well you know who we are
Står på scenen og vi tør	On the stage and we dare
Poesi og **harmoni**	**Poetry** and **harmony**
Gangsterrap **lad mig være fri**	Gangster rap **spare me**

These lyrics are about being a competent rapper, being yourself and and not being an aggressive gangster. The linguistic features are predominantly standard, and the vocabulary includes examples of academic expressions, 'argue' and 'irresistible', as described explicitly by the adolescents in interviews and essays (Møller and Jørgensen 2011; Madsen 2013). These co-occur with expressions that certainly do not index streetwise toughness, such as 'clean', 'nice', 'friendly' or 'poetry'; and in particular the chorus with the 'Gangster rap spare me' reflects associations with a relatively traditional and 'posh' register in a Danish context. In the critical hip hop studies hybrid, non-standard linguistic practices are considered closely related to hip hop practice and valued for improving linguistic skills and creativity by expanding traditional linguistic models (see overview of this research in Alim 2011). The change of linguistic style illustrated in these two excerpts exemplifies a more general tendency in our data towards the use of more standard language in the hip hop productions (Stæhr and Madsen 2015). This tendency differs strikingly from what is observed in other language and hip hop studies. To explain this we need to contextualise our observations. We do not jump directly to a discussion of, for instance, societal language ideologies and potential assumptions about seriousness and standard language. With the LE approach we can combine our longitudinal ethnographic observations with micro-analysis of situated interactions and take into account normativities and connections in speech events across time and space (Agha and Wortham 2005).

Hip hop and education

A possible first step towards a better understanding of the topical and linguistic development in the hip hop music is to ask the participants themselves what happened between the two different productions, and our colleague from the research team, Andreas, did so (see also Stæhr 2010):

Excerpt 3: 'Rap saved us'

1 Andreas: what's happened
2 Bashaar: **we've become more mature**
3 Isaam: yes we've begun to **take it seriously the rap (music)** before we
                 were
4   just some kids trouble makers but **now we don't want to play
                 smart**
5   **and be aggressive**
6 Bashaar: and before I remember in the fourth grade that eh we skipped
7   classes all the time we ran away from [name]'s classes and stuff
8 Isaam: we were like real brats but now (.) after (.) the rap (.) **rap**
9   **saved us you can say**
10 Bashaar: have saved us also **school itself we've taken more seriously**
11 Isaam: mm so
12 Andreas: really
13 Bashaar: yes
14 Mahmoud: [before I didn't do] much homework before
15 Bashaar: [for example I I]
16 Isaam: **we can thank our manager Joseph Mbida for this**
17 Bashaar: **listen I've gone from zero to ten and twelve** (1.3) just from
18   fourth grade and here and and now

(Translation of Group-interview, May 2009)

The most significant point to make from the participants' expressed understandings in the interview is that the trajectory towards maturity and seriousness in relation to rap music is presented as closely related to improvement of school performance (lines 10 and 17). The boys express this connection between their popular culture engagement and education as being 'saved by rap' and even express thanks to their manager. Thereby they appear to draw on an understanding of leisure activities and mentor-relationships as important for their educational development, and this is a well established understanding within voluntary association and community work in Denmark and elsewhere (Madsen 2012). Educational aspects of hip hop are also emphasised by the grassroots organisation the boys are involved in. The rap academy the adolescents attended was described as follows on the web page of the Ghetto Gourmet:

The rap academy.

An academy is a kind of educational institution. In contemporary modern society the academy is typically connected to higher education, like universities. But back in antique Greece the *Academy* was a place for the goddess Athea who among other things represented wisdom, inspiration, strength, courage, crafts and skills. It is these completely basic ideas we take back from the ivory tower and out to the street.

(Translation from Danish by Lian Malai Madsen; the web page of the Ghetto Gourmet organisation, quoted in this chapter, was closed down by September 2013 and instead a Facebook page remained. Educational aspects are also prevalent on the Facebook page e.g. featuring a link to a guide to become a better poet.)

The quote illustrates how the local hip hop organisation argues for an 'education of the streets' in opposition to the 'ivory tower' of traditional educational institutions and thereby points to two contrasting cultural models. At the same time, the linguistic register employed strongly signals a traditional formal educational model, for instance, with the linguistic standard form and the reference to ancient Greece. The observations from the hip hop lyrics of the adolescents, the link between school performance and serious engagement with hip hop they expressed, and the linguistic practices involved in the presentation of Ghetto Gourmet all point to the same conclusion: that it is perhaps not as much the academy that has been taken back to the streets as it is the street-associated cultural genre that has approached 'the ivory tower' – linguistically, stylistically and content-wise. Yet, before we reach a conclusion it is worth taking a closer look at some interactional episodes where the link between hip hop culture and education is enacted outside and in the school setting.

Interaction around hip hop

The first such episode we will discuss is a self-recording made by Mahmoud and Bashaar. It illustrates a hip hop oriented activity in the youth club where the boys usually spent a few hours after school. They are writing a climate rap, which is homework for school, but the activity takes place in a leisure context in which they often worked on their hip hop music. This makes the setting for the activity somewhat hybrid and the linguistic practices they deploy during this sequence relates to similar hybrid relationships between popular and school cultural resources. The two boys jointly create the lyrics and Mahmoud writes them down. Before this sequence the writing has led Bashaar to make fun of and correct Mahmoud's spelling of the word 'temperature'. So the school-oriented frame, including a norm of correctness, has indeed been made relevant. In this excerpt a third participant joins the conversation, Madiha, a girl, who is also a regular to the youth club (see transcription key in appendix).

Excerpt 4: 'Do your homework'

1	Mahmoud:	den stiger] ((rapper))	[it rises] ((rapping))
2	Madiha:	[Koran xxx kom nu] lav jeres	[Koran xxx come on] do your
3		lektier få jer en uddannelse (.)	homework get yourself an education
4		↓rap Koran tror I I får	(.) ↓rap Koran do you think you'll
5		penge [for det]	get money [for it]
6	Bashaar;	[HVOR MEGET] HVAD	[HOW MUCH] WHAT
7		HVAD TROR DU JEG FIK I	WHAT DO YOU THINK I GOT IN
8		FRANSK I DAG (.) <u>TI</u>	FRENCH TODAY (.) <u>TEN</u>
9		HISTORIE FIK JEG TOLV	HISTORY I GOT TWELVE
10		MATEMATIK FIK JEG <u>TI</u>	MATH I GOT <u>TEN</u>
11		LAD VÆRE MED AT SNAKKE	DON'T TALK
12		WALLAH	WALLAH
13		(2.0)	(2.0)
14	Madiha:	(ej hvor skulle jeg vide det fra)	(well how would I know)
15	Mahmoud:	[tempera<u>tur</u>en (.) den stiger]	[The tempera<u>tur</u>e (.) it's rising]
16		((rapper))	((rapping))
17	Madiha:	[øh JA I FORHOLD TIL ANDRE]	[eh YES COMPARED TO OTHERS]
18		HVAD FIK DU MOUD	WHAT DID YOU GET MOUD
19	Bashaar:	Mahmoud fik sgu også ti	Mahmoud also got bloody ten
20	Mahmoud:	<u>TI</u> I FYSIK OG	TEN IN PHYSICS AND
21		KE↑MI (0.3) <u>TOLV</u> I	CHEMIS↑TRY (0.3) TWELVE IN
22		BIOLO↑GI	BIOLO↑GY

Madiha interrupts Mahmoud's rap with the suggestion that the boys do homework instead of rap music in order to get an education (lines 1–6). Thereby she seems to articulate an assumption that rap does not lead to income (as education does) and that there is a contradiction between youth cultural practices such a rap music and general measures of societal success. However, to do so, she employs non-standard linguistic features such as a prosodic pattern characteristic of the aforementioned street language and the slang expression *koran* used as intensifier (line 2 and 4). Bashaar does not argue against the expressed assumption or claim that they are in fact engaged in doing homework. Instead he defensively and loudly asks Madiha a rhetorical question about his educational achievements and continues by listing a range of the high marks he has recently received as an answer (line 6–12). This seems to function as a demonstration of his academic capabilities, and a way of positioning himself as school-skilled (in line with his earlier spelling corrections). Still, similar to Madiha, he deploys linguistic features associated with street language. These are both prosodic and lexical (e.g. the expression *wallah*, line 12). Finally, Mahmoud, too, lists high marks in several subjects using the same intonation (lines 22–22). Excerpt 4 thereby illustrates how the boys defend their school competence as a reaction to the articulation of an assumption of an opposition or at least lack of connection between rap-culture and school success. The example shows that the close relation between school competence and hip hop activities expressed by the boys, and significant to the ideologies of Ghetto Gourmet activities, is not uncontested – in this case it has to be defended. But it is also a typical example of how these boys creatively, and in many ways successfully, blend dominating educational norms and positive school orientation with peer and popular cultural norms and semiotic activities such as linguistic vernacular forms and hip hop.

The example makes clear that to understand how hip hop was appropriated by the boys in this context it is necessary to take into consideration the local, socio-cultural meanings given to particular cultural resources. Such socio-cultural meanings can be accounted for through the notion of indexicality (Ochs 1992; Silverstein 2003). Indexicality refers to the associations between forms and (typical) usage, contexts of use and stereotypes of users that are (re-)created in communicative encounters through linguistic and other signs. Indexical associations are termed metapragmatic because they typify and otherwise characterise signs' links to pragmatically usable systems of signs or 'metapragmatic models' (Agha 2003, 2007). In the data so far we have seen explicit metapragmatic commentary in the rap lyrics (e.g. typifying 'our language' in Amager as characterised by mixing of linguistic resources in Excerpt 1). In Excerpt 4 Madiha's actions typify hip hop cultural resources as incompatible with education and success. Bashaar and Mahmoud, though, challenge this metapragmatic model through their simultaneous orientation to hip hop and school norms.

Indexicality plays a central part in our analysis. The relevance and presence of contrasting norms and centres of authority in interactional encounters are indexically pointed to through language-in-use. Centres of authority influence linguistic and other semiotic conduct. They also motivate moral evaluations of semiotic conduct in terms of 'good' and 'bad' (Silverstein 1998: 406). Yet, centres of authority are connected to specific socio-cultural domains and spaces, and in fact a multiplicity of such centres co-exist. This co-existence of norm centres is referred to as polycentricity (Blommaert, Collins and Slembrouck 2005; Silverstein 1998: 405). Polycentricity implies that what is considered valuable and prestigious in one domain and by some individuals may be stigmatised in another domain and by other individuals – or in fact by the same individuals – and the evaluation of particular signs or resources depends highly on the particular normative centre that the individual orients to. For instance, in the excerpt above we have seen how hip hop was a way for the boys to show themselves to be school oriented in a non-nerdy way, while for others (here Madiha) it indexed educational non-achievers. All situated encounters are potentially polycentric, even those not obviously so; there are always 'multiple – though never unlimited – batteries of norms to which one can orient and according to which one can behave ... ' (Blommaert 2010: 40). Participation in popular cultural activities involves orientation to multiple norms, both within and across domains, and for pupils a pertinent implication of the existence of multiple centres of authority is that they need to learn to recognise and juggle different sets of norms of expectations, maybe even simultaneously (Blommaert et al. 2005: 207). Excerpt 4 suggests that the adolescents in our study successfully manage to do so, but we shall now turn to a final example illustrating the challenges related to bridging popular culture and education.

During the first year of our fieldwork hip hop came to play an increasingly important role in the educational activities not only for the *boys engaged in the rap band,* but for their classmates as well. The final excerpt we include is from a Danish lesson a couple of weeks after the encounter in the youth club. At this point the entire class had participated in a rap workshop, which was an element of a larger initiative by, mainly, Ghetto Gourmet, the city council of Copenhagen and the music venue Vega. The aim was to enhance young Copenhageners awareness of citizenship, diversity and identity and to give them the chance to express themselves on these topics in performances of rap, among other genres. Fifteen schools in Copenhagen, typically from less privileged areas, participated.

The quotes from the field diary and Excerpt 5 are from a preparation phase where the teacher linked hip hop to poetry and linguistic elements of poetry in general:

Excerpt 5: Support teacher

Inger announces that some rappers will visit next week and that the students have to make their own rap lyrics. They will also go to Vega to perform their rap (possibly battle). Inger addresses Mahmoud and Isaam, when she has rap specific questions. For instance she asks them if one uses 'linguistic mechanisms' in rap lyrics. Isaam says that one does.

(...)

Isaam tells Inger that he thinks it is better to choose a beat for their rap before they write the lyrics. Inger replies that they cannot choose the beats before the rappers join the class. Isaam offers to bring some beats. It is not clear to me whether Inger agrees or not, but she says: 'there is no doubt that you will be support teacher during this course and so will Mahmoud' because – as she says – they know more about hip hop and rap than she does.

(Translated excerpt of field diary, 21.10.09, Lian)

Excerpt 6: 'Linguistic mechanisms'

1	Inger:	det er noget med hvad for nogle rim	it's something about what rhymes
2		man kan bruge i en raptekst det papir	one can use in rap lyrics you'll get
3		får I og så har jeg nogle	that sheet and then I have some
4		papirer (.) eller det er	sheets (.) or it's
5		kun et to papirer og de er om	just one two sheets and they're about
6		sproglige virkemidler i lyrik i det	linguistic mechanisms in poetry in
7		hele taget I kan måske også bruge det	general perhaps you may also be able to
8		i rap eller det ved jeg ikke bruger	use that in rap or I don't know does one
9		man sproglige vir virke[mid]ler	use linguistic me me[chanisms]

10		((henvendt til Isaam og Mahmoud)	((addressing Mahmoud and Isaam))
11	Isaam:	[mm]	[mm]
12		((bekræftende))	((confirming))
13	Inger:	i rap hvad hvad kunne det være giv	in rap what what could that be give
14		mig et eksempel	me an example
15	Mahmoud:	[ø:h (°et eksempel°)]	[e:h (°an example°)]
16	Isaam:	[ø:h xxx eksempel]	[e:h xxx example]
17		(2.2)	(2.2)
18	Tahir:	xxx xxx	xxx xxx
19	Mahmoud:	hvad [siger du hhh]	what [are you saying hhh]
20	Inger:	[ikke dig Tahir] ikke dig Tahir	[not you Tahir not] you Tahir
21		jeg spurgte Isaam ikke	I asked Isaam right
22	Mahmoud:	(jeg kan ikke finde et ordentligt)	(I can't find a proper)
23	Inger:	I kan ikke lige finde på noget	you can't think of something
24	Mahmoud:	[nej]	[no]
25	Isaam:	[nej] nej men man bruger meget (.)	[no] no but one uses a lot (.)
26		det der	that thing
27	Inger:	hvad er det nu sproglige	so now what is it linguistic
28		[virkemidler er]	[mechanisms is]
29	Mahmoud:	[forskelligt]	[different]
30	Inger:	kan vi lige få nogle (.) sproglige	can we just have some (.) linguistic
31		billeder kalder vi dem også	figures we call them as well
32	Isaam:	ja dø døden banker på døren	yes dea death knocks on the door

From the accounts in the field diary as well as from the transcript of the interaction it is clear that the engagement with hip hop culture shifted the relations of authority in this teaching situation (Karrebæk 2012). The teacher positioned Mahmoud and Isaam as experts (lines 8–9, 11–12, 18). The boys reflected this positioning by suggesting a different order of tasks and offering to bring beats. There seems to be an opposition here between the teacher's authority in terms of institutional classroom hierarchy and traditional curricular knowledge and the boys who have authority in terms of knowledge about hip hop. Slowing down and looking into the details of this classroom interaction also highlights some challenges of trying to connect popular cultural expertise and traditional curricular knowledge (Lefstein and Snell 2011). In this sequence, the teacher links what she refers to as 'linguistic mechanisms' in poetry to hip hop, as she asks if such effects are used in rap. This term is generally used by the Danish teachers when teaching of literary analysis. Both Isaam and Mahmoud react as respondents to her question to Isaam in line 18, but the hesitation markers and the relatively long silences suggest that they have some problems providing an example. Isaam's response (lines 22–23), 'no but one uses a lot (.) that thing' suggests that he is not comfortable with the term 'linguistic mechanisms'. When the teacher rephrases 'linguistic mechanisms' as 'linguistic figures' Isaam seems to realise what she is talking about and suggests 'death knocks on the door' as an example. This textbook example of a linguistic figure is highly conventional and widespread in Danish teaching of metaphors and poetry. It is unlikely to be related to the kind of rap that these boys practice and listen to, and the attempt from the teacher to position the boys as experts and connect the poetry and hip hop genres somehow fails here. Excerpt 6 provides a contrast to Excerpt 4 from the youth club as it points to the limitations of creatively mixing cultural forms in this polycentric encounter. We find only standard near linguistic forms including features indexing academic models (such as the vocabulary items 'poetry', 'linguistic mechanisms') throughout this example. So carrying out rap-related tasks for school purposes clearly seems enacted differently in the leisure setting from in the school setting when guided by the teacher.

Concluding discussion

In this chapter we have discussed the relationship between peer-cultural and academic orientation in leisure settings and formal educational settings. We documented that the young hip hop-practitioners creatively enacted hip hop streetwise and school-positive personae, and we showed how hip hop-cultural practices in the context of the mentors' hip hop pedagogical framework to some extent bridged a gap between education and popular culture, but we cannot categorise them as counter-hegemonic. The regular teacher brought the boys' interest and skills for rap music into the classroom, yet her efforts to manage a bridging of traditional curricular activities and hip hop had certain limitations. The hip hop pedagogy of the grassroots organisation aimed to empower youth, but still seemed to rest on traditional educational models and standard linguistic norms in contrast to similar projects documented elsewhere (Alim 2011). So in fact this became a process of domestication of the adolescents. However, it is worth noting that the young rappers in this context did not necessarily experience a gap between education and hip hop. Traditional educational models appeared to be part and parcel of being a serious rapper in this local hip hop environment. This explains why the rap group used more standard linguistic practices when they left behind 'gangster rap' and become more serious.

While the situated negotiations we have discussed have some element of creativity, we have also shown that there may be certain limitations to the local appropriation of popular cultural resources. It is clear that the centres of authority and the directions of normativity are neither obvious nor easily predictable. Initiatives aimed at including popular culture phenomena in the classrooms often argue that by combining activities and practices that students engage in outside the classroom with activities of importance inside the classroom, teachers can demonstrate recognition of students as individuals with a legitimate place in a school context, as well as offering them ways to contribute with something valuable to the school based activities (e.g. Gutiérrez et al. 1995; Dyson 1997; Harklau and Zuengler 2004; Rymes 2004; Cowan 2005; Fast 2007). However, to the issue of popular culture our study has added dimensions of peer culture, social dynamics and – slightly paradoxically maybe – reproduction of dominating normative models within a genre more often associated with opposition to standard cultural models. Popular culture is as much about differentiation as it is about integration and our study raises the question of how far and in what ways these powerful but complex cultural processes can be accommodated within national systems and philosophies of education. As Hill (2009: 97) notes:

> The effective use of culturally relevant curriculum and pedagogy inevitably creates new relationships between teachers, students, and the classroom context. Despite the well-documented virtues of such a shift, we must resist the urge to romanticize the relocation of previously marginalized cultural artifacts, epistemologies, and rituals into formal academic spaces. While such processes can yield extraordinary benefit, we must also take into account the problematic aspects of 'culture' and the underside of 'relevance'.

We have argued that the combination of methods that characterises Linguistic Ethnography has proven fruitful in our attempt to elucidate the polycentricity related to popular culture in education (see also Lefstein and Snell 2011). This could not have been done building on an approach solely focussed on language and interaction nor with a purely anthropological approach disregarding linguistic mechanisms and indexicalities. Our longitudinal ethnographic work has enabled us to notice activities and actions and to recognise these as, exactly, practices; ethnographic insight has also been essential for knowing relations between the individuals that take part in the field that we studied. By means of interviews and informal chats we have elicited individuals' own views on practices and incidents, or at least their construction of a situated meta-pragmatic understanding of these. We used sequential micro-analysis on audio-recorded material to uncover the situated performance and construction of identities, activities and understandings. The combination of an LE approach and different sources of data has enabled us to explore the significance of linguistic indexicality and polycentricity, to combine micro-analysis of situated language use with larger social and contextual analysis, and to answer the micro-analytically always pertinent question 'why that now?' and, in addition, the equally relevant question 'and so what?'.

Appendix

Transcription:

[overlap] overlapping speech
LOUD   louder volume than surrounding utterances
xxx   unintelligible speech
(questionable)   parts uncertain about
((comment))   transcriber's comments
:   prolongation of preceding sound
↑↓   local pitch raise and fall
(.)   short pause
(0.6)   timed pause
Stress   stress
hhh   laughter breathe

References

A. Agha (2003) 'The social life of cultural value', *Language & Communication* 23, 231–273.

A. Agha (2007) *Language and Social Relations* (Cambridge: Cambridge University Press).

A. Agha and S. Wortham (eds) (2005) 'Discourse across speech-events: intertextuality and interdiscursivity in social life', Special issue of *Journal of Linguistic Anthropology* 15/1.

H. S. Alim (2011) 'Global ill-literacies: hip hop cultures, youth identities and the politics of literacy', *Review of Research in Education* 35, 120–147.

H. S. Alim, A. Ibrahim and A. Pennycook (2009) *Global Linguistic Flows: Hip Hop Cultures, Youth Identities and the Politics of Language* (London: Routledge).

S.C. Andersen (2010) *Mehmet og Modkulturen: En undersøgelse af drenge med etnisk minoritetsbaggrund* (Copenhagen: Rambøll Management Consulting).

A. Appadurai (2004) 'The capacity to aspire: culture and the terms of recognition' in V. Rao and M. Walton (eds) *Culture and Public Action* (Stanford: Stanford University Press), pp. 59–84.

J. Blommaert (2010) *The Sociolinguistics of Globalization* (Cambridge: Cambridge University Press). J. Blommaert, J. Collins and S. Slembrouck (2005) 'Polycentricity and interactional regimes in "global neighborhoods"', *Ethnography* 6(2), 205–235.

P. Bourdieu and J.-C. Passeron (1977) *Reproduction in Education, Society and Culture* (London: Sage Publications).

H. E. Bruce and B. D. Davis (2000) 'Slam: Hip-hop meets poetry – A strategy for violence intervention', *The English Journal* 89(5), 119–127.

M. Bucholtz (2011) *White Kids: Language, Race and Styles of Youth Identities* (Cambridge: Cambridge University Press).

P. Cowan (2005) 'Putting it out there: revealing Latino visual discourse in the Hispanic academic program' in B. Street (ed.) *Literacies across Educational Contexts: Mediating Learning and Teaching* (Philadelphia: Caslon Publishing), pp. 145–169.

A. Creese and A. Blackledge (2011) 'Separate and flexible bilingualism in complementary schools: Multiple language practices in interrelationship', *Journal of Pragmatics* 43, 1196–1208.

G. Dimitriadis (2001) *Performing Identity/Performing Culture: Hip-hop as Text, Pedagogy, and Lived Practice* (New York: Peter Lang).

A.H. Dyson (1997) *Writing Superheroes: Contemporary Childhood, Popular Culture, and Classroom Literacy* (N.Y. and London: Teachers' College Press).

N. Egelund, C.P. Nielsen and B.S. Rangvid 2011 *PISA Etnisk* (2009). *Etniske og danske unges resultater i PISA 2009*. http://www.akf.dk/udgivelser/container/2011/udgivelse_1041/; accessed 06-07-11.

C. Fast (2007) *Sju barn lär sig läse och skriva: Familjeliv och populärkultur i möte med förskola och skola* (Acta Universitatis Upsaliensis, Uppasala Studies in Education 115. Uppsala: Uppsala Universität).

S. Fedorak (2009) *Pop Culture: The Culture of Everyday Life* (Toronto: University of Toronto Press).

J. Gumperz (1982) *Discourse Strategies* (Cambridge: Cambridge University Press).

K. Gutierrez, B. Rymes and J. Larson (1995) 'Script, counterscript, and underlife in the classroom – James Brown versus Brown v. Board of Education', *Harvard Educational Review* 65(3), 445–471.

S. Hall (1985) 'Popular culture as a factor of international understanding: the case of reggae'; public lecture; accessed at http://unesdoc.unesco.org/images/0006/000650/065008eb.pdf

L. Harklau and J. Zuengler (2004) 'Introduction to proposed special issue: Popular culture and classroom language learning', *Linguistics and Education* 14, 227–230.

D. Hebdige (2006) 'Reggae, Rastas and Rudies' in S. Hall and T. Jefferson (eds) *Resistance through Rituals: Youth Subcultures in Post-war Britain* (London: Routledge), pp. 113–130.

M. L. Hill (2009) *Beats, Rhymes and Classroom Life: Hip Hop Pedagogy and the Politics of Identity* (New York: Teachers College Press).

A. Ibrahim (1999) 'Becoming Black: Rap and hip-hop, race gender, identity and the politics of ESL learning', *TESOL Quarterly* 15(3), 349–369.

J. Jaspers (2005) 'Linguistic sabotage in a context of monolingualism and standardization', *Language and Communication* 25, 279–297.

M. S. Karrebæk (2012) 'Authority relations: the mono-cultural educational agenda and classrooms characterized by diversity', *Naldic Quarterly* 10(1).

D. Kulick and B.B. Schieffelin (2004) 'Language socialization' in A. Duranti (ed.) *A Companion to Linguistic Anthropology* (Oxford: Blackwell), 349–368.

A. Lefstein and J. Snell (2011) 'Promises and problems of teaching with popular culture: a linguistic ethnographic analysis of discourse genre mixing in a literacy classroom', *Reading Research Quarterly* 46(1), 40–69.

L. M. Madsen (2011) 'Interactional renegotiations of educational discourses in recreational learning contexts', *Linguistics and Education* 22(1), 53–68.

L. M. Madsen (2012) 'Discourses on integration and interaction in a martial arts club'. In M. Theeboom, B. Vanreusel, C. Timmerman and B. Segaert (eds) *Sports, Stakeholder in Society? Sports Community Building and Corporate Social Responsibility* (Oxford: Routledge), pp. 74–88.

L. M. Madsen (2013) '"High" and "low" in urban Danish speech styles', *Language in Society* 42, 1–24.

L. M. Madsen, M.S. Karrebæk and J.S. Møller (2013.) 'The Amager Project'. Tilburg Papers in Culture Studies.

C. McCarthy, M. D. Giardina, S. J. Harewood, J. K. Parket (2003) 'Afterword: Contesting Culture: Identity and curriculum dilemmas in the age of globalization, postcolonialism and multiplicity', *Harvard Educational Review* 73 (3), 449–465.

J. S. Møller and J. N. Jørgensen (2011) 'Enregisterment among adolescents in superdiverse Copenhagen' in J. S. Møller and J. N. Jørgensen (eds) *Language, Enregisterment and Attitudes* (Copenhagen: University of Copenhagen), pp. 99–122.

E. Ochs (1992) 'Indexing gender' in A. Duranti and C. Goodwin (eds), *Rethinking Context: Language as an Interactive Phenomenon* (Cambridge: Cambridge University Press), pp. 335–358.

OECD (2006) *Where Immigrant Students Succeed – A Comparative Review of Performance and Engagement in PISA 2003* (Paris: OECD Programme for International Student Assessment).

A. Pennycook (2005) 'Teaching with the flow: fixity and fluidity in education', *Asia Pacific Journal of Education* 25(1), 29–43.

A. Pennycook (2007) *Global Englishes and Transcultural Flows* (Abingdon: Routledge).

B. Rampton (1995) *Crossing: Language and Ethnicity among Adolescents* (London: Longman).

B. Rampton (2006) *Language in Late Modernity: Interaction in an Urban School* (Cambridge: Cambridge University Press).

B. Rymes (2004) 'Contrasting zones of comfortable competence: popular culture in a phonics lesson', *Linguistics and Education* 14, 321–335.

B.B. Schieffelin and E. Ochs, (eds) (1986) *Language Socialization across Cultures* (New York: Cambridge University Press).

M. Silverstein (1998) 'Contemporary transformations of local linguistic communities', *Annual Review of Anthropology* 27, 401–26.

M. Silverstein (2003) 'Indexical order and the dialectics of sociolinguistic life', *Language & Communication* 23, 193–229.

A. Stæhr (2010) *Rappen reddede os. Et studie af senmoderne storbydrenges identitetsarbejde i fritids- og skolemiljøer* (Copenhagen: University of Copenhagen).

A. Stæhr and L. M. Madsen (2015) 'Standard language in urban rap – Social media, linguistic practice and ethnographic context', *Language and Communication* 40, 67–81.

H. Vigh (2008) 'Crisis and chronicity: anthropological perspectives on continuous conflict and decline', *Ethnos* 73(1), 5–24.

14
Metacommentary in Linguistic Ethnography

Angela Creese, Jaspreet Kaur Takhi and Adrian Blackledge

In the introduction to this volume, Rampton, Maybin and Roberts suggest that: 'Ethnographies involve rhetorical forms, such as vignettes and narratives (Hymes 1996: 12–13), that are designed to provide the reader with some apprehension of the fullness and irreducibility of the 'lived stuff' from which the analyst has abstracted structure.' This reminder is useful in discussion of linguistic ethnography. Researchers' records of their observations are fundamental to ethnography because they document 'some slice of experience' (Heller 2008: 250). Ethnographies are typically full of rich descriptions which document the researcher's account of 'being there' (Geertz 1988). These accounts take many different forms, including fieldnotes, diary extracts, vignettes, interview transcripts, and participants' oral and written stories. In this chapter we focus on fieldnotes, and in doing so we adopt the concept of metacommentary (Rymes 2014) as a mechanism with which to understand how people make sense of one another, given the multiplicity of semiotic resources available in interaction. That is, we attend to comments about language, or, more precisely, comments about signs, to understand how certain elements of repertoires become meaningful in interaction.

We conduct our research in ethnographic teams, observing simultaneously in multiple sites, and often more than one researcher observing in the same site at the same time. According to Eisenhart, collaborative approaches involve 'more different kinds of people' (2001: 219) in designing the research process and creating the final product, and require researchers to disclose more about their own views, commitments, and social positions. Such approaches make clearer 'the social position, cultural perspective and political stance' (Eisenhart 2001: 219) of the researcher and how these influence subsequent actions. A further dimension of ethnographic team research is its affordance of multisite ethnographic investigation, which enables us to examine mobilities and linkages and helps get at the nature of contemporary social, economic, and political processes (Heller 2011). Bourdieu argued that in working in ethnographic teams we must 'relinquish the single, central, dominant, in a word, quasi-divine, point of view that is all too easily adopted by observers ... we must work instead with the multiple perspectives that correspond to the multiplicity of coexisting, and sometimes directly competing, points of view' (1999: 3). In this chapter we explore the different perspectives brought to the table by two researchers. We consider whether representing the voices and perspectives of individuals in a team of researchers can add complexity and richness to ethnography. In doing so we argue that reflexivity is a crucial dimension of team ethnography, and 'the collective work of critical reflexivity should enable scientific reason to control itself ever more closely, in and through conflictual cooperation' (Bourdieu 2000: 122). Metacommentary offers a lens with which to make visible critical reflexivity.

Our focus in this chapter is on fieldnotes as metacommentary. We propose that an analysis of fieldnotes which focuses on metacommentary illuminates the process of linguistic ethnographic research. A fieldnote is an ethnographic account which describes 'the units, criteria, and patterning of a community' (Hornberger 1995: 238). In effect this means there is really no such thing as 'a' fieldnote because patterning can only be established iteratively over time. Extensive sets of fieldnotes are required to identify patterns. Fieldnotes are accounts of time invested in the field. They have a special place in ethnography because of their role in documenting the complexity of social life. In writing fieldnotes, ethnographers engage in observation, choosing to describe what appears significant to participants. Fieldnotes also record the researcher's emotions, feelings, values and beliefs. The often-hidden nature of fieldnotes in ethnography has come in for some criticism. Silverman (2001) points out that observational studies rarely provide readers with anything other than brief, persuasive data extracts. Bryman (1988) notes that ethnographic accounts do not normally offer full versions of original fieldnotes. He argues that 'these would be very helpful in order to allow the reader to formulate his or her own hunches about the perspective of the people who have been studied' (p. 77).

A further key dimension of ethnography, according to Heller (2011), is telling our (researcher) story of other people's lives. She describes the need to find our own researcher voice, to reflect on this, and to take responsibility for what we say. However, achieving this as an author is not entirely straightforward. Geertz points out that within anthropology, 'Explicit representations of authorial presence tend to be relegated, like other embarrassments, to prefaces, notes or appendixes' (1988: 16), and he describes the tension of finding a place in the text which achieves both 'an intimate view and a cool assessment' (1988: 10). We take up this challenge. We hope to illustrate how fieldnotes have a central role to play in linguistic ethnography, not only in making ethnographies more open and accessible through making audible researcher voices, but also by making the case that linguistic ethnographic analysis should be rigorous and reliable. One way to do this is to subject fieldnotes, like other data sets, to a linguistic analysis of the rhetorical forms which holds them together.

Fieldnotes in linguistic ethnography

As we have established, fieldnotes have a secure place in ethnography. But the topic we take up in this section is about their place in linguistic ethnography. In this section we highlight the 'linguistic' in fieldnotes, and make the argument that fieldnotes are as central to linguistic ethnography as any other data set. But before we do this, we will make explicit our own understanding of the conjoining of 'linguistics' and 'ethnography' in the phrase 'linguistic ethnography'.

We do not view linguistic ethnography as the welding together of two separate disciplines. This would be an orientation which takes the view that linguistics and ethnography are two separate disciplines, with their own community of scholars and histories of practice. In such a definition, boundaries are maintained and knowledge ordered so that some minor borrowing across borders may take place, but disciplinary orientations remain in place. Rather, we view linguistic ethnography in the tradition of linguistic anthropology, which over the last hundred years or so has been drawing across disciplines to address cultural, social and communicative phenomena, and to seek answers to complex social issues. Our view is that the study of language and social life should be viewed as unitary. Dell Hymes (1968, 1974) argued that because linguistics was too narrowly defined, and ethnography did not make enough of speech, a new orientation was required. Hymes called this 'Ethnography of Communication'. Linguistic ethnography shares many antecedents with Hymesian Ethnography of Communication, which is 'concerned with the situations and uses, the patterns and functions, of speaking as an activity in its own right' (Hymes 1968: 101). Hymes saw the Ethnography of Communication as filling the gap between what is usually described in grammars and what is usually described in ethnographies. He saw its interdisciplinary contribution as making links between 'the ordinary practices of the disciplines [linguistics, anthropology, sociology, psychology] to answer new questions' (1974: 32). We share Hymes' advocacy of an interdisciplinary approach. Like Blommaert (2007), we engage critically with traditions in linguistic anthropology which have viewed research on language and culture as two distinct phenomena. Because the focus of ethnography is on situatedness and dynamics, it lends itself well to an interdisciplinary approach. A linguistic perspective can make a significant contribution to an interdisciplinary agenda. As Rampton (1997: 12) points out, being 'specialised enough to make a distinctive contribution' must inform any attempt at interdisciplinarity.

Blommaert and Dong (2010: 37) point out that fieldnotes provide us with invaluable information, 'not only about *what* we witnessed in the field, but even more importantly about *how* we witnessed it'. Emerson, Fetz and Shaw (2011: 15) similarly point out that '*what* the ethnographer finds out is inherently connected with *how* she finds it out'. Linking method and substance builds sensitivity to the multiple, situational realities of those studied into the core of fieldwork practice. Fieldnotes tell us a story about the way in which we tried to make new information understandable for ourselves. They are written accounts that filter research participants' experiences and concerns through the person and perspective of the ethnographer. By explicitly attending to our own written commentary on the action we are observing – including linguistic action – we begin to understand our journey as linguistic ethnographers understanding and making sense of the social world. Emerson et al. (2011: 80) refer to 'asides and commentaries' as interpretive writings composed while the ethnographer is actively composing fieldnotes. Asides and commentaries may convey the ethnographer's personal or emotional response to events, shifting the focus from the observed action to the feelings and reflections of the researcher.

In the analysis of the fieldnotes which follows, we make use of foundational work in linguistic anthropology. Silverstein (1981) makes it clear that we cannot rely on the linguist's limited interpretation of cultural action, but we must also draw on the anthropologist's model and 'its program of understanding the properties of ideologies that guide participants in social systems' (1981: 21). We also find useful Hymes' reminder that 'how something is said is part of what is said' (Hymes 1972: 59), and that this means examining evidence for both expression and content, or put another way, for both discourse and theme. Our analysis of filednotes is therefore both linguistic and ethnographic because it looks at how researchers use language to interpret the social context, and how they place themselves in the interpretive process.

Metacommentary

To achieve this we draw on Betsy Rymes' recent work on metacommentary (Rymes 2014). Rymes adopts Silverstein's work on metapragmatic function (1993) to make visible to self and others the salient features of the social context by paying attention to how language comments on itself. Her work is of particular relevance to our own because we share with her a focus on linguistic diversity and communicative repertoire. Rymes asks 'how do people make sense of each other?' 'How do people interacting know what counts as a communicatively relevant repertoire element?' (2014: 302). She proposes that using the concept of meta-commentary – that is, comments *about* language – offers a new order-ing principle for understanding heteroglossic communication. Rymes points out that while disciplinary linguistics has traditionally sorted languages into discrete codes, sociolinguistics has identified dialects and registers that vary across contexts. Linguistic anthropology has exam-ined how forms become enregistered (Agha 2005) over an accumulation of linked interactions. Even here, though, it is necessary to identify distinct forms in order to analyse how they cohere and sediment in the repetitions of social life. Rymes takes a different approach, looking at interactions 'not to characterise codes or departures from them, but to identify how people draw attention to those communicative elements that make meaning in the moment' (2014: 302). In this chapter we adopt this approach.

In her research Rymes sets out to capture the 'baroque complexity of interaction between people on different historical and biographical tra-jectories' in a time of 'massive multilingualism' (p. 304). Rymes argues that metacommentary can be a useful analytical tool because it sign-posts what is socially salient to participants. In such phrases as 'I meant that as a compliment', or 'Don't call me guy, I'm your mum' and 'I love your accent', language comments on itself. Rymes describes metacom-mentary as an ordering principle which social actors can draw upon to make sense of the 'idiosyncratic accumulation of experiences and expressions' which make up individuals' communicative repertoires (2014: 301). In the next section we explore the analytical potential of metacommentary in fieldnotes.

Researching multilingualism in multilingual teams

For the last 12 years we have been researching language practices in community-run language schools. These are known in the UK as 'complementary' or 'supplementary' schools, and in the US as 'heritage language' schools. Complementary schools are grassroots institutions which have developed with very little government funding. In many ways financially vulnerable, and surviving from hand to mouth, they are nonetheless sites which have a political role in countering the monolingual orientation of mainstream schooling, providing young people with an opportunity to resist ethnic categories and social stereotypes associated with static identity markers. These non-statutory and voluntary schools provide a community resource for young people, parents and teachers to network, and to support positive student learner identities. They also create spaces where young people and their teachers are able to negotiate identities through the performance of diverse linguistic repertoires.

We have conducted ethnographies in eleven British complementary schools, spending on average one year in each site collecting data for projects which last approximately two years each (for more information see Blackledge and Creese 2010). We have also worked in collaboration with European sites investigating similar phenomena (Blackledge et al. in press). The schools we investigated taught Bengali, Cantonese, Gujarati, Mandarin, Panjabi, and Turkish, to mainly British-born young people. We negotiated access to the schools through contacts made by researchers who for the most part already had excellent community networks. We then observed, recorded, interviewed, and collected field documents, often with more than one researcher on site at the same time.

Funding from the UK and European funding councils has allowed us to work in multilingual, multisite and increasingly multidisciplinary research teams, and this has become our default approach of conducting linguistic ethnography. We will refer to one research project in this chapter. We discuss the 'European' project, which spanned four contexts in Denmark, Sweden, The Netherlands, and the UK. The UK case study of the project investigated Panjabi complementary schools. These were community-run, often small-scale organisations staffed by community groups for the purpose of teaching Panjabi. The particular school we worked in met on Saturdays in two sites. The case study team comprised three researchers, Jaspreet Kaur Takhi (JKT), Adrian Blackledge (AB), who was also project leader for the wider European team of fourteen researchers, and Angela Creese (AC). As field researchers Jaspreet and Angela visited the Panjabi school most Saturdays for a year, where we observed classes, wrote fieldnotes and set up audio-recordings both during class time and at home and elsewhere. We separately visited all classes over the initial four months of the project, before deciding as a team on two focal classrooms for more detailed observation and recording over a further four months. Our data sets include fieldnotes, interviews, audio- and video- recordings, and field documents. In this chapter we refer mainly to fieldnotes.

Fieldnotes as metacommentary

In this section we turn to our fieldnotes to consider metacommentary as an analytical tool for understanding the process of what is recorded during participant observation. Our interest is in how some social practices (and not others) are noticed during observations in the field. What we offer here might be described as a second order analysis of fieldnotes. This is because the fieldnotes have already gone through a first round of analysis. We originally produced 42 sets of fieldnotes between us, with each set consisting of between two and nine pages of single-spaced (typed) observational notes. In our original analysis we generated 18 themes, grouped together under four broad categories (see Copland and Creese, 2015 for full account). Our approach followed the ethnographic process of 'finding data' in which we searched, defined, and identified categories and themes which were 'statable' (Erickson 2004a).

The second order analysis reported on here constitutes a return to our fieldnotes to ask new questions about knowledge construction in linguistic ethnography. We adopt Rymes' concept of metacommentary to understand this process and to make the interpretive exercise of linguistic ethnography more comprehensible, robust and reflexive. We think this is important because it requires ethnographers to consider their role in the 'games of truth' that produce knowledge (Guta et al. 2013: 308).

In her work Rymes describes six types of metacommentary, which range from explicit metapragmatic discourse to less overt commentary. We illustrate each by drawing on our fieldnotes (and occasionally on audio and interview transcripts) from the Panjabi complementary school study. The initials of each researcher and date follow the extracts.

Metacommentary Type 1: Marking code

This is 'probably the most obvious kind of metacommentary' (Rymes 2014: 305). Obvious, because a comment can be easily identified as a remark about a linguistic entity. It is commentary which points out the boundaries between languages. This usually takes the form of highlighting one linguistic code rather than another, or marking language x from language y. The first example below is a prototypical example which we came across routinely in the complementary school classroom, and noted time and again in our fieldnotes. Here Jaspreet records teacher SU's comments about language use in the classroom:

> In SU's class the children are told they must only speak in Panjabi and must ask questions in Panjabi. However, they are also told if they cannot speak Panjabi properly they are not to worry as that is what she is there for – to teach them and get them up to GCSE exam level. (JT, 18/9)

Over the last twelve years we have made many fieldnote entries of this kind of directive in the complementary school classroom, as students are told to use one language and not another (e.g. 'speak Bengali, you are Bengali', 'don't speak English'). As teachers make this plea it often takes the form of a mild reproach. Such warnings have the metapragmatic function of attempting to banish English from the heritage language classroom. The invocation 'only speak in Panjabi' indexes an ideological orientation to a particular pedagogy, a particular model of language teaching and learning. In our observations in the fifteen classrooms of the Panjabi school this was by no means the only ideology or pedagogy in play. In some classrooms there was an explicit orientation to bilingual (Panjabi and English) pedagogy. In others, while the explicit message was 'only speak in Panjabi', teachers and students alike departed from the message where necessary. In the direction 'only speak in Panjabi' the notion of language-as-code is invoked to distinguish one language from another. The category of 'different languages' reinforces the 'sense of nation-state-bounded linguistically distinct code' (Rymes 2014: 307).

Metacommentary on code is very common in language classrooms, and the heritage language classroom is no exception. However, the marking of code does not always have to be about the teacher enforcing linguistic boundaries. In the next example Angela records a teacher commenting about code in a way which breaks down boundaries:

> The teacher then addresses the class with a story – hopefully this has all been recorded because it's very interesting. She talks about how she was doing a translation and she gave the Panjabi word for 'community' but nobody recognised it, and so she translated 'community'

as 'community'. 'Some words' she explains 'are easier to say in English'. (AC, 19/2)

As the fieldnotes indicate, the teacher was being recorded simultaneously while Angela sat in class making notes. Below is a transcript of the relevant section of the audio file:

I will share one thing with you. Last week I was doing a translation for somebody. Er, it was a gurdwara <Sikh temple> and there was a leaflet. A couple of lines only I had to translate for some, er babaji <grandfather>, like bazurgh <elderly person> yeah? Elderly person. Er, and the word was 'community', yeah? And, I was doing the translation and I said 'samhudai' <community> yeah? Community means samhudai. He couldn't understand! Ah then I tried to make this word more easier. No! Then I was thinking 'hunh mein ehnoo ki dasaa?' <what shall I tell him now?> 'what shall I tell him now?' Then I said shall I say the word 'community'? I said 'community'. It was fine! [laughter] He did understand, because some words like, they are so familiar right? The people, the people are living with those words, right? He easily understood what I'm talking about. 'Community haa puth, tu community kehna si, community kehna si menoo!' <yes child, you should have said community, should have said community to me!> I said ok. I was 'uncleji <uncle> I was doing word to word translation'. Ok? Some words they are more easier to understand if you say them in English. Ok?

(classroom audio-recording)

This narrative includes metacommentary, in which the teacher talks about language use and community change. In her short narrative, the teacher uses her story of translation to make several points to her class of students. First, languages change – so whereas 'samhudai' may have been appropriate at one point in the community's history, 'community' is appropriate now. Second, languages do not own words, but people do. 'Community' isn't the property of English, just as 'samhudai' is not owned by Panjabi. The words serve as sign tokens for people to use. Interestingly, the teacher evokes the voice of the elderly 'bazurgh' to legitimise her point, 'yes child, you should have said community to me'. Finally, in the telling of the story her communicative repertoire endorses a flexible bilingualism rather than a separate bilingualism. She translanguages effortlessly, ignoring code boundaries, and gives her students permission to do the same. A re-examination of our fieldnotes taking metacommentary as an analytical category reveals how our participants' 'small stories' (Georgakopoulou, 2007) about code become patterned as a theme in our fieldnotes. Rymes (2014: 303) points out that in any inter-action metacommentary signals an understanding of what a sign means by pointing to that sign's situated communicative value. Here the teacher does exactly this, explicitly pointing to the value of particular signs.

Metacommentary Type 2: Marking the sounds of language

Rymes' second metacommentary type is enacted when people com-ment on accent or pronunciation. Our fieldnotes are full of entries about accent. Often this takes the form of participants commenting on good and bad pronunciation in the learning of Panjabi. The teachers have clear views of what is appropriate and use the regular drills of class-room pedagogy to enforce linguistic standards and social norms. In our fieldnotes and interviews participants commented regularly on varieties of Panjabi. For example, varieties include 'posh', 'rough', regional varie-ties, 'Pakistani Panjabi', 'African Panjabi', 'English Panjabi', and 'decent Panjabi'. The Principal of the school mentioned that Panjabi families at the school pass on a 'rough' variety of Panjabi:

> over time I've found that some of the families here whose ancestors I would say or grandparents came from really rural backgrounds – from villages. They passed on the language, very rough, very – not very posh language to their next generation and next generation passed it onto the young children. (Interview)

He describes this variety as 'not very respectful', and 'not very nice Panjabi', and says that he has to stop the children at the school from speaking in this way. He makes a further distinction between the Panjabi spoken by people born and raised in the Panjab and the Panjabi spoken by people born in the diaspora, saying 'whoever is born over here they speak actually Panjabi in an English accent'. Here the school Principal distinguishes between groups of Panjabi speakers by marking their accent through metacommentary. A pedagogic rationale of the school appeared to be to counter the spread of non-standard varieties of Panjabi. Fieldnotes recorded the teachers' commentary on pronunciation:

> The teacher speaks to students about phonemes. She tells them 'there are meaningful differences and pronunciation makes a difference'. One girl asks why there are so many different 'g' sounds. This makes

the teacher laugh. 'I don't know', she says, 'It's just the way it is'. (AC, 19.2)

However, the students too had firm views about pronunciation. The next example comes from a set of fieldnotes in which the researcher had noticed that the accent of one of the teachers was attracting attention.

Teacher Narinder is reading to the class, but her accent appears to cause the children some problems. She checks that they understand 'her' Panjabi accent. (AC: 12. 5)

A child asks teacher Narinder for clarification about her translation from Panjabi to English. He wants to know if she said 'eating'. She repeats and says 'knitting', but with a very long /i/ sound. The young man still looks a bit perplexed and so Narinder writes the word on the board. She writes 'kneeting'. This causes the class to snigger. (AC, 19.3)

In these fieldnotes the researcher makes a number of entries about the different values vowel sounds have in the classroom. Metacommentaries about accent are rife in the data.

The distinction between the English phonemes /i/ and /ɪ/ is problematic for Narinder, and results in the incorrect written representation of the word 'knit' as 'kneet'. Just as a yawn may signal boredom, the students' snigger is a metacommentary on the authenticity of the teacher. The students impose their own benchmarks of authenticity and legitimacy, and their sniggers indicate that at this moment Narinder has not met them. Our analysis across data sets attends to linguistic signs where small units of meaning, like phonemes, come to have powerful social significance (Blackledge and Creese 2014). Here the mispronunciation of the phoneme in the English word 'knitting' has real consequences for the teacher. By attending to explicit comments on the situated value of particular signs we can make not only visible but also meaningful and relevant the 'communicative layers that exist in an interaction' (2014: 314).

Narinder's illegitimacy as a teacher does not necessarily reside in the students' expectation that she should be able to produce correct Standard English. The regular class teacher, Hema, herself of Panjabi heritage, often spoke to the students in a non-Standard variety of English: 'when somebody's talking you', 'you look people's lips', 'where I'm taking my tongue?' and so on. Hema had been a teacher in the school for many years, and spoke with an accent that might be described as Birmingham Asian Vernacular English. The dialect was recognisable to the students, even if they tended to use a more Standard variety of English themselves. In the eyes of the students the distinction between Hema's non-Standard speech and Narinder's confusion with the sound and spelling of the word 'knitting' was that while Hema's Birmingham Asian Vernacular English was familiar, and so indexed the local, Narinder's attempt at Standard English pronunciation and spelling indexed an identity as newly-arrived and 'fresh'. Talmy (2004) refers to the discursive construction of the newly-arrived, 'fresh-off-the-boat' student, relationally defined against an unmarked, idealised 'native' speaker (see also Blackledge and Creese 2010, Creese et al. 2006, and Martin et al. 2004 for discussion of 'freshie' subject positioning in complementary schools in UK). Talmy refers to 'linguicism' at work in the social practice of 'the public teasing and humbling of lower L2 English proficient students by their more proficient classmates', which 'was one of the primary ways that students produced and reproduced the linguicist hierarchy' (2004: 164). In the case reported here students humble not each other, but the assistant teacher. The distinctions are relatively subtle, but immediately recognisable to the students. The legitimacy of the teacher at least partly depends on the production of speech and writing which the students recognise as authentic. The students' sniggering metacommentary points to distinctions and hierarchies which are at once nuanced and, for Narinder, consequential.

Metacommentary Type 3: Marking address terms

Rymes suggests that 'Names, nicknames, and terms of address often proliferate like mushrooms. As such, probably the most obvious form of metacommenatry about names is the comment of what you can "call me" ' (2014: 309). In our observations in the Panjabi school over the course of a year we saw many examples of address terms in use. Of special value in the complementary classroom was the teaching of kinship terms, as this appeared to be an important dimension of heritage and culture. Fieldnotes record Jaspreet and a student talking together about how to address family members:

Just as the break is over the kids are chatting. Manika calls her sister, but instead of calling her by her name she says 'Penji' which is Panjabi for big sister. She calls her sister this out of respect. I comment on how nice that is and she said that she has always called her Penji. I am the same with my sister. Except I call her 'Dedee' rather than Penji, which means the same thing. This is definitely something that is culturally instilled by her family rather than taught at Panjabi school. (JT, 19.3)

In what we might call 'meta-meta-commentary' the researcher's own commentary on Manika's address term is recorded in her fieldnotes. The interaction she has with Manika involves commenting on and evaluating the appropriateness of forms of address, including her own. Jaspreet notes the importance of this kind of language for herself, and she records these comments in her notes. A secondary analysis of fieldnotes which attends to metacommentary identifies Jaspreet's commentary on her own comment as a site of alignment with the student.

In another example, a teacher, MS, is reinforcing the importance of 'respect':

> MS says, 'Tell me what 'ji' stands for?' A child volunteers, 'respect'. MS is happy with the answer and says 'to show respect'. He illustrates this by saying 'Hello Baba and Hello Mama, doesn't sound good'. He tells them you need to say 'ji' and then you are being a respectable family as well. (AC, 9/10)

One of the functions of the complementary school, visible here, is to transmit to the next generation forms of address which signal respect. This appeared to be supportive of the efforts of the students' parents to instil values of respect. The forms of address are heavily symbolic and they serve as a metapragmatic function for heritage and identity maintenance. Rymes (2014: 310) points out that while students do not always comment on terms of respect such as 'ji', 'there is implicit metapragmatic negotiation about their function, or when it is ok to say them'. A more *explicit* metapragmatic negotiation of the same term of respect is evident in *Metacommentary Type 6*, below. While the maintenance of heritage and identity may be a function of the complementary school, this is not an uncontested process, as students have their own ideas about the kinds of heritages and identities to which they orient.

Metacommentary Type 4: Gesture

Rymes describes how 'gesture, eye gaze and body comportment' can all be powerfully used to mark forms of speaking which can provide an additional layer of metacommentary. She also shows how gesture itself can become the object of metacommentary in examples such as 'Sit up straight!' which Rymes argues show how gesture becomes stereotyped. Illustrations from our research are limited because the topic was not in our research questions. However, 'body comportment' did attract some attention in our fieldnotes, particularly in relation to the teaching of pronunciation. Our fieldnotes include description about the tongue, lips and mouth, with regard to teaching pronunciation:

> She tells them off (gently) for not distinguishing sounds. 'Look at me. Take your tongue to the top. OK, now say this five times. Come on, all together.' (AC, 18/9)

Students in class are encouraged to watch the teachers' mouths, 'Take your tongue to the top', 'you look people's lips', 'where I'm taking my tongue?', 'my tongue is going the top, yeah?'. Teachers embody authentic pronunciation, moving their tongue and lips in an authentic way. That is, their historical body (Scollon and Scollon 2004), or their bodily hexis (Bourdieu 2008), is assumed to equip them with the cultural capital to produce authentic pronunciation of Panjabi. This authenticity appears to be linked to their status as native speakers, and to the students' (perceived) status as non-native speakers. The teacher's commentary on the students' failure to move their mouths in a way that will produce authentic pronunciation of Panjabi words points to the teacher's view of the importance of 'correct' pronunciation.

In another example the teacher's gesture is a form of metacommentary, as he makes the students laugh by commenting physically on his use of language:

> They now review the Sihari sound. It has the same phonetics as the 'i' in the 'hit'. Teacher MS asks for examples and says 'shit' as one of them. This makes the kids laugh and MS covers his mouth in mock embarrassment, it's clear that he said this on purpose to get a reaction from the children. (JT, 17.10)

The teacher's gesture, covering his mouth in mock embarrassment, marks his use of the word 'shit' as both inappropriate and humorous.

Metacommentary Type 5: Comments on clothing, appearance

Just as there can be nonverbal commentary on verbal tokens, 'there is also verbal commentary on nonverbal communicative displays' (Rymes 2014: 311). Blommaert and Varis (2011) point out that identities are clarified – i.e. offered for inspection to others – by referring to forms not only of language, but also preferences for forms of art, music, food, and appearance. Blommaert and Varis (2012: 4) propose that fashion, and consciousness about appearance, have extended into an immense terrain of social and cultural life, and in commentary on clothing and appearance we witness the emergence and consolidation of complexes of instruction and prescription, management and monitoring, and identity effects (Blommaert and Varis 2012: 4). At the same time commentary on clothing and appearance becomes a space of social evaluation, something about which others can pass judgment, and about which we may articulate anxiety. Blommaert and Varis (2012) note that such judgments are fundamentally rooted in 'recognizability' – that is, appearance; the clothes we wear, our hairstyle, the colour of our nail varnish, recognisably index particular identities. Recognisability is an important dimension of social and cultural life: 'We strive towards maximum recognizability in most of what we do and our worst anxieties are often about not being recognized as that which we aspire to be' (Blommaert and Varis 2012: 5). In this way the smallest details of appearance are metonymically inflated so as to stand for something far bigger. We extend this argument to suggest that recognisability, indexicality, and evaluative judgment become visible in people's comments on others' (or their own) clothing and appearance. Just as comments about language offer a new ordering principle for understanding linguistic signs, so comments about non-verbal communication offer a means for understanding non-linguistic signs.

We often noticed young people's metacommentary about appearance, particularly in relation to girls talking about hair. We recorded this in both our fieldnotes and audio-recordings. In the next two examples, both recorded in fieldnotes, Jaspreet and Angela note appearance as salient both to themselves and their participants:

> The girls are talking about hair (such a common topic) and complimenting each other on their hair. Simran says that she doesn't leave the house without straightening her hair (neither do I on most days) and how much of a pain it is (another sentiment I also share with her). (JT, 21/5)

Here we see two layers of metacommentary. The girls comment on each others' appearance, and Jaspreet comments not only on their talk about their hair, but also on her own appearance. Jaspreet's metacommentary aligns herself with the student, Simran. Jaspreet demarcates her commentary on herself with parentheses, signalling what becomes almost a dialogue between her semi-public researcher self and her private self. Angela's fieldnote also moves subtly between commentary on the subject of the research and commentary on her private self:

My attention on the teaching activity is wandering. I notice that all the girls have got long hair. I make a note of [teacher] Hema's green nail varnish and think that I need to start wearing more colour! (AC, 25/9)

Angela similarly comments on herself in relation to the teacher. Blommaert (2012) argues that it is through attention to such habitual, low-key, routine and ritual identity work that we can see how complicated and dynamic the demands are on such work. He points out that we should not overlook the ordinary routines of social life, what people do in the pursuit of happiness, for reasons no more elevated than merely to be happy, to avoid having to perpetually play for big stakes, to feel good, and to give others similar feelings. In the deployment of non-verbal signs we see the appearance of micro-hegemonic norms and standards. In focusing on comments *about* such signs we come closer to understanding how verbal and non-verbal signs intersect in identity work.

Metacommentary Type 6: Irony

Rymes argues that this is probably 'the most widespread form of communicative meatcommentary these days' (p. 312). She illustrates this category by looking back at the other five types to show how each can be given an ironic spin. We can find similar examples from our own fieldnote entries. The term of respect 'ji', normally deployed in a conventionally respectful way (see *Metacommentary Type 3*), on occasion became a candidate for ironic metacommentary. When a boy has come to class late, Angela notes:

A boy enters the room and says very loudly (too loudly and class laugh) 'Sorry I am late ji'. The teacher says to him 'you are always late. Please come on time – exactly ten'. (AC, 2/10)

The boy's ironic deployment of 'ji' to perform disrespect to the teacher provides a metacomment on the school's highly prized practice of teaching forms of address to show respect. Rymes points out that while ironic metacommentary on language, accent, address terms, gesture, or clothing can function as mockery, ironic metacommentary can also display appreciation for people's knowing use of their repertoire range. In our observations we frequently heard students ironically adopting a stereotypical 'ethnic Indian' accent. The ironic, stylised 'ethnic Indian' accent adopted by the (all British-born, Indian-heritage) students on a number of occasions probably points to a range of social identifications.

They are ironic versions of stereotypical voices which rely on interlocutors' common knowledge of the stereotype as a resource. In the many stylised representations of the 'ethnic Indian' voice we heard, the social, political, and historical ideologies associated with, or represented by, the stylised word were recognisable and shared by the recipients. They were often nuanced, as on the one hand a stereotype was portrayed and evaluated, and on the other hand an ironic distance from the 'Indian' voice was maintained, and the stereotype perpetuated.

Conclusion

Fieldnotes provide evidence of the lived stuff from which the analyst abstracts structure. They remind us that doing linguistic ethnography is about making observations and authoring the texts we produce. We believe that in linguistic ethnography fieldnotes should be made visible for the following reasons. First they produce varied and protean accounts to alleviate a tendency in social research to produce 'squeaky-clean', realist accounts of truth. Instead fieldnotes reveal contrast, difference, and diversity. In publishing them we can make visible the 'experiences, struggles, and histories' (Foley 2002: 486) which have gone into authoring them. Second, like any data set they can be subjected to thematic and linguistic analysis to show how researchers discursively construct the social world they are observing. Fieldnotes are primary data sets, and like other kinds of data, including transcripts, should be rigorously analysed alongside other kinds of evidence collected in the field. Third, allowing the reader access to fieldnotes provides a picture of the social context, its participants, interactions, rituals, routines, systems and structures. An analysis of fieldnotes which attends to what both researchers and those they research say about language, and how they say it, brings into focus what situated communicative repertoires mean in action.

We agree with Rymes (2014: 314) that the meaning of the experiences and phenomena we investigate 'is often made visible to self and others through metacommentary', enabling us to notice the nuances of someone's unique repertoire. Rymes (2014: 302) asks, given the infinite variability in play when people on different biographical and historical trajectories interact, 'how do people in interaction – and how do we, as sociolinguists, linguistic ethnographers, or linguistic anthropologists – figure out which of these accumulated details are relevant?' One of the ways in which we figure these things out is through analysis of our own – and our team-mates'– written comments about language. Through an analysis of metacommentary, Rymes(2014: 304) points out, we can go beyond simply observing that people speak multiple languages, to 'accounting for their facility with the multiple and nuanced functions languages take on in context'. Analysis of fieldnotes alongside other data types offers us the means to develop such accounts.

Transcription conventions are used as follows:

(.)	pause of less than a second
(1.5)	length of pause in seconds
speech	transcribed speech
<speech >	translated speech
CAPITALS	loud
(XXX)	speech inaudible
[]	'stage directions'

References

Agha, A. (2005) 'Voice, Footing, Enregisterment', *Journal of Linguistic Anthropology* 15(1): 38–59.

Blackledge, A. and Creese, A. (2010) *Multilingualism. A Critical Perspective.* London: Continuum.

Blackledge, A. and Creese, A. (2014) 'Heteroglossia as practice and pedagogy', in A. Blackledge and A. Creese (eds), *Heteroglossia as Practice and Pedagogy.* New York: Springer. pp. 1–20.

Blackledge, A., Creese, A. and Takhi, J.K. (in press) 'Emblems of identities in four European urban settings', in J. Nortier and B.A. Svendsen (eds), *Multilingual Urban Sites. Structure, Activity, Ideology.* Cambridge: Cambridge University Press.

Blommaert, J. (2007) 'On scope and depth in linguistic ethnography', *Journal of Sociolinguistics,* 11 (5): 682–688.

Blommaert, J. (2012) 'Complexity, accent and conviviality: Concluding comments', *Tilburg Papers in Cultural Studies* 26.

Blommaert, J. and Dong, J. (2010). *Ethnographic Fieldwork. A Beginner's Guide.* Bristol: Multilingual Matters.

Blommaert, J. and Varis, P. (2012) Culture as accent. *Tilburg Papers in Cultural Studies* 18.

Blommaert, J. and Varis, P. (2011) 'Enough is enough: The heuristics of authenticity in superdiversity', *Tilburg Papers in Cultural Studies* 2.

Bourdieu, P. (2008) *The Bachelors' Ball: The Crisis of Peasant Society in Bearn* Chicago: University of Chicago Press.

Bourdieu, P. (1999) *The Weight of the World: Social Suffering in Contemporary Society.* Cambridge: Polity.

Bourdieu, P. (2000) *Pascalian Meditations.* Cambridge: Polity.

Bryman, A. (1988) *Quantity and Quality in Social Research.* London: Unwin Hyman.

Copland, F. and Creese, A. with Rock, F. and Shaw, S. (2015) *Ethnography and Language in the Social Sciences: Collecting, Analysing and Presenting Data.* London: SAGE.

Creese, A. and Blackledge, B., with Bhatt, A., Jonsson, C., Juffermans, K., Li, J., Martin, P. Muhonen, A. and Takhi, J.K. (2015) 'Researching bilingual and multilingual education multilingually: a linguistic ethnography', in W.E. Wright, S. Boun and O. Garcia (eds), *Handbook of Bilingual & Multilingual Education*. Malden, MA and Oxford, UK: Wiley/Blackwell, pp. 127–144.

Eisenhart, M. (2001) 'Changing Conceptions of Culture and Ethnographic Methodology. Recent Thematic Shifts and Their Implications for Research on Teaching'. In *Handbook of Research on Teaching*. 4th edition. V. Richardson (ed.) Washington, DC: American Educational Research Association. pp. 209–225.

Emerson, R., Fetz, R. and Shaw, L. (2011) Writing *Ethnographic Fieldnotes. 2nd Edition*. Chicago: The University of Chicago Press.

Erickson, F. (1990) 'Qualitative methods', in R.L. Linn and F. Erickson (eds), *Research in Teaching and Learning: Volume Two*. New York: MacMillan. pp. 77–194.

Erickson, F. (2004a) 'Demystifying data construction and analysis', *Anthropology and Education Quarterly*, 35(4): 486–493.

Geertz, C. (1988) *Works and Lives: The Anthropologist as Author*. Cambridge: Polity Press.

Georgakopoulou, A. (2007) *Small Stories, Interaction and Identities*. Amsterdam/Philadelphia: John Benjamins Publishing Company.

Heller, M. (2008) 'Doing ethnography', in L. Wei and M.G. Moyer (eds), *The Blackwell Guide to Research Methods in Bilingualism and Multilingualism*. Malden, MA: Blackwell. pp. 249–262.

Heller, M. (2011) *Paths to Post-Nationalism: A Critical Ethnography of Language and Identity*. New York: Oxford University Press.

Hornberger, N. (1995) 'Ethnography in linguistic perspective: understanding school processes', *Language and Education*, 9(4): 233–248.

Hymes, D. (1968) 'The ethnography of speaking', in J. Fishman (ed.), *Readings in the Sociology of Language*. The Hague: Moulton. pp. 99–138.

Hymes, D. (1972) 'On communicative competence', in J.B. Pride and J. Holmes (eds), *Sociolinguistics*. Harmondsworth: Penguin. pp. 269–293.

Hymes, D. (1974) *Foundations in Sociolinguistic: An Ethnographic Approach*. Philadelphia, PA: University of Pennsylvania Press.

Hymes, D. (1996). *Ethnography, Linguistics, Narrative Inequality: Toward an Understanding of Voice*. London: Taylor and Francis.

Miles, M.B. and Huberman, A.M. (1994) *Qualitative Data Analysis*. 2nd edn. London: Sage.

Rampton, Ben. 1997. 'Retuning in applied linguistics', *International Journal of Applied Linguistics*, 7: 3–25.

Rymes, B. (2014) 'Marking communicative repertoire through metacommentary', in A. Blackledge and A. Creese (eds) *Heteroglossia as Practice and Pedagogy*. Dordrecht: Springer Science+Business Media. pp. 301–316.

Scollon, R. and Scollon, S.W. (2004) *Nexus Analysis: Discourse and the Emerging Internet*. London, UK: Routledge.

Silverman, D. (2001) *Interpreting Qualitative Data*. 2nd edn. London: Sage Publications.

Silverstein, M. (1993). 'Metapragmatic discourse and metapragmatic function', in Lucy, J. (ed.) *Reflexive Language*. New York: Cambridge University Press.

Tierney, W. (2002) 'Get real: representing reality', *Qualitative Studies in Education*, 15(15): 385–398.

Subject Index

CPSIA information can be obtained at www.ICGtesting.com
Printed in the USA
LVOW10s1741090816

499678LV00012B/350/P